THE
HISTORY OF
ETHIOPIA

ADVISORY BOARD

THE HISTORY OF ETHIOPIA

Saheed A. Adejumobi

The Greenwood Histories of the Modern Nations
Frank W. Thackeray and John E. Findling, Series Editors

Greenwood Press
Westport, Connecticut • London

Library of Congress Cataloging-in-Publication Data

Adejumobi, Saheed A.
  The history of Ethiopia / Saheed A. Adejumobi.
     p. cm.—(The Greenwood histories of the modern nations, ISSN 1096–2905)
  Includes bibliographical references and index.
  ISBN 0–313–32273–2 (alk. paper)
  1. Ethiopia—History. 2. Ethiopia—Politics and government. I. Title.
  DT381.A45 2007
  963—dc22   2006027877

British Library Cataloguing in Publication Data is available.

Copyright © 2007 by Saheed A. Adejumobi

Library of Congress Catalog Card Number: 2006027877
ISBN: 0–313–32273–2
ISSN: 1096–2905

First published in 2007

Greenwood Press, 88 Post Road West, Westport, CT 06881
An imprint of Greenwood Publishing Group, Inc.
www.greenwood.com

Printed in the United States of America

The paper used in this book complies with the
Permanent Paper Standard issued by the National
Information Standards Organization (Z39.48–1984).

10 9 8 7 6 5 4 3 2 1

Central cover image: Ethiopian Orthodox Christians wear ceremonial clothing
during the Timkat Festival. Behind them is the 12th century rock-hewn Beta Giorgis
Church. Lalibela, Ethiopia, ca. January 2000. © Earl & Nazima Kowall/CORBIS

Dedicated in affectionate greeting to my father,
Kazeem Adegbenro Adejumobi,
who lately transcended and joined the ancestors.
Omo Sobaloju, sun re o

Contents

Series Foreword

The *Greenwood Histories of the Modern Nations* series is intended to provide students and interested laypeople with up-to-date, concise, and analytical histories of many of the nations of the contemporary world. Not since the 1960s has there been a systematic attempt to publish a series of national histories, and, as editors, we believe that this series will prove to be a valuable contribution to our understanding of other countries in our increasingly interdependent world.

Over thirty years ago, at the end of the 1960s, the Cold War was an accepted reality of global politics, the process of decolonization was still in progress, the idea of a unified Europe with a single currency was unheard of, the United States was mired in a war in Vietnam, and the economic boom of Asia was still years in the future. Richard Nixon was president of the United States, Mao Tse-tung (not yet Mao Zedong) ruled China, Leonid Brezhnev guided the Soviet Union, and Harold Wilson was prime minister of the United Kingdom. Authoritarian dictators still ruled most of Latin America, the Middle East was reeling in the wake of the Six-Day War, and Shah Reza Pahlavi was at the height of his power in Iran. Clearly, the past 30 years have been witness to a great deal of historical change, and it is to this change that this series is primarily addressed.

With the help of a distinguished advisory board, we have selected nations whose political, economic, and social affairs mark them as among the most important in the waning years of the twentieth century, and for each nation we have found an author who is recognized as a specialist in the history of that nation. These authors have worked most cooperatively with us and with Greenwood Press to produce volumes that reflect current research on their nations and that are interesting and informative to their prospective readers.

The importance of a series such as this cannot be underestimated. As a superpower whose influence is felt all over the world, the United States can claim a "special" relationship with almost every other nation. Yet many Americans know very little about the histories of the nations with which the United States relates. How did they get to be the way they are? What kind of political systems have evolved there? What kind of influence do they have in their own region? What are the dominant political, religious, and cultural forces that move their leaders? These and many other questions are answered in the volumes of this series.

The authors who have contributed to this series have written comprehensive histories of their nations, dating back to prehistoric times in some cases. Each of them, however, has devoted a significant portion of the book to events of the last thirty years, because the modern era has contributed the most to contemporary issues that have an impact on U.S. policy. Authors have made an effort to be as up-to-date as possible so that readers can benefit from the most recent scholarship and a narrative that includes very recent events.

In addition to the historical narrative, each volume in this series contains an introductory overview of the country's geography, political institutions, economic structure, and cultural attributes. This is designed to give readers a picture of the nation as it exists in the contemporary world. Each volume also contains additional chapters that add interesting and useful detail to the historical narrative. One chapter is a thorough chronology of important historical events, making it easy for readers to follow the flow of a particular nation's history. Another chapter features biographical sketches of the nation's most important figures in order to humanize some of the individuals who have contributed to the historical development of their nation. Each volume also contains a comprehensive bibliography, so that those readers whose interest has been sparked may find out more about the nation and its history. Finally, there is a carefully prepared topic and person index.

Readers of these volumes will find them fascinating to read and useful in understanding the contemporary world and the nations that comprise it. As series editors, it is our hope that this series will contribute to a heightened sense of global understanding as we embark on a new century.

Frank W. Thackeray and John E. Findling
Indiana University Southeast

Preface and
Acknowledgments

Narratives of modernity are often canonized in forms that are culturally and politically exclusive and thus hegemonic. The African continent is yet to be allowed to enter fully into the modern world's political consciousness as an equal in the family of nations. Even though Ethiopia has had a recorded history and a thriving civilization for more than 3,000 years, no other country in the twentieth century has been so completely defined by the narrow scope and idiosyncrasies of the modern and dominant popular media. Newsreel footage showing the Italian army invading Ethiopia in 1935 was a popular yet under-appreciated cataclysmic prelude to World War II. Ethiopia's image has also suffered from its description as the alter ego of Western modernity in the pro-liferation of Western narratives and literary canons rooted in the predilections of colonial encounters. Evelyn Waugh's popular reportage from Ethiopia has been commended for its lightheartedness, acute observations, and jolly nar-ratives, though the literary iconography he bequeathed us was also riddled with biases and stereotypes. Waugh's "primitive" gaze upon Ethiopia led him to express an admiration for fascist modernity as he described the war be-tween Ethiopia and Italy as a conflict between barbarism and civilization. His writings on Ethiopia and Africa are still being reproduced without a consid-eration of their historic context and, worse still, they are often cited as an apt prognosticator of contemporary Africa's political and economic backward-ness. Regarding Ethiopia and the world in general, the intellectual brunt of Cold War politics has also resulted in the marginalization of the progressive voices of the anti-fascist internationalist Left such as Sylvia Pankhurst, Joel T. Rogers, George Steer, and W.E.B. DuBois, to name a few. Post–World War II academic publications have since enabled a critical appreciation of the nuances and complexity of the Ethiopian polity under the Solomonic and postimperial regimes.

Ethiopia has also been betrayed from within. Many Ethiopian political leaders have ruled as claimants to absolutism over the relationship of humans and society. Inequality in Ethiopian monarchical structure also acquired a new significance with the onset of European colonialism in Africa. Thus, the failure to place the supreme quality of life for every individual at the center of state policies has engendered the perennial presence of international actors and social engineers under the rubric of seductively universalist frameworks of liberal imperialism, Cold War politics, humanitarian interventions, and global theocracy. Regardless of Ethiopia's location, contribution to human civilization, and unique trajectory into the modern era, its iconic images in the second half of the twentieth century are firmly rooted in that geopolitical spatial concept of "sub-Sahara Africa" and its pathologies: famine, war, poverty, and political instability.

Ethiopia's history has, however, been important for the critical understanding of modern global relations and paradigms such as the evolution of the concepts of international lobby, postwar reconstructions, boundary disputes, and international socialist and liberalization reforms. Also of significance is the emergence of modern African Diaspora intellectual and political traditions: as Ethiopia's influence waned in European courts—and its autonomy became progressively undermined by the latter's political and economic imperatives—a transnational black canon responded with a broad-based critical analysis of racial and economic imperialism. The black nationalists celebrated Ethiopian civilization and independence from both a religious and secular humanist perspective, within essentialist and interracial configurations, and from structuralist and humanist frameworks. However, both the colonial inflected narratives and nationalist historiographies failed to fully appreciate the complexity of the Ethiopian modernist project. Many of the post–World War II narratives have underscored these shortcomings even when they still bear the burden of the Cold War analytical paradigms that favor structural analysis, power, and identity politics over critical evaluations of African subjectivities and the interrelationship between the concepts of local and global justice.

The History of Ethiopia focuses on the three interrelated themes of politics, economy, and intellectual forces that have shaped the history of Ethiopia since the late nineteenth century. I explore shifting local and global power configurations from the late nineteenth century to the twentieth century and the related implications in Ethiopia and the Horn of Africa region. Against this background, the book evaluates Ethiopia's precarious balancing act of upholding a modernist project tethered to the idea of divine Christendom. I evaluate how Ethiopian regimes managed the secular realities of sustained management of resources, planning, and priorities while engaged with international, regional, and local politics. In addition, the book explores Ethiopia's efforts at charting an independent course in the face of imperialism, World War II, the Cold War, and international economic reforms. I also examine the complexities, paradoxes, and pragmatic challenges of imperial and postimperial Ethiopia related to social, political, and economic reforms. Of utmost significance is a renaissance at home and abroad in the arts, theater, Orthodox Coptic Christianity, Islam, and ancient ethnic identities. The book paints a vivid picture of a dynamic and compelling country and region for scholars, policymakers, and general readers seeking to understand the historical context of global relations as we begin the twenty-first century. Finally, the work provides a timeline of events in Ethiopian history, brief biographies of key figures, and a bibliographic essay.

Many people have helped me complete this task. I thank Professor Frank. W. Thackeray and Professor John E. Findling; the series editors of the Greenwood Histories of the Modern Nations, Kevin Ohe, Steven Vetrano, Sarah Colwell, and the rest of the Greenwood crew have been very helpful. From my sojourn at the University of Texas at Austin, I am grateful to Dr. Toyin Falola, Dr. Christopher Adejumo, Dr. John Lamphear, Dr. Berndth Lindfors, Drs. Kevin K. Gaines and Penny Von Eschen, Dr. Sheila Walker, Betty Nunley, and Jenni Jones. At Wayne State University in Detroit, Michigan, I also received tremendous assistance from Drs. Melba Joyce Boyd, Beth Bates, Ollie Johnson, Eboe Hutchful, and Perry Mars. I have enjoyed the warm support of Malam Olufemi Taiwo, Drs. Jason and Elizabeth Sikes-Wirth, Dr. Wallace Loh, and the faculty and staff of the Global African Studies Program and History Department at Seattle University. Inestimable forms of affection and comfort came from members of my family: my wife, Alea Adejumobi, and our children, Adenike and Aderemi. I am grateful to my mother, Omolara, and my siblings, Abiodun, Aderonke, Adedapo, and Adesola. Additionally, I have been blessed by the encouragement of an extended community from Dr. Quintard Taylor, Dr. Chidi Nwaubani, Dr. Onaiwu Ogbomo, Dr. Jerry Dibua, Dr. Hakeem Tijani, Kevin Washington, Simon Olufemi Allen, Rafiu Lawal, Wole Akande, Ehije Aire, Jide Johnson, Mark Radermacher, Toyin Alade, Augustine Agwuele, and Margo Ramsing. I would also like to acknowledge the Pepes, Jane Palmer and Jeff Dewhirst, and the Blochs, Merlos, Allens, Berkeys, Descantes, Comiskeys, Owosekuns, Igerias, Lewises, Cokers, Obitades, Eblens, and Sanyas. Last but not least, I thank my kola nut suppliers, Mr. Alimi of Austin and Mr. Syla of Seattle. I join the Ethiopian community here in the Northwest and other parts of the Diaspora in wishing the Ethiopian nation, the Horn of Africa, and the continent as a whole peace, progress, prosperity, and good health for all in the new millennium.

The book is dedicated to my father, Kazeem Adegbenro Adejumobi, who passed on during the writing process. His illness and the year he spent with me and my family in Michigan may have delayed the project somewhat but certainly furthered my comprehension of the cosmopolitanism, humanism, and fortitude inherent in African cultures. In spite of being ravaged by illness, he replenished us with a regular analysis of globalization as theorized by himself and his grassroots "think-tank groups" back home in Africa. One favorite epigram revolves around how he had once funded a special prayer at his local mosque to be invoked on behalf of former President Bill Clinton for the travails he was enduring toward the end of his tenure in the White House. As I tried to suppress the instinct to query my father for an enumeration of the particular African policy that best justified this act of benevolence and, more importantly, to question whether this dedicated sum had come out of the remittances I was sending home to supplement his meager pension, I wondered if he was merely employing a transnational framework to remedy postcolonial national frustrations. He explained, however, that his action was based on a belief that the beleaguered president was a person of good heart who was being unfairly persecuted. This was, after all, the leader of the country in which his son (myself) now bore residency, he concluded. Regardless of the merit of his action, my father, a retired journalist, was neither conflicted about his spirituality nor was he demeaned by his corporeal marginalization as an African in a global modern world. Rather, he represents the passing generation that combines a strong appreciation for the power of positive ideas and rituals, recognizes the interconnectedness of global welfare, and believes with fortitude that what goes around comes around. I hope that *The History of Ethiopia* equally allows us some lessons for our universe: appreciation of those forces that recycle local and global inequalities, the importance of power and its corollary freedom, the urgency required to address the quantitative loss of humanity and African subjectivity, especially within the drama of the globalization phenomenon, and the relevance of historical and cultural particularisms in the application of what we might ordinarily consider universal narratives of modernity.

Saheed Adeyinka Adejumobi
Seattle, Washington

Timeline of Ethiopian History

2nd century A.D.	Semitic people from the Arabian Peninsula establish the kingdom of Aksum.
4th century A.D.	Coptic Christianity is introduced to the region via Egypt.
1530–31	Ahmad Gran, a Muslim leader, invades Ethiopia and gains control of most of the territory.
1818–68	Lij Kasa conquers Amhara, Gojjam, Tigre, and Shoa.
1855	Lij Kasa is renamed Emperor Tewodros II.
1868	Emperor Tewodros II is defeated by British expeditionary forces. He decides to commit suicide rather than be captured.
1872	Tigrean chieftain becomes Yohannes IV.
1889	Yohannes IV is killed while fighting Mahdist forces. He is succeeded by the king of Shoa, who becomes Emperor Menelik II.

1889   Menelik II signs a bilateral friendship treaty with Italy at Wichale. Italy now considers Ethiopia to be one of its own protectorates.

1889   Addis Ababa is named the capital of Ethiopia.

1895   Ethiopia is invaded by Italian forces.

1896   Italian forces are defeated by the Ethiopians at Adwa; the treaty of Wichale annulled; Italy recognizes Ethiopia's independence but retains control over Eritrea.

1913   Menelik dies and is succeeded by his grandson, Lij Iyasu.

1916   Lij Iyasu is deposed and is succeeded by Menelik's daughter, Zauditu, who rules through a regent, Ras Tafari Makonnen.

1930   Zauditu dies. Her successor, Ras Tafari Makonnen, becomes Emperor Haile Selassie I.

1935   Italy invades Ethiopia.

1936   Italians capture Addis Ababa, and Haile Selassie flees. The king of Italy is made emperor of Ethiopia. Eritrea, Italian Somaliland, and Ethiopia together form Italian East Africa.

1941   With the help of Ethiopian resistance fighters, British and Commonwealth soldiers defeat the Italians. Haile Selassie reclaims his throne.

1952   The United Nations federates Eritrea with Ethiopia.

1962   Haile Selassie annexes Eritrea and claims the territory as an Ethiopian province.

1963   The Organization of African Unity (OAU) holds its first conference in Addis Ababa.

1973–74 Some 200,000 people perish in the Wallo province due to famine.

1974   Haile Selassie is deposed in a coup led by Teferi Benti.

1975   Haile Selassie dies in mysterious circumstances while in custody.

1977   Teferi Benti is assassinated and replaced by Mengistu Haile Mariam.

1977–79	Mengistu Haile Mariam orders the death of thousands of government opponents. The collectivization of agriculture begins. The Tigrean People's Liberation Front starts a war to obtain regional autonomy.
1977	Ethiopia's Ogaden region is invaded by Somalia.
	The Soviet Union and Cuba offer Ethiopia assistance and help defeat Somali forces.
1985	Western countries send food aid to stave off the worst famine in 10 years. Thousands of people are forced to resettle from Eritrea and Tigre.
1987	With a new constitution, Ethiopians elect Mengistu Haile Mariam to serve as their president.
1988	Ethiopia signs a peace treaty with Somalia.
1991	The People's Revolutionary Democratic Front of Ethiopia captures Addis Ababa, and Mengistu Haile Mariam flees the country. Eritrea, awaiting independence, establishes a provisional government.
1992	The remains of Haile Selassie are discovered under a toilet in the palace.
1993	Eritrea gains independence.
1994	Ethiopia's new constitution divides the country into regions based on ethnicity.
1995	Tamrat Layne is named prime minister, and Meles Zenawi becomes president.
1998	The border dispute between Ethiopia and Eritrea leads to violent clashes. War is declared the following year.
April 2000	Three years of drought leave more than eight million Ethiopians facing starvation.
May 2000	Ethiopia seizes control of the Eritrean town of Barentu.
June 2000	Ethiopia and Eritrea sign a cease-fire agreement. The United Nations oversees the withdrawal of Ethiopian troops from Eritrea.
November 2000	The late Haile Selassie is reburied in an official ceremony in Addis Ababa's Trinity Cathedral.

December 2000

Ethiopia and Eritrea end two years of conflict by signing a peace agreement in Algeria. The agreement forms organized commissions to define the disputed border. Prisoners and displaced people are allowed to return home.

February 24, 2001

Ethiopian withdrawal from Eritrea is officially completed in accordance with a U.N.–sponsored agreement.

March 2001

Meles Zenawi claims that he prevented a potential coup by a dissident group in the dominant Tigrean People's Liberation Front.

April 2001

Thousands of demonstrators clash with police in Addis Ababa in protest against police brutality and in support of calls for political and academic freedom.

May 12, 2001

Intelligence and security chief Kinfe Gebre-Medhin, a key ally of President Meles Zenawi, is assassinated upon entering an armed forces officers' club in Addis Ababa.

May 21, 2001

Ethiopia and Eritrea agree to let a U.N. independent commission demarcate the disputed border.

April 2002

Nearly one year later, Ethiopia and Eritrea accept a new common border. Both sides still lay claim to the town of Badme.

April 2003

An independent boundary commission decides that the disputed town of Badme is part of Eritrea. Ethiopia refuses to accept the ruling.

January–February 2004

Ethnic clashes break out in the isolated western region of Gambella. Nearly 200 people die and tens of thousands choose to flee from the violence.

March 2004

A resettlement program is enacted to move more than two million people away from the Ethiopian highlands, which are experiencing drought-like conditions.

November 2004

Ethiopia says it accepts "in principle" a boundary commission's ruling on its border with Eritrea.

March 2005	The Human Rights Watch, a U.S.–based organization, accuses the Ethiopian army of "widespread murder, rape and torture" against the Anuak people of Gambella. Ethiopia's military reacts with defiance.
April 2005	The first section of the Axum obelisk, looted by Italy in 1937, is returned to Ethiopia from Rome.
May–June 2005	The third round of multiparty elections take place, revealing initial results that the ruling party and its allies have won the majority in parliament.
June 2005	Protesters accuse the ruling party of electoral fraud. Thirty-six people are shot dead in clashes with the police in the capital.
August–September 2005	Electoral fraud complaints lead to reruns in more than 30 seats. Election authorities say that final results give the ruling party enough seats in parliament to form a government.
November 2005	Forty-six protesters die during renewed clashes between security forces and opposition supporters over May's elections. Thousands of people, including opposition politicians and newspaper editors, are detained.
	Amid reports of troop build-ups along the disputed Ethiopia-Eritrea border, the U.N. Security Council threatens both countries with sanctions unless they return to the 2000 peace plan.
December 2005	An international commission, based in the Hague, rules that Eritrea broke international law when it attacked Ethiopia in 1998. It says that the attack could not be justified as self defense.
	More than 80 people, including journalists and many opposition leaders, appear in court on charges of treason and genocide relating to November's deadly street clashes.
May 2006	Six political parties and armed groups form an opposition alliance, the Alliance for Freedom and Democracy, at a meeting in the Netherlands.

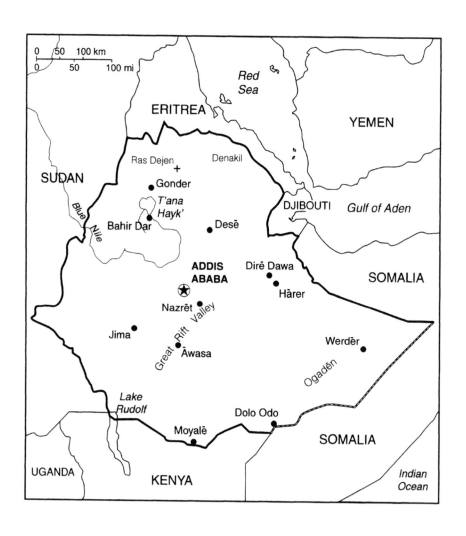

1

Ethiopia: Intellectual and Cultural Background

INTRODUCTION: ETHIOPIA IN PERSPECTIVE

This twenty-first-century narrative history of modern Ethiopia traces the major events of an ancient African civilization in engagement with the global community in which powerful cultural, political, and religious forces helped shaped the evolution of a very significant and viable nation state, one primed to face equally significant problems associated with the modern era. The modern reader's conception of Ethiopia has no doubt been shaped by stories of wars and natural disasters including the latter-day famine crisis. In fact, Ethiopia's history stretches back to antiquity, with references to Ethiopia in the Bible and classical Greek literature. Later, between 1855 and 1974, the state witnessed events that culminated in the emergence of a centralized modern bureaucratic state. Alongside Haiti and Liberia, Ethiopia maintained her status as one of the three historical independent black nations and, with the exception of a five-year occupation by Italy under Benito Mussolini, successfully defended herself against the European colonization of Africa. The modern history of Ethiopia also provides a glimpse of global African cultural, intellectual, and political history. Ethiopia is prominently featured in the iconography of both classical and modern era cultural, religious, and political development and therefore is fertile territory for the enthusiast of both ancient and modern Africa.

Ethiopia has held a profound cultural significance for the black diaspora as one of the world's—and, to say the least, Africa's—oldest independent republics, which provided an (admittedly idealized) inspiration for the dream of black independence throughout the world. Indeed, the name *Ethiopia* had emerged as a near generic term for the whole universe of dark-skinned people in Western narratives, including Shakespearean literature. Some scholars have argued that the Ethiopian identity was virtually a Western imposition on African Christians. African slaves in the New World adopted "Ethiopia" as a hallmark of religio-cultural identity because Europeans used it to describe black Africa. Similarly the concept was introduced into the vocabulary of African peoples on the continent with Portuguese contact in parts of "Ethiopia." In later centuries, the scriptural prophecy of how Ethiopia would reach to God for succor was commonly used as a slogan with the European missionary movement to energize efforts for the conversion of Africa. As a result, African Christians could readily appropriate Ethiopia as a symbol of identity and readily embrace Ethiopianism as an intellectual movement of religious nationalism and grassroots activism. For these reasons, Ethiopia's cultural legacy came to embody the concepts of black freedom and independent black nationhood and, as we shall see, influenced generations of prominent black intellectuals in the new world.

ETHIOPIANISM AND ITS INFLUENCE ON THE AFRICAN DIASPORA

Before the twentieth century, some observers have described Ethiopia as "the Hidden Empire" because of its relative isolation and feudal autocracy. Others have mythicized the Ethiopian state as the epitome of African independence and self-determination as a result of having defeated an invading Italian force in 1896 at Adwa. Noted intellectual and activist W.E.B. DuBois expressed this anticolonial sentiment in 1935 when he stated that "unlike other parts of colonized Africa, Ethiopia . . . had kept comparatively free of debt, had preserved her political autonomy, had begun to reorganize her ancient policy, and was in many ways an example and a promise of what a native people untouched by modern exploitation and race prejudice might do."[1] DuBois' evocation was not only a reflection of the ancient state's historical background and Africa's transition into modernity, it was also a reflection of *Ethiopianism*, which had emerged as an Afro-Atlantic literary-religious tradition common to the English-speaking world originating out of shared political and religious experiences of the late eighteenth and early nineteenth centuries. Ethiopianism had also found expression in the slave narratives, in the exhortations of conspiratorial slave preachers, and in the songs and folklore of the slaves of the Old and the peasants of the New South. As a literary tradition it later became part of the sermons and political tracts of a sophisticated urban elite. Practitioners of Ethiopianism found inspiration in the biblical passage, "Princes shall come of Egypt; Ethiopia shall soon stretch out her hands unto God" (Psalms 68:31). The verse was seen by those who associated modernity with Western traditions as a prophecy that Africa would through Christianity "soon" be saved from "heathenism" and was a prerequisite for a dramatic political, industrial, and economic renaissance. For cultural nationalists however, the scripture is a prophecy that some day the black man would rule the world. "Ethiopian" traditions often lay claim to African genius, aspirations which, they argued, were undermined by the cultural dependency borne out of slavery and colonialism. This tragic racial experience, they concluded, carried a profound historical value that endowed the African with presumed moral superiority.

In addition, the rise of modern black internationalism—a combination of intellectual and political protests and lobbying—arose out of the global powers' ambivalence to the plight of Africa in the face of Italian transgression of what was considered the black man's last citadel. Ethiopia thus became the trigger for a modern black political tradition, which combined political activism with trade unionism and anticolonialism with early civil rights initiatives. Ethiopia's regional significance in the northeast region of Africa known as the "Horn," so called because of the horn-shaped tip of the continent that marks off the Red Sea from the Indian Ocean, also provides a window into the twentieth-century economic, political, and cultural evolution of modern African societies. Ethiopia is bounded by Sudan in the west, Djibouti in the east, Eritrea in the north and northeast, Somalia in the southeast and Kenya to the south. Ethiopia's population is estimated at more than 76 million, making it the third most populous African country after Nigeria and Egypt. Its modern ethnic composition includes a number of groups: the Oromo 40 at percent; Amhara and Tigre at 32 percent; Sidamo 9 at percent; Shankella 6 at percent; Somali 6 at percent; Afar 4 at percent; Gurage at 2 percent; and 1 percent other.

Two important phenomena helped define the setting for the unfolding history of the modern Ethiopia. The state went through a series of changes, from its status as a powerful state in ancient and medieval times to social and political decline in the middle of the eighteenth century. Domestically, Ethiopia suffered rapid political fragmentation fueled by the usurpation of civil and political powers and zero-sum conflicts between monarchs and emergent feudal lords. Ethiopia's centralized government was replaced by a decentralized provincial autonomy of rulers, many of whom had social, political, and economic relations but also often warred among themselves. From the late nineteenth into the twentieth century Ethiopia's modern external relations were unique yet symbolic of modern Africa's political and economic history as the continent was subsumed by shifting global power configurations. The importance of the Red Sea in global affairs was increasing, given its triadic significance of cultural, political, and economic activities. From the late nineteenth century to the latter half of the twentieth, the impact of Western colonial and Cold War ideologies also had considerable ramifications upon territorial configurations and social, political, military, and economic affairs in the northeast region of Africa. Following the overthrow of colonialism throughout the continent, African nationalists expressed the aspirations of their people for an economic, political, and cultural renaissance by creating a movement of independent states called the Organization of African Unity. The first conference was held at its new headquarters in Addis Ababa, the capital of modern Ethiopia, in 1963. Other relevant themes in the history of modern Ethiopia include modernization reforms in the educational, military, and political realms and constitutional sectors. The sum of these concepts is emblematic of African transition into the modern era. Regrettably, Ethiopia's simultaneous development of independence with cultural and intellectual advancement was not accompanied by corollary economic development or a considerable rise in the status of the peasantry class, a theme that we shall explore in greater detail over the course of this book.

We shall also analyze efforts directed toward the management of natural disasters by the creation of state bureaucracies and the development of non-state actors in Ethiopia as she deals with natural disasters, political irredentism, and economic development. We will also deal with what some have described as an Ethiopian renaissance fueled by a political intelligentsia and popular culture shaped by traditional Ethiopian communities and their emergent Diasporic returnees. The literary renaissance of ancient Ethiopian scripts, such as the thousand-year-old *Kebra Negast* described by some as the lost Bible of Rastafarian wisdom, and the popular yearning for similar ancient manuscripts locked away in European museums not only served as a testament to the common experience of colonialism but also as evidence of the refashioning of ancient tools for the modern nation-building process. This becomes more significant with the latter-day regeneration of the Ethiopian state in political and cultural terms, and also in the sheer population size of the state as a modern entity.

GEOGRAPHY, CULTURE, AND POLITICAL BACKGROUND

Ethiopia, described by ancient chroniclers as a land of awe-inspiring mountains, isolated plateaus, and precipitous valleys, owes its name to the Greeks, who referred mainly to the black population living south of Egypt. Ethiopia's geography, like its people, has a long and dynamic history, resulting in a scenic landscape of variety and splendor unique to the whole of Africa. The highlands of present-day Ethiopia are dissected by enormous gorges and canyons thousands of feet deep, the largest and most spectacular of which is the valley of the Abbai. Except where piles of volcanic lava formed great mountain ranges, the intervening areas were left as flat-topped plateaus, called *ambas* by the Ethiopians. Many of these plateaus remain completely isolated from one another, some being joined only by the narrowest necks of land between great precipices.

The fragmented nature of Ethiopia highlands played an important part in the country's political and cultural history. Isolated and mountainous plateau massifs have proven to be almost insurmountable obstacles to political leaders who have sought to unify the country, to the invaders who desired to conquer it, and to those who have sporadically attempted to develop its economic resources. Ethiopia is divided topographically into three major zones: *daga* (the cool highlands where the annual average temperature is about 16 degrees centigrade), *wayna daga* (the intermediate zone where most of the settled population lives), and *qolla* (the hot valleys and plains, which are dependent on the desert conditions of the northeastern end of the Rift Valley for their hotness or coolness). The climatic designations have over time assumed broader significance for their impact on the distinctive ways of life, culture, means of existence, and social temperaments.

Ethiopia contains four major rivers systems. The first system consists of the Takkaze (also known as the Atbara), the Abbay (Blue Nile), and the Baro (Sobat), originating in Sudan and flowing westward into the Nile. The Abbay is the most famous, deriving its source from Lake Tana. In the second group is the Ganale, which is also known as Juba, and the Wabe Shabale, and these two rivers both flow towards the Indian Ocean. The Gibe, also known as Omo in its lower course, flows through the southwestern highlands, with the Turkana, also known as Lake Rudolph, on the Ethio-Kenya border as its terminus. The Awash sets off from the highlands west of Addis Ababa, Ethiopia's capital, streams across the Rift Valley, and vanishes in its northeastern sands. The Rift also play host to Ethiopian major chain of lakes. These include Lakes Zway, Langano Abyata, Shala, and Awasa in the north, Abbaya and Chamo in the middle, and Lake Rudolf at the southern tip. A string of volcanic crater lakes can be found around the town of Dabra Zayt, formerly known as Beshoftu, about 31 miles south of Addis Ababa.

The main growing season in Ethiopia is known as *keramt* for the "heavy rains" that fall between June and September. The *balg* or "little rains" occur between March and May. These are caused by monsoon winds blowing from the Indian Ocean into the low-pressure area of the Sahara desert and Arabia. The temperate conditions of the northern and central highlands have permitted abundant agricultural productivity. The most important of this is *tef (Eragrostis tef)* a small cereal indigenous and peculiar to the country that is processed into the distinctive bread, *enjara*, the staple diet of a large proportion of the country's population. In the southern part, *ensat*, a root vegetable, is the staple crop.

Geographic isolation also created a spirit of relative independence in many areas where the pattern of life has remained unchanged for hundreds of years, and where the central government still has only limited influence. The nomads of the Danakil deserts; the farmers of the cool mountains of Shewa, Gojjam, and Tigre; the fishermen of the coast of Eritrea; the collectors in the coffee forests of Jimma; and the hunters in the wet tropical forests farther southwest are as varied in their customs and livelihood as the scenery itself. Nowhere are the human and scenic contrasts more marked than along the edges of the vast Rift Valley escarpments. To the northeast, the Rift Valley broadens like a funnel to join the Red Sea, and part of this region, the Danakil Depression, lies below sea level. The Danakil, or Afar Desert, separates Ethiopia from similar deserts and mountain terrain in Arabia, but, as we shall see, this did not preclude early cultural contacts with the Islamic world.

Ethiopia's contribution to the development of world religions is also evident in the evolution of early Christian traditions. In the fourth century, the Christian Church, influenced by the great Middle-Eastern academies, developed two separate schools of thought on the nature of Christ. The Greek and Roman churches held that a divine and a human spirit had been brought together and fused in the body of Christ. Alternatively, many of the representatives of the Syrian and Egyptian churches believed in the singular, divine nature of Christ. Their attitude came to be described as Monophysite, Jacobean, or Coptic. Ancient Ethiopia had followed the lead of Alexandrian Egyptian, and to this day remains Coptic. The church emphasizes that all concerning Christ should be applied to his entire person as one Lord. The seven sacraments (mysteries)—baptism, confirmation, penance, Holy Communion, unction of the sick, matrimony, and holy orders—are important in the teaching of the Ethiopian Orthodox Church. Sacraments are holy ordinance through which the believer receives an invisible grace under the form of an outward sign. In the performance of each sacrament the Divine Majesty himself is present. The church also teaches five other pillars of mysteries: the mystery of the Trinity, incarnation, baptism, Eucharist, and the resurrection of the dead. These mysteries are regarded by the church as basic knowledge for all faithful, and every Christian must know this. Fasting is strictly observed by all baptized members above the age of seven years. During lent, meat and meat products are prohibited. The Old and New Testaments were translated into Ge'ez as early as 615, emphasizing Ethiopia's relevance to the biblical narratives of human creation. Significantly, although Ethiopia became a land mostly populated by Christian churches, it continues to play host to a fairly large Muslim population as well.

THE PEOPLE

Ethiopia plays host to a mosaic of nationalities speaking a multiplicity of languages that fall into four major categories. Three of these languages could be traced to a common ancestry linguists call proto-Afroasiatic. These are known as Cushitic and include the Agaw, the Beja, the Somali, the Afar, the Saho, the Hadiya, the Kambata, the Gedeo, and the Oromo, who now constitute the largest single nationality in Ethiopia. A second category is the Omotic, who derive their name from their location on both sides of the Omo River and consist of the Dorze, Janjaro, Kafa, Walayta, the Dizi or Gimira, and Maji. While the Cushitic and Omotic are the most ancient in the Ethiopian region, the Semitic languages are most recent and have played the most dominant role in the country's history. The oldest of the Semitic languages, Ge'ez, is now confined to ecclesiastical use. Other Semitic languages include Tegra, Amharic, Gurage, and Harari. The Nilo-Saharan language group is an independent strain found in the western fringes of the country and includes the Kunama in southwestern Eritrea, the Gumuz in Matakkal in western Gojjam, the Manjangir, the Anuak, and the Nuer.

In addition to linguistic evidence, archeological research suggests that the beginning of Ethiopian history lies in the prehistoric period. Some of the earliest evidence of human existence has been found in the vast array of stone tools and other functional implements and worked artifacts found throughout Ethiopia. Examples include the flanks of Wachacha, a vast volcanic mountain near Addis Ababa in the Ethiopian Lake District. Early humans had also settled on the rims of the volcanic craters found in several areas not far south of the capital and used the black volcanic glass "obsidian" to create razor-sharp tools while camping near the Rift Valley lakes. In southwest Ethiopia, decorated ceramics and metal implements have been found in association with stone tools. Other evidence of stone industries has been found in Djebel Djinn in the Horn. In 1974, one of the earliest hominids was found in Hadar, in the Afar desert. Named "Lucy" by foreigners and "Denqenash" by Ethiopians, this female ancestor of the human race has been determined by archaeologists to have lived three and a half million years ago.

Village farming communities developed in Ethiopia during the Neolithic period. In the fourth millennium B.C., agriculture, which may well have emerged independently in several places in the world, extended to Ethiopia from the western Sudan, possibly as part of the expansion of this knowledge into the northeastern region of Africa from Egypt. There is also the possibility that after 3,000 B.C. peoples to the west of the area moved into what is now Wellega, and thence onto the plateau, bringing agriculture with them. There is abundant evidence that there were different durations of the Ethiopian Stone Age cultures. For instance, the Watta people of Ethiopia were related to the hunting groups of northeastern and eastern Africa. The Agau are an example of an early population found today in the northern and central areas of the Abyssinian highland plateau. The Agau are noted for their pioneering discovery and development of new strains of plants and the domestication of the donkey and breeding of mules in the region.

The plateau peoples diversified into three main groups, which linguistic and other anthropologists refer to as the Central Agau and the Western and Eastern Cushites. Towards the end of the second millennium a population explosion occurred in Ethiopia, a result of the introduction of new techniques to overcome problems associated with the changing physical environment. As a result, the Cushitic population who resided in the southern fringes expanded and fanned out through Uganda, Kenya, Tanganyika, and beyond. Subsequent migrations of the Bantu-speaking peoples also changed the population dynamics of Ethiopia and all other African societies to the south. Scholars have argued that the Cushitic people are the architects of the phallic stones found between southern Ethiopia and the coastal territories of northeast and eastern Africa. These developments served as the basis for the emergence of states in the Ethiopian region.

THE OROMO

The Oromo of Ethiopia, lived in the highlands of Bali and, more likely, in areas now within the borders of the Somali Republic. Oral traditions carried out by the Oromo ascertain that they came from the Borana region of southwestern Ethiopia, and many go on pilgrimages to the "Land of the Abba Muda," the home of their spiritual leader, in the northern Borana region of southwestern Ethiopia. Oromo traditions also attest to population translocations to southern parts of Ethiopia. The Azebu and Raia Oromo are thus believed to have moved west from the coast of the Gulf of Aden to their present home. By the fourteenth and fifteenth centuries, strong Abyssinian monarchs pressured the Oromo to move west and southwest into relatively inhospitable saltpans and lava fields and towards the boulder and sand deserts in the vicinity of Lake Rudolph. Another Oromo group migrated in a southerly direction, leaving descendants along present-day Kenya's Tana River. Some Oromo groups, however, did develop into powerful monarchical states. The Oromo have remained notable for their cavalry, whose exploits are featured in the literature and oral fables of Ethiopian military and political tales. The relationships between the different Oromo or Galla peoples have been very complex, and some have argued that, despite numerous similarities, there is also a great deal of difference between the Wallegga Galla, the "Ittu" Galla of Arusi, and the "Cottu" Galla of Harar. Essentially, the Galla are an assembly of various peoples. Many Galla groups acted either independently or in alliance with the Ethiopian provincial nobility—and often in the service of the sometime hapless throne—reinforcing the centrifugal tendencies of provincialism and internecine struggles. The absence of a central authority made these communities vulnerable to invading forces, ultimately leading to new population dispersal. In 1766, civil war broke out, resulting in the beginning of the "age of the princes," which lasted until 1855. During this time, the state dissolved into its provincial components. These components in turn became involved in an endless and ultimately inconclusive struggle for supremacy. This period was followed by the rise of numerous provincial dynasties, which competed fiercely for national ascendancy until the middle of the nineteenth century. During this period, each province had its own king, and people felt loyalty to their own province, not to a country called Ethiopia.

The decline of the Gondar monarchy, noted for its establishment of the city that represented a new chapter in Ethiopian urban culture, especially in the construction of impressive castles and churches, also led to an increase in Galla influence and domination. Once Ethiopia's largest city and a center of religion and art, Gondar served as the capital of Ethiopia from ca. 1635 to 1867. In order to cement its alliance with certain Galla groups, the royal family resorted to political marriages. The legitimacy of the Gondar monarchy, already weakened by the religious apostasy of earlier emperors, was eroded further by the monarchy's connection with the Galla and Islam. Some Ethiopian nobles occupying their Christian Solomonic throne were unhappy with the affiliation to the Galla, since the latter were becoming predominantly Muslim. When it became obvious that the throne had become an instrument of Galla power, the position of the monarchy became untenable. The last emperor with any semblance of power was Iyoas (1755–69), who was half Galla and entirely dependent on Galla support.

THE SHOA

One province remained aloof from the internecine warfare occurring throughout this period and thus profited in political terms, as the province was able to produce a dynasty that eventually laid claim to the Solomonic throne. Shoa, also spelled Shewa, is the southernmost province of Ethiopia and was the most heterogeneous of the ancient Ethiopian provinces, with several ethnic and religious groups striving to maintain a precarious political balance. The unification of the province was accomplished under a Christian dynasty, which waged hegemonic warfare until the end of the eighteenth century. During the reign of Sahle Selassie (1813–47), Shoa incorporated large territories to the east, west, and south, and its ruler styled himself "King of Shoa and the Galla." The Christian rulers of Shoa, seeking to minimize resistance, abandoned a policy of punitive excursion, substituting it with one of inducements designed to persuade local chiefs to accept Christianity. Christian converts were abundantly rewarded with gifts and recognition of their local status. On the other hand, where Islam had deep roots, local Muslim chiefs were allowed to retain their position as long as they acknowledged the overall supremacy of the Christian rulers of Shoa.

The Shoa "age of the princes" came to a close in the middle of the nineteenth century. A new emperor, Tewodros, bore the responsibility of ending the internecine struggle by restoring the authority of the Solomonic throne over the provincial dynasties while emerging as the unchallenged ruler of Ethiopia. Tewodros successfully broke down the traditional divisions of Ethiopia into smaller administrative units governed by officials of his choice. He also realized that the strength of the nobles rested on their control of local army units who made up a national Ethiopian army. These units comprised soldiers from different provinces who served under crown appointees and received salaries from the imperial treasury. Although Tewodros was a devout Christian, he often collided with powerful and profoundly conservative forces including the Ethiopian Church and clergy. Hard-pressed for the funds he needed to maintain his large army, Tewodros curtailed the privilege of tax exemption enjoyed by the church. He also faced new challenges from the Galla, who resumed their raids to lay claim to the Ethiopian countryside. After a brief provincial contest, the Solomonic throne was claimed by the ruler of the Tigre province, who was crowned king of kings in 1872 under the title of Yohannes IV. Yohannes as the king of kings reigned in both provinces of Shoa and Gojjam.

During what some describe as the Ethiopian Dark Ages, ca. 960, a non-Christian princess, Yodit ("Gudit"), usurped the Ethiopian royal throne and reigned for 40 years over the kingdom; she transmitted the crown to her descendants. During the next century, the last of Yodit's successors were overthrown by Mara Takla Haymanot, an Agaw overlord who founded the Zagwe dynasty and married a female descendant of Axumite monarchs ("son-in-law") or previous ruler. One of the highlights of this dynasty was the reign of Gebre Mesqel Lalibela, in whose reign the stone churches of Lalibela were carved. The Zagwe dynasty's capital was in Roha, also referred to as Lalibela in honor of the city's most famous monarch and saint. Lalibela remains important in modern day Ethiopia for its religious and architectural contributions. The churches of Lalibela were excavated from blocks of rock left isolated by deep surrounding trenches. Constructed ca. 1250, the 11 churches are found in 3 distinct groups, each church differing widely in size, color of rock, and style of architecture, and can be reached in modern era by subway, bridges, and tunnels. The Ethiopians believed that the difficult and complicated feat of excavating as opposed to constructing a church was possible with the help of holy angels.

Archeological finds, monuments, and some short inscriptions dating from the fifth or the sixth century B.C. have shown a succession of civilizations existing in northern Ethiopia even before the rise of the famous Aksumite civilization. Yeha in northern Tigre and Matara are examples of the several important sites where monuments, inscriptions, pottery, and bronze tools have been found. The craftworks of Yeha, like that of Aksum, and other historical cultural features of ancient Ethiopia, such as the monolithic churches of Lalibela and the castles of Gondar, were all works of local craftsmen.

CULTURAL INFLUENCES FROM ARABIA

The Ethiopian cultural heritage, epigraphy, and languages have also been influenced by migrations and "invasions" from southern Arabia, although this proved secondary to Bantu migration from the south. Movements of people from Arabia began in the first millennium B.C. These migrations were preceded by several centuries of influx of Sabaen traders and farmers from across the Red Sea into northern Ethiopia, or what is present-day Eritrea. The remains of old cities and trade routes are scattered throughout the culturally synonymous Eritrea and northern Tigre.

Following the rise of Islam in Arabia, Muslim power spread via the Red Sea coast and lowlands, forcing the Aksumites to retreat into mountainous strongholds. As Islam spread northward into Egypt, the Ethiopian Christian empire became increasingly politically if not culturally and commercially isolated from the outside world. Other examples of cross-cultural impact were the Alexandrian influences found at Yeha. Ancient Greek and Egyptian literature referred to the Ethiopian region as the land of Punt, a semimythical source of gold and riches somewhere in or near the eastern Horn of Africa. The literature, objets d'art, and inscriptions from Middle Eastern countries banish any doubt of the significance of Ethiopia to its neighbors. Recent works also reveal that there was also considerable trade with Arabia and the kingdoms of the Upper Nile.

The legend of the Queen of Sheba is also of high significance in Ethiopian history. While in Ethiopia, she was revered as an Ethiopian queen named Makeda; in ancient and medieval Palestine and Arabia it was widely believed that the renowned Queen of Sheba was actually an ancient Arabian queen named Belkis, and that the Yemenite Kingdom of Himyar was her ancestral domain. However, Ethiopian legends, archeological discoveries, and various historical tracts leave little doubt that Ethiopia was in fact the motherland of the Queen of Sheba, one of history's most regal figures and the source of the ruling dynasty in Ethiopia at that time. Her legacy as an historical phenomenon will be further examined, as her significance or relevance to modern Ethiopia can hardly be overemphasized.

The *Kebra Negast*, or *Book of the Glory of Kings* described how the Ark of the Covenant was brought to Ethiopia, and how Solomon seduced Sheba, who, according to the story of Amlak's mother, Queen Makeda, was called to the throne in the tenth century B.C. Feeling inadequate for the task, she journeyed to Jerusalem to observe and learn from the wise and beneficent rule of King

Solomon. The two royalties had a relationship, and the product was a son, Menelik I. Menelik in turn traveled to Jerusalem twice—when he became of age and when Solomon as the king of Ethiopia anointed him. Because of these events, Ethiopians became "the chosen people," an honor reinforced by their acceptance of Christianity. The offspring of Solomon and Sheba, Menelik I, was the founder of the Aksumite civilization. The restored Solomonic lineage started in 1270 with Emperor Yekuno's declaration to be the lineal descent Menelik I, offspring of King Solomon and Queen Makeda (Queen of Sheba or Queen of Saba). All succeeding Ethiopian rulers confirmed having full filial rights and obligations by birth to Yekuno Amlak and, by that means, to King Solomon and Queen Makeda. During the high point of the restored Solomonic dynasty, strict regulations were set over all the Christian territorial division of the kingship and its surrounding areas. A series of successful military operations against Muslim provinces gave the dynasty power over the trade routes to the Red Sea. The political and economic achievements of this dynasty continued until the modern era. It should be noted that Haile Selassie, the last emperor of Ethiopia, traced his heritage back to Menelik I.

THE IMPACT OF CHRISTIANITY AND ANCIENT AKSUM

The core of the traditional state of Ethiopia originally centered on the ancient city-state of Aksum in what is the present-day Tigre province. Sometime between the first and third centuries A.D., *The Periplus of the Erythraen Sea*, an ancient writing of global significance consisting of 66 chapters written by a Greek sailor, a Roman subject living in Egypt, provided an insight into the rich commercial heritage of Africa, notably Azania. The text included in the log of the journeys of his vessels, notes on trade, and other first-hand description also included a vivid description of Aksum's port of Adulis. The writer of the *Periplus* cited the considerable imports, which included sheets of soft copper, small axes, a little wine from Italy, gold and silver plates for the kings, military cloaks, Indian iron, steel, and cotton cloth. The text described the totems of lions along with ceremonial umbrellas as having important political symbols. At its greatest extent Aksum was able to unify the principalities of north Tigre, and toward the end of the third century A.D., three regions of western Arabia were included in the Aksumite Territory. The empire also controlled shipping in the Red Sea, especially when the kingdom of Meroe to the west was destroyed in war. Meroe, which had thrived before Aksum, did not fully recover.

King Ezana of Aksum (320–356 A.D.) occupies a vital place in Ethiopian history. Near the end of his reign the Aksumite king converted to Christianity, thus becoming the first African king to embrace this faith and to have made

Christianity the official religion of his empire. The story is rooted in the rule of Ezana's father, King Ella Amida, who had raised his totemic symbol in the form of black basalt steel in the capital city of ancient Meroe. The kings of Aksum produced coins in bronze, silver, and gold. Precious crowns of former emperors were kept in the cathedral church of St. Mary of Zion. The emperor Yohannes presented most of these in the nineteenth century. The church was destroyed by marauding Muslim warriors in the sixteenth century and was not rebuilt until the seventeenth and eighteenth centuries. Other illustrations of Aksumite civilizations include the large irrigation reservoir of Mai-Shum, locally known as the Queen of Sheba's pool. There are also sites of tombs; one, which lies to the west of Aksum, is ascribed to the legendary monarch Menelik I.

Aksum eventually fell into decline but the Christian church it had adopted survived the ruin. Contact with the rest of the world in early times came through the trade routes. Because these routes had always been the lifelong routes of progress, without the free interchange of ideas nations stagnated and development stopped. The trade market declined with the expansion of Persian influence over the Red Sea. The rise of Islam and the jihad, or holy wars, which followed also contributed to the decline of Aksum. As the lineal predecessor of modern Ethiopia, Aksum was based on trade and conquest, rose to prominence in the first two or three centuries of the Christian era, came into major focus during the sixth century B.C., flourished between the first and eighth centuries A.D., and was finally decimated in 970 A.D. by hostile neighboring groups. It was during the Aksumite era that the inhabitants of the state began to refer to themselves as Abyssinians and their preeminent leader as the king of kings or emperor. The Aksumites comprised an amalgam of the Cushite inhabitants of northern Ethiopia and the "Semite" colonizers who had crossed the Red Sea from southern Arabia to settle in the area. Abyssinia maintained relatively close trading links with the Roman Empire, and this might have contributed to the adoption of Christianity as the official religion during the middle of the fourth century. From this period onwards, the Christian religion and the Ge'ez language—the language of the church—became the vehicles through which Abyssinian culture was spread to conquered peoples towards the southern region, the center of the plateau where a fusion of Aksumite and Cushite population resided and also the large population of Agaw-speaking people. The society that emerged was commonly referred to as Abyssinian. Ge'ez, the precursor of Ethiopia's three major Semitic languages and the liturgical language of the church, as earlier indicated is no longer in popular use. The relation of Ge'ez to the Amharic, the modern lingua franca, is rather like that of Latin's relation to Romance languages.

From the time of its initial collapse in 970 until 1135, the Christian empire fell on hard times. From the north came new threats from Muslim Arabs; Muslim Somalis threatened it from the southeast and from the south; and other civilizations in their adherence to the worship of traditional gods also threatened the Ethiopian Christian state. By 1135, the original state has been pushed to the south and west but was able to reconstitute itself, albeit in a weakened form. Between the early fourteenth and fifteenth centuries, the state once again became strong enough to embark on political and cultural expansion. In this phase, dominated by Amhara kings, the Amhara-Christian culture was diffused to all regions of the state where the conquered were forcibly Amharized and forced to abandon animist beliefs and embrace Coptic Christianity. Amharic remains the first official language of Ethiopia today (English is the second). The Ethiopian state and the northeast African region remains the only place on the African continent where Christianity emerged and survived as a truly indigenous creed. European missionaries introduced the religion to other parts of the continent.

The Abyssinian society came into historical focus through the writings of its own clergy towards the end of the thirteenth century. By this time, the integration of the Agaw had progressed enough to make possible the creation of an Agaw political dynasty. The dynasty was called Zagwe and was to rule the highland kingdom from about the middle of the eleventh century until 1270. Another dynasty, which was based in the Amhara province and claimed descent from Solomon, attempted to gain control of Aksum. In 1270, the Zagwe were overthrown and the historical reign of the Solomonic dynasty began. During these centuries, Ethiopian power for the most part proved adequate in repelling attacks on its own territory. From time to time, it brought large areas of the south and southeastern parts of the plateau under the sway of the Solomonic throne. In many instances, however, this influence was indirect and did not last for a long period.

MAPPING ETHIOPIAN CULTURE: ICONOGRAPHY AND LITERATURE, ART, AND MUSIC

Until recently, the traditional art of Christian Ethiopia has remained relatively unknown beyond the confines of its borders. The earliest known specimens of pictorial art in Ethiopia are the rock carvings of animal scenes found in some northern parts of the country, including Gobedra and Kohaito. Ethiopian artists have produced a unique and prodigious body of church murals, manuscripts, miniatures, and panel paintings on wood. Ethiopian icons depict a wide variety of sacred images used for devotional purposes both as apotropaic objects, that is, having the power to ward off evil or bad luck, or as the significant part of votive offerings, expressing a desire or a pledge to a specific saint or the Virgin Mary. The small folding panels and diptychs in textile or leather bags were also worn suspended from the neck to ward off negative forces. From the seventeenth century onwards, the practice of taking an oath before an icon became commonplace. In the seventeenth and eighteenth centuries, double-faced diptych pendants or two painted or carved panels hinged together with suspension cylinders emerged.

Beginning with the introduction of Christianity in the fourth century, the evolution of Ethiopian Christian owed much to the church, which commissioned painters, many of whom were also ecclesiastics. As early as the seventh century, wall paintings and hagiographic narratives often depicted the Virgin Mary and the saints as living objects with the power to see, talk, and take action like cure the sick or protect the weak. By successfully repulsing all attempts at permanent conquest by external powers, Ethiopian creativity has continued to flourish against all odds, providing uniquely African forms even while responding to a variety of outside influences.

Ethiopian art also reveals evidence of both the Eastern and Western worlds that include Byzantine, Greek, Coptic, Nubian, and Armenian cultures. It also featured elements of Indian and Islamic cultural influences. Although active manuscript illustration began at about the fourteenth century, between fifteenth and twentieth centuries several developments, including the arrival of the Jesuits and the discovery of new maritime routes, helped stimulated the growth of Ethiopian art with the introduction of Western European cultural influences and iconography. Some of these Ethiopian icons were featured in the sacred painting and interpretations of the art expressed in fervent confirmation of the Christian faith. The thwarting of Muslim invaders also led to a reconstruction project that featured the rebuilding of churches and monasteries and a renewed vigor for strong-colored, proportioned paintings and illustrated manuscripts, especially beginning in the second half of the fifteenth century. Some of the large churches and monasteries also possess precious processional crowns, giant crosses, prayer sticks with intricately patterned handles, beautifully ornamented censers, processional umbrellas, sistra, and metal book covers.

Ethiopian art is didactic, driven by a desire to convey to believers the drama and narratives of the gospels and the activities of the hallowed personages, and is handed down from one generation of painters to another by training, then augmented and expanded through local oral traditions. The combination of continuity and flexibility resulted in a cultural renaissance, or Ethiopianization. By the mid-fifteenth century, the translation of homilies in honor of saints and patriarchs venerated by the Coptic Church combined with collections of miracles wrought by saints and several biographies of the Zagwe kings all contributed immensely to the flourishing of Ethiopian literature. These manuscripts are also often accompanied by beautifully colored paintings. The later nineteenth and early twentieth century, often described as the last phase in the development of traditional Ethiopian art, saw the flourishing of illuminated manuscripts, illustrated books on parchment, a tradition that has endured for centuries. Ethiopic manuscript art reached a high degree of perfection between the fourteenth and eighteenth centuries both in calligraphy and illustration. These consist of vellum—fine parchment made from animal skin.

Literature, art, and music and most facets of organized expression were dominated and shaped by the ecclesiastical, as the religion of the state largely determined the scope of artistic creation. Hymns were composed in honor of Christ, the virgin, saints, and angels. There were also many secular poems and songs and other forms of oral traditions, which have suffered from a relative lack of critical appreciation as a result of the hegemony of Christian written literature. In this category are exhortations and panegyrics, laudatory songs and poems in honor of imperial rulers or as forms of social commentary, and other forms of affectations. Although Christianity was not the only source of Byzantine and Ethiopian art, it not only helped mold it but also prescribed its task and purpose. The popularity of musical genres such as the *deggwa* church music or chants and the *janhoy* or royal chants suggests that Ethiopian music, liturgical chant, and hymnography still require better appreciation. The musical instruments of Ethiopia include the *Kerar* "lyre" of 6 or 10 strings. There is the one-string *masanko,* and the *Kabaro,* or tambourine was one of the earliest and most widespread instruments. Ethiopian musical occasion is incomplete without the prayer-stick or *Makwamiya,* which plays a prominent part in beat, alongside the rhythmic hand clapping.

Until the early twentieth century, formal education was confined to a system of religious instruction organized and presented under the aegis of the Ethiopian Orthodox Church. Such schools were also responsible for preparing individuals for the clergy and for other religious duties and positions. In the major centers of Amhara and Tigre, the schools also provided religious education to the children of the nobility and to the sons of peasants associated with elite families. Islamic schools, however, provided education for some members of the Muslim population. A few missionary schools had been established in the late nineteenth century, and these were often accessible to interdenominational and multireligious communities.

LITERATURE

Until the nineteenth century, when books and literature in Amharic began to come off the printing presses, the term "literature" was reserved only for literary production in the Ge'ez language. The Red Sea served as the conduit for Egyptian, Hellenistic, and Byzantine influence upon Ethiopian literary beginnings. The introduction of Christianity into Ethiopia saw the religion emerging as the focus and expression of all literary creation. Christianity also became the filter through which both old and new facets of thought had to pass or gain acceptance. The Ethiopianization of literature included translations, adaptations, and transformation into the spirit and ambience of Christian Abyssinian. The *Fetha Nagast (Legislation of the Kings)* is one of such documents subjected to a very high level of rethinking and modification and have to this day retained their value and practical importance in Ethiopia. The *Fetha* forms the basis of the customary law in some regions and has also inspired some of the civil and penal law that has been enacted in Ethiopia over the years. The *Fetha Negest* remained the official supreme law in Ethiopia until 1931, when Emperor Haile Selassie I helped enacted a modern-style constitution.

Although written Amharic literature became widely recognized in the seventeenth century, it only achieved full emancipation during the nineteenth century, when King Theodore gave the greatest impulse and encouragement to its production. Created as a plank in his general program of imperial unification, this development also affected government policies for a long time. As the influence of Amharic spread, Ge'ez was relegated to the liturgical sphere. By establishing a major printing press in Addis Ababa, Emperor Menelik II had opened the door for the subsequent proliferation of printing establishments in the major cities of Addis and Asmara. The presses have turned out books, pamphlets, periodicals, and newspapers.

Notable authors of the early modern era include Ato Kebbede Mikael and Ato Mangestu Lemma, who wrote on education, health, and other social and political issues of the day; Aleka Tayye authored the popular *The History of the People of Ethiopia*; Afework wrote *Life of Menelik II*; Lebb Walad Tarik authored a pioneering novel in Amharic; Heruy Walda Sellasie created a study of the reign of King John IV coupled with biographical sketches and political reflections of notable Ethiopians; Blatta Mars'e Hazan published a series on Amharic grammar; Ato Ba'emnal Gebre-Amlak wrote on the linguistic origins and growth of Amharic. Other notable contributions came from Ras Bitwodded Makonnen Endalkatchew, a former prime minister. Both Germatchew Tekla-Hawaryat and Kebbede Mika'el devoted their talents to the theatre and the novel. Ato Mangestu Lemna also made notable contribution to Ethiopian poetry.

Ethiopians have also critically engaged with the best of European literature and intellectual traditions. The writings of popular figures such as William Shakespeare and Johann Goethe, and other works like *Aesop's Fables*, *The Arabian Nights*, and *Pilgrim's Progress*, were all translated into Amharic and made available for educational purposes. Other popular publications in Ethiopia included literary features on global figures such as Mahatma Gandhi. Other popular subjects of the modern era that Ethiopian publication circles have focused on include such international issues as race, identity, power relations, civil rights, diplomatic history, and Ethiopia's place in modern African global experience. Amharic newspapers and periodicals also include *Aimero* and *Berhanenna Salam*. The first official gazette is *Negarit Gazeta*. Contemporary daily newspapers of Addis Ababa include *Addis Zaman* and *Ya-Ityopya Dems*.

Ethiopia is also notable for its architectural distinctiveness, of which the Ethiopian stelae rank as highest of the land's indigenous art. The multistoried towering structures are pre-Christian, serving as gravestones and memorials. Working, moving, and erecting these beautifully sculptured richly decorated structures required immense technical skills. The largest obelisk standing at Aksum is nearly 70 feet high, while the biggest of all measured about 110 feet in height and thus was once the largest upright monolith in the world. An Aksum obelisk of 24 meters was taken to Rome in 1937 and erected at the Piazzadi Porta capena. The fascist dictator Benito Mussolini, in his effort to create a new Roman Empire, had removed the tallest of the famous historic Axum obelisks and placed it in front of what became the Ministry of Italian African Territories. The obelisk was part of Ethiopian treasure that remain confined to European museums, library, and art collections. Citizens, scholars, and friends of Ethiopia have launched modern-day lobby groups to clamor for the return of this heritage and iconography of the origins of Ethiopian civilization. The obelisk was in Italy for more than 70 years until it was returned in 2005.

The elaborate architecture of the Aksum monoliths and churches was exclusive to the ecclesiastical and royal prestige buildings. The average community members in smaller settings such as the villages live in modest huts—the round *tukul* or *agdo* with cone-shaped roofs. Relatively prosperous folks live in *tukuls*—more elaborate cylindrical wooden structures that are often strengthened by stones. Village chiefs and political elites have been known to favor elaborate houses with upper stories. In the major towns, officials, ministers, and noted citizens have often invested in European-style modernist structures.

The national dress of Ethiopia is the toga-like white *shamma*, a rectangular shawl of usually more than three feet in width, hand-woven and made of cotton. Both men and women wear the shamma, although the manner in which it is draped by women differs from that of men. Men wear white jodhpurs, which are tight fitting from knee to ankle. Women on the other hand wear shirt-like dresses with very full skirts of ankle length. Both dresses are often made of beautifully colored materials. On feast days, the same outfit is worn but adorned with a wide red stripe close to the hem and called the *jano*. Underneath the shammas, men of distinction wear a silk tunic, or *kamis*, stylized with embroidery. Both men and women may wrap a cloak, or *barnos*, over their shoulders, especially in cool breezy atmospheres.

The Ethiopian national dish is *injera*, a local bread, and *wat ot zegeni*, which is a kind of curried stew made of beef, mutton, or chicken to which some hard-boiled eggs have been added and which has been seasoned with red pepper or *berbere* and other spices. This is on occasion served with the *tedj* or *mies*, a honey-mead fermented drink, or the *tall*, a popular Ethiopian beer.

Names or naming ceremonies are very important in Ethiopian traditions. Children in the Tigrinya-speaking areas generally received a baptismal name. Amharas often bear their father's name as the second element. They also receive in addition a secular and a baptismal name. If a child has died or some other disaster has befallen the family, the newborn baby will be called Kassa, meaning compensation. Common secular names for men include Hagos—joy, Desta—pleasure, Mebrahtu—light, and Tesfaye—my hope. For women, favorite names include Ababa—flower, Terunesh—you are pure, Hagosa—joy, Zawditu—crown, and Belainesh—you are superior. Typical Christian names are compounds with Gebre—servant of, Walda—son of, Amete—maid of, Walatta—daughter of, Tefa—hope of, Teklam—plant of, Haile—power of, and Habte—gift of. Popular examples of such names include Gebre-Yesus—servant of Jesus, Amete-Maryam—maid of Mary, Walatta-Sion—Daughter of Zion, Habte-Mikael—gift of Michael, and Walda-Ab-son—son of Ab-son.

NOTE

1. W.E.B. DuBois, "Inter-racial Implications of the Ethiopian Crisis. A Negro View," *Foreign Affiars* 4, no. 1 (October 1935): 85–86.

2

Globalization and Modernization to Late Nineteenth Century

From the middle of the seventh century A.D., the rise of Islam and the subsequent disruption of the Red Sea trade triggered the decline of Aksum. Islam continued to pose a great threat from the southeast in the form of a string of Muslim principalities that had emerged from the ninth century onwards. The series of military clashes between Christian Ethiopia and these Islamic forces served as the most important factor in Ethiopian history prior to the fifteenth century. By the end of the fifteenth century, the Christian kingdom had for all practical purposes imposed its will over its enemies. Around the same time, an international quest commenced for a legendary Christian king of superlative wealth and power believed to rule somewhere beyond the Muslim crescent, which shut Europe off from Asia. The legend of King Prester John contributed to the construction of a national image of Ethiopia in the international arena by providing an impetus for crusading powers to intervene against the spread and influence of Islam and in the process to lay claim to the vast riches of the hidden kingdom. This intervention was to lead several European observers to play a part in the history of Ethiopia during this period, through diplomatic and religious correspondence as well as the exchange of emissaries between Ethiopia and Europe. In addition to the unifying character of the Ethiopian monarchy, which was reinforced by the Christian faith, an indelible sense of identity manifested itself in the form of a continued general unity and in the fight for an independent Ethiopia. Except for the Italian invasion and occupation from 1936–40, this attitude prevailed in Ethiopia throughout the era of colonialism in Africa.

Among the many merchant visitors to Ethiopia in the fourteenth and fifteenth centuries were the Venetians, who facilitated the availability in Europe of geographical information about northeast Africa. A popular geographical document of 1457 known as the Fra Mauro's map and a succession of writings of the classical era all bore evidence of Ethiopia's political and commercial notoriety. The papacy tried to establish contact through Ethiopian monks in Jerusalem. A Spanish king wrote to Emperor Zara Yakob (1434–68), described as a fanatical Christian who not only encouraged the writing of books, the building of churches, and the instruction of the public through teaching but also helped established religious nationalism and Ethiopian identity. Yakob was a prolific author of numerous theological and philosophical books. He was also noted for reorganizing the government, suppressing a provincial rebellion, and forming an army of spies used to seek out those who were opposed to his convictions. His influence was felt even in the most distant and independent regions of ancient Ethiopia. The chiefs and kings in the south and east were obliged to acknowledge him with tribute.

THE PORTUGUESE AND JESUIT FACTOR

The legend of Prester John was of great interest to the kings of Portugal from the time of Prince Henry the Navigator, and they soon established diplomatic relations with Ethiopia. Their ambassador, Peros da Covilha, reached Shewa in 1493. In 1509, the Empress Helena sent an Armenian, "Matthew," back to Portugal as her ambassador. However, the desire to foster combined operations against Islam was to give way to misconceptions in Lisbon and Rome that the Ethiopian Church was anxious to accept papal jurisdiction. This led to a disastrous phase in Ethio-European relations, a legacy of which was the lack of trust between Ethiopians and foreigners for a long period. This suspicion was borne out in its most vivid form at the time of the nineteenth century European scramble for Africa by a series of Italian invasions and a short period of British military administration, which immediately followed the collapse of the Italian occupation.

The period from 1529 to 1632 was an extremely turbulent one for the "Solomonic" state of Ethiopia. In 1557 the Turks captured the Eritrean seaport of Massawa, penetrating the frontiers of the Tigre highlands. The Turks also provided groups such as the Afar and Somali peoples with arms, thus enabling their ability to pressure Abyssinia from the east. The Eastern Cushitic Oromo also penetrated as far north as Shoa and into Begemder and Gojjam. Firearms were first introduced into Ethiopia during the reign of Emperor Lebna Dengel (1508–1540), a factor that played an important role in the outbreak of fighting in the sixteenth century.

In the first half of the sixteenth century, Ethiopia suffered a devastating Muslim invasion led by Ahmad Ibn Ghazi (1506–43) also known as Ahmad Gran (or Gurey) ("Ahmed the left-handed"), who declared a jihad (holy war) against the Ethiopians. The Ethiopians sought military assistance from Portugal to repel the Islamic invaders, but the latter group subsequently sought to impose Catholicism on the country. Led by Christopher da Gama (son of Vasco da Gama, discoverer of the route around South Africa to India), a Portuguese force of 400 soldiers arrived in 1541 and successfully repelled Ahmad Gran. Jesuits missionaries, who had hoped to make religious capital out of the atmosphere of Aksumite-Portuguese friendship, entered Ethiopia and were well received by its grateful rulers, but subsequently became embroiled in social and political struggles in the period between 1606 and 1632. Emperor Za Dengel (Asnaf Sagad II 1603–1604) and Susenyos (1607–1632) were secretly converted, but under the rule of Emperor Fasiladas (1632–1667), the Jesuits fell out of favor and were expelled. Although the future of Ethiopian allegiance to Alexandria was secured, the Jesuit interim (1500–1633) continued to influence the course of Ethiopian history. Pedro Páez (1564–1622), the Jesuit missionary who was described as "gentle, learned, considerate," was highly influential in facilitating the spiritual and intellectual engagement of Ethiopian rulers with Catholic traditions. Some of the Catholic churches he designed are still standing and were an influence on Ethiopian architecture. His replacement, Alfonso Mendez, who arrived in January 1624, proved to be less tolerant of Ethiopian traditional practices, and he soon proclaimed the primacy of Rome while condemning local practices.

Between the seventeenth century and the middle of the nineteenth century, regional controversies reigned over the Catholic infringement on Ethiopian Orthodox traditions and most importantly over the diverse doctrines regarding the nature of Christ. Two of the traditions introduced by the mission of the Portuguese Jesuits included the Qebat (anointing), which states that Jesus became a perfect man and a perfect God by the anointing of the Holy Spirit in the Jordan River and not upon the incarnation. The Tsegga (son of grace) on the other hand, expressed the view that Christ had undergone three births—eternal birth, of the Son from the Father; genetic birth, of the Son from the Virgin Mary; and birth from the Holy Spirit during baptism. This controversial distinction continued until the reign of Emperor Tewodros II (1855–1868), who tried to forge Ethiopian unity by enacting a decree banning the politics of religious doctrinal crisis. The final resolution of this theological dispute came during the reign of Emperor Yohannes IV (1872–1889). As is true with all Oriental Orthodox churches, the teachings of the Ethiopian Church are founded on the apostles' experience of the Lord Jesus Christ as the Creator and Saviour of the World.

Although Ethiopia was ultimately able to repress a series of Islamic jihads in 1843, this merely cleared the way for massive immigration by the Galla people, whose adherence to either Christianity or Islam was nominal and whose pressure on the Ethiopian state continued for many decades. The Galla settled extensively all over the empire, including the homeland area of the Amhara, the dominant ethnic group in Solomonic times. The reign of Fasiladas (1632–1667) marked a significant departure from tradition for the Ethiopian monarchy, as the quasi-nomadic mode of life customarily led by Ethiopian emperors was abandoned and the royal court came to rest at a fixed site, the city of Gondar. The state apparently flourished from its capital at Gondar down into the early eighteenth century. However, the period from 1706 into the 1760s was marked by decline and eventual collapse. Fasiladas also began the processes of development that was to make Gondar the most important city in Ethiopia until the founding of Addis Ababa at the close of the nineteenth century. Fasilidas's rule forms the prelude to the modern history of Ethiopia. Historian Bahru Zewde has argued that the Industrial Revolution that transformed European society, starting from the end of the eighteenth century, ushered in a new pattern of relationship between Europe and Africa. In this regard, he continued, there were four distinct yet interrelated facets of European interest in Ethiopia—the commercial, the official, the missionary, and the scientific. With the advent of nineteenth-century imperialism, these European interests developed a rationale for colonial behavior in the guise of social Darwinism. The subsequent application of unequal military and scientific power had major implications upon the structuring of race, commerce, and international diplomacy throughout Africa. The theory that the capacity of the nation-state to compete in the modern world was dependent on the evolutionary "fitness" and "development" of its human and technical resources made Ethiopia an anomaly in a world that had defined Africa and Africans as the ward of the great European powers.

The period between 1769 and 1855 is known in Ethiopian history as the "age of the princes" (Zemene Mesafint), an era dominated by political crisis and provincialism. The decentralization of political power saw a decisive shift in power from the monarchy into feudal, regional compartments as local warlords and traditional nobility competed for supremacy. Some scholars have described the role of the emperor in the mid-nineteenth century as that of a puppet. Political power was divided among the nobles, led by the rulers of Begemder, of Gojjam, and of Simien men who sought to enlarge their territorial control. The level of civil strife also increased as the empire disintegrated into a series of pseudo-independent feudatories whose main allegiance was directed not to the monarchy, but rather to the Christian Church. As a result of these cultural, political, and military developments, Ethiopia entered the nineteenth century as a deeply divided political entity, facing challenges against traditional Abyssinian values and related specific politico-religious institutions. Although Orthodox Christianity was a dominant force among the ruling class, possession cults, headed by the *ibede gudo*, the supreme spiritual leader, predominated among the masses. The spread of Islam also continued in the areas under the influence of Galla migrants. In spite of these revolutionary changes, the most important development on the horizon was the expansionist influence of Egypt and Western European forces from the 1820s, especially on the western and northern borders. Between 1830 and 1900, Protestant and subsequently Catholic missionaries also established new links between Ethiopia and Europe.

By the 1770s the principal institutions of the Ethiopian state had collapsed. These institutions owed their ultimate origins to a classical period associated with the Aksumite Empire in the early centuries of the Christian era. They had evolved through an obscure period late in the first millennium and early in the second millennium A.D., to emerge under the Solomonic dynasty in the late thirteenth century. The Solomonic kings presided over an expanding and flourishing empire into the sixteenth century, profoundly influencing the Ethiopian state and church.

In 1855, the governor of Ye-Maru-Qimis defeated Ras Ali of Shoa, marking the beginning of the end of close to a century-long fratricidal conflict in the Abyssinian core. Kasa dedicated himself to crushing the kings of Tigre and Shoa. He subdued Tigre in 1855 and had himself crowned "King of Kings" in the traditional manner. He took the title of Emperor Theodore, claiming, according to one of the religious documents that form the basis of Ethiopian myth and the custom *Fikkere Iyesus* (the interpretation of Jesus), that he was a righteous, just, and popular king who would come to the throne after a period of divine punishment had been heaped upon the Abyssinians for their evil deeds. It was prophesied that this king would be called Theodore and that he would rule for 40 years, restoring Abyssinia to its former unity and greatness. This was the beginning of the modern Ethiopian Empire. Theodore or Tewodros began a process of imperial reconstruction, the primary stage of which was not concluded until 1878.

TEWODROS II (1855–1868)

Tewodros II embarked on reunification and development of the country by restoring one rule in the ancient heartlands of Ethiopia. He also developed a close relationship with the Christian Church with the ultimate goal of securing control of the monarch, the civil society, and national wealth. Tewodros' reign, however, witnessed tension between the church and the state over the disbursement of land tributes, a development that later broadened into a general dispute over the nature and scope of royal authority.

The emperor instituted two measures geared towards strengthening his imperial sovereignty. First, he fragmented traditional administrative divisions and thus deprived many local princes and kings of their bases of power. He also chose administrators for the reconstituted units among trusted officers in his military or members of the royal family. Second, Emperor Tewodros created a disciplined, professional state army equipped with modern firearms and artillery who drew regular salaries, clothes, and equipment for the first time. He often employed Europeans and Turks with military expertise to train his men. Tewodros' successful reign was ultimately defined by landmark achievements, including the introduction of administrative reforms and effective management of feuding nobles. He also initiated road construction and was recognized as a shrewd actor in matters of foreign policy. Some of his efforts included the attempt to preempt the spread of then British colonial sphere of influence in the Horn, and more importantly he was able to break the Egyptian hold on the economically vital Massawa, an Aksumite-era port on the Red Sea.

Eager to introduce European technology into his country, he initiated a series of diplomatic contacts with Europe, especially with Queen Victoria of England. He exploited the history of the Ethiopian Church to appeal to European Christendom to send Protestant missionaries. On the other hand, based on his fears of Catholic influence eroding his authority in the northern fringes of Ethiopia, Tewodros was repulsed by and expelled members of this latter Christian sect and their major allies, the French. Although his relationship with the Protestants was more amicable, his intensions were not entirely altruistic. He employed them in the manufacturing of armaments and restricted their proselytizing activities among the non-Christian Falashas. Some of the missionaries did not endear themselves to the king based on their cultural biases or insensitivity. Unable to effectuate his modernizing impulses, with his political fortunes and popularity waning, Tewodros expressed his frustration by holding British missionaries and diplomats captive in Magdala. The British sent an expedition of 32,000 soldiers led by General Napier, which clashed with Tewodros' army led by his general, Dejazmatch. Though the Ethiopian army, which numbered close to 3,000, was armed with matchlocks and percussion guns and put up a great fight beneath the towering rock face of Amba Magdala, they were no match for the rockets and Snider breech-loading rifles of the British. The British had also secured valuable support from Kasa Mercha of Tigre (the future Emperor Yohannes IV), who supplied the expedition with provisions and transportation. After securing victory in the battlefront, the British loaded 200 mules and 15 elephants with gold crowns, swords, altar slabs, and more than 400 manuscripts before burning Magdala to the ground. Tewodros, however, denied the British the satisfaction of capturing him by committing suicide. Some scholars argue that Tewodros did not lose to General Napier. Rather, they claim, the vast untamed country he had built defeated him as he had lost relevant influence over his officers and men in the provinces. The most significant political consequence of General Napier's campaign and the British triumph in the battle of Amba Magdala was the emergence of a new age of European colonial presence in northeast

Africa. In the face of these infringements, Ethiopia's diversity and extensive territoriality remained a vibrant aspect of its national history.

The reign of Emperor Tewodros II, which is still widely recognized as the precursor to the foundation of modern Ethiopia, was also marked by a conscious effort to strengthen the army's firepower. The emperor began the production of weapons in the country to complement the concentration of armory in Tigre. Defeat at the hands of British troops on April 17, 1868, led to the destruction of Ethiopia's arsenal and consequently the expansion of European imperial encroachment in northeast Africa. Upon Tewodros' defeat in 1868, Ras Kassa was crowned Emperor Yohannes IV in 1872. Yohannes' foremost general, Ras Alula, who became governor of the province of Hamasien and prince of Eritrea, also emerged as a very important figure in the modern history of Ethiopia and Eritrea as he helped undermined the ever-threatening Mahdist army. His role in Ethiopia's successful resistance of European imperialism is further examined below. In synopsis, Tewodros was unsuccessful in securing diplomatic recognition from the European powers that were already beginning to expand their interest in the northeastern region also known as the Horn of Africa.

YOHANNES IV

Theodore's centralization policies were continued by his successor Yohannes IV. Ethiopian supplies of arms and ammunitions increased tremendously during the reign of Yohannes IV (1872–1889). He purchased arms from both public and private European agents. Reports held that the emperor received a gift from European powers of 6 mortars, 6 howitzers with 400 rounds of ammunitions to match, 850 muskets and bayonets, 40,000 rounds of small arms ammunition, and 28 barrels of gunpowder as a reward for his signatory to treaties of neutrality and friendship. Growing firepower enabled Yohannes to achieve major victories in numerous military confrontations. Most of his efforts were directed towards territorial expansion; he pushed the periphery of his domain to the west from his capital in the Tigre region. He defeated a reputable Egyptian army at the battles of Gundet in November 1875 and Gura in March 1876. When another batch, this time a force of 15,000 well-armed troops with the support of the British, showed up an Ethiopian force of 60,000 men, most of who were at this time armed with rifles, routed them. The Ethiopian emperor captured about 20,000 Remingtons, the most modern rifles of the day, as well as a considerable amount of artillery, horses, mules, camels, and food supplies. Although he was able to impose his hegemony over much of the kingdom with the support of a strong, modern army, Yohannes' most outstanding achievements were in the field of foreign policy. He was ultimately able to secure a peace treaty with Egypt and subsequent trade agreements with Britain, whose colonial authority was dominant in the region. Yohannes also became a serious power to be reckoned with in the Horn of Africa, where he deterred European adventures into Ethiopia during the nineteenth-century European scramble for the continent.

The opening of the Suez Canal in 1869 brought dominion over the Red Sea coast into dispute as local authorities in the area of the canal and foreign interests struggle for its control. As a result, the Ottomans, the Egyptians, the British, and ultimately the Italians all laid claim to parts of Ethiopian territory. In spite of external encroachment in northeast Africa, domestic rivalry between the various royal households and provinces of Ethiopia continued unabated. While Emperor Yohannes and his general Ras Alula battled Islamic, European, and other foreign incursion, Menelik of Shewa Province, who had signed a treaty of friendship with the Italians and received a large consignment of rifles, was biding his time. The mounting costs of defending against Mahdist military expeditions into the kingdom continued, and in 1889 Emperor Yohannes was wounded and later died from a sniper's bullet during one such military confrontation. The throne passed on to the most powerful of the provincial rulers, Menelik II of Shoa, as decreed by the late ruler before his death.

During his reign, Yohannes IV tried but failed to establish a fully centralized monarchy. From his power base in the province of Tigre, he imported firearms by exploiting his proximity to the Red Sea coast. Ironically, this location also exposed the territories to external influence, especially with the emergence of European imperial interest in Africa in the second half of the nineteenth century.

MENELIK II OF SHOA

The period of Menelik's reign (1889–1914) is another important milestone in modern Ethiopian history. Not only did the era coincide with the consummation of European theories of imperialism and the scramble for African territories, with the partition sanctioned at the Berlin Conference, but the era was also marked, ironically, by the large-scale unification of Ethiopian national territory. Between 1872 and 1896, Menelik was able to double the territory under his control, occupying as many areas as were seized by European powers in the scramble for territories in the northeastern region. A combination of military and diplomatic campaigns in the Galla region, the sultanate of Harar, and the regions of Wellega, Wellamo, Jimma, Kaffa, and Gomma, led to their annexation and political realignment as part of Christian Ethiopia.

Menelik of Shoa, formerly known as Prince Sahle Mariam, was the most powerful and least tractable of the emperor's vassals. His reign was notable for the construction of a powerful army equipped with arms procured through numerous agents who were engaged in the extensive arms trade of his era. Menelik began to import arms fairly early in his career as the ruler of Shoa, and by the 1880s the trade had reached stupendous proportions, with weapons coming from the Italians and, later, the French. He then began the conquest of Galla territories to the east, west, and south of Shoa. The British ultimately opposed the arms trade between Europe and Ethiopia, as this ran counter to the crown's imperial ambitions in northeast Africa. The European powers also quarreled over suppression of the arms and slave trade to the Somali coast. The Italians emerged as the most aggressive imperial power coveting Ethiopia as a strategic outpost for her ambitions. Although Italy had concluded several independent treaties of "friendship and commerce" with King Menelik of Shoa between 1883 and 1887, there was disagreement over the implications of the agreement. Italy saw the treaties as a means of playing off one Abyssinian power against another, while Menelik on the other hand saw the arrangement as another vital avenue for securing much-needed arms and ammunition. In 1889, Menelik concluded the Treaty of Wichale with Italy, which officially recognized Menelik as emperor of Abyssinia and also granted his state duty-free privileges for any goods passing through the port of Massawa, a substantial loan, and a promise of future arms and military supplies. Portions of Ethiopia, namely the states of Bogos, Hamasen, Akale-Guzai, and parts of Tigre, were also ceded for Italian activities in return for financial and development assistance to Ethiopia.

Although the Treaty of Wichale appeared to be useful for both powers, Italy began to penetrate into Abyssinian territories from its base in Eritrea. Menelik later discovered that the treaty he had signed in both Italian and Amharic contained differing clauses relating to the disposition of diplomatic relations between the two states. While the Amharic version suggested that Abyssinia could use Italy as an agent in foreign relations if it desired, the Italian version claimed that Abyssinia was obliged to go through Italy in its foreign relations. Ethiopia had been duped into becoming a protectorate of the Italian nation.

On February 27, 1893, Menelik informed the European powers of his decision to reject the Italian proclamation. He declared, "Ethiopia has need of no one; she stretches out her hands unto God." When a war with Italy seemed imminent, Menelik issued a mobilization proclamation calculated to strengthen, in his words, the religious solidarity of the Ethiopian Church and the general community in the face of Italian aggression:

> Enemies have now come upon us to ruin the country and to change our religion . . . . Our enemies have begun the affair by advancing and digging into the country like moles. With the help of God I will not deliver up my country to them . . . . Today, you who are strong, give me of your strength, and you who are weak, help me by prayer.[1]

In response to this call, every *tukul* (hut) and village in every far-off glen of Ethiopia sent out his or her warriors. The first skirmish occurred in December

1895, and by March 1, 1896, at the battle of Adwa, the Ethiopians had gathered at least 70,000 rifles and 42 canons in the field. Described as one of the worst colonial disasters of modern history, 25,000 Italian army troops were defeated by the Ethiopians, who were able to raise a 100,000-strong diverse yet coherent military force. Victory for Ethiopia at the Battle of Adwa gave Menelik both domestic and international prestige and won the state new allies and admirers. The victory sent shock waves throughout Europe, causing the demise of the Italian government. The event also rendered Ethiopia exempt from the type of nineteenth-century colonial wars that raged all over Africa. Menelik also struck an alliance with the French, a diplomatic move that was followed by larger arms gifts from France to Ethiopia. At the end of the nineteenth century, not only the standing army but also the farmers of northern Ethiopia had been equipped with modern breach-loaders and plenty of cartridges and could be mobilized rapidly.

Ethiopia thus witnessed the culmination and consolidation of its vast territorial expansion into an empire, further reinforcing a traditional reputation entrenched in biblical and other narratives of antiquity. Ethiopia had also become the strongest indigenous power in Africa by far, with the potential to disturb the balance of power in the region, severely taxing the human and financial resources the various European metropolitan governments could afford on such excursions. Some have suggested that Ethiopia's foreign policy under Menelik is better understood as an aggressive or an equally imperial campaign of territorial acquisition along the western frontier of Ethiopia. They cite the 1889 Treaty of Ucciali (or Wichale), by which Emperor Menelik not only accepted Italy's colonization of Eritrea but also joined the Great Powers (Britain, France, and Italy) in expanding their territorial control. In this regard, the emperor's influence reached beyond Gondar and Shoa to include the Ogaden. Others suggest that Menelik's ambition was to secure his people's confidence and Ethiopian self-preservation on the one hand and the diplomatic support of European powers on the other. Menelik, however, subordinated his territorial aspirations in the Nile Valley for the promotion of good relations with the Islamic Khalifa, while frustrating European colonial designs for the Nile and its surrounding environs. Another counterargument on the parallels between European and Ethiopian imperialism suggest that the Coptic Church, as a transnational Christian body to which the Ethiopian authorities owed its religious hegemonic sanction, never raised an army to enforce Christianity outside of its territorial purview. Of greater relevance, the northeastern region of the continent, which played host to the intersection of ancient African, Islamic, and Christian religious and cultural civilizations, engendered constant territorial and political disputes and compromises. Certainly any attempt to distill from these equations an essential definition of "imperialism" is sure to come to grief. For the purpose of this "national" study such a definition can hardly be justified by this reductionism. Yet there are some shared features that have been put under the rubric of "imperialism" for analytical purpose in understanding the power and cultural relations in the region. Examples include the socioeconomic damage wrought by Ethiopian armies in transit upon the civil societies throughout the nineteenth century. Predatory soldiers, in state's service and freelancers, plundered many surrounding communities and took control of new lands and properties of both loyal and rebel territories alike. The armies collected free provisions (dirgo), often through forceful measures. Some rural peasants mounted opposition to the imposition of taxes and the orderly levying of supplies for military campaigns. The mountaineers of Simien and the peasants of Dembya in the district of Gonder also provided local resistance to military excursions. These activities, combined with European colonial state formation and divergent politico-economic goals, laid the foundations for the modern irredentist movements and civil conflicts that continue to plague Ethiopian, Somalian, and Eritrean relations in the Horn of Africa.

Remarkably, by signing of the Peace Treaty of Addis Ababa, Italy renounced the Treaty of Wichale and recognized the absolute and complete independence of Ethiopia. In spite of the double stroke of military victories and a series of diplomatic coups, Menelik did not consider himself capable of insisting on an Italian withdrawal from Eritrea, though he had often expressed a desire to obtain access to the sea through the region. In the months following the signing of the treaty, the French and the British governments all sent diplomatic missions to sign treaties of friendship with Menelik. Other diplomatic entreaties came from the Sudanese Mahdists, the sultan of the Ottoman Empire, and the Tsar of Russia. Addis Ababa thus emerged as a regular diplomatic center where several important foreign powers had regular legations. The relative military and political success of Ethiopia also led to the expansion of European chancelleries, many of whom for a period came to terms with the idea of Ethiopian independence and its achievements. Ethiopian history was "Aryanized" so as to further distinguish it from that of the rest of the African continent. The lofty achievements of the empire, it was argued, could only be attributed to a people superior to the rest of the Africans even if they are not as good as the Europeans. Some Ethiopian officials equally made arguments of Ethiopian exceptionalism, albeit on religious as opposed to racial grounds.

In late nineteenth-century Ethiopia, the military emerged as one of the few careers of promise open to enterprising young men, many of whom of very humble origin emerged as significant political figures. Martial life offered a place among the privileged and a new means of livelihood and power. The life of a common soldier was, however, quite difficult, as many were exposed to diseases and lacked proper protection from the dangerous war terrain of northeast Africa. In addition to its religious heritage, the military also helped in the geopolitical and psychological construction of modern Ethiopian nationalism, as different ethnic groups were unified under the umbrella of nationhood. The realpolitik practiced by Ethiopian emperors laid the foundation for a problematic political future of Ethiopia, a fact evident in the development in which the Oromo cultural group became the emperor's preferred auxiliaries to oppose rebellious nobilities. For other, smaller ethnic groups, (other than the Amhara and Tigreans), there were minimal opportunities in Christian armies. Military activities also led to the evolution of modern Ethiopian ethnography. Military lords and powerful men who have been granted the use of land and military service over local subjects are often referred to as *"Amhara"* or *"Sidama,"* which could interchangeably mean Christian or alien. These appellations were, however, neither so homogenous nor so distinct as to always distinguish the intruders from the conquered, as these misapplied ethnic terms suggest. Another important dynamic in this era was that of forced assimilation into new social groups, as witnessed in the "Amharization" of Oromo migrants to the native Amhara. In nineteenth-century Ethiopia, religion continued to play a major role in legitimating political and economic transformation as the influence of colonial capitalism gradually spread from one society to another. Ethiopia was the only country to preserve its independence throughout the period of the European scramble and partition of Africa. The possession of arms and ammunitions, the development of a professional army, and the nurturing of ancient powerful religious and political institutions were factors that were instrumental in allowing Ethiopia to maintain its independence. Hence colonized and marginalized Africans in general from the nineteenth century onwards proclaim Ethiopia as a liberator, a monument, and a living exponent and testimony of African political freedom.

Menelik also established a permanent administrative presence as a buffer against foreign aggression. He appointed his most trusted generals as governors general of the provinces, which constituted the largest administrative division in the empire. Below the governor of a province were the district governors, who were also appointed by the emperor. The district governors in turn appointed the heads of the lowest administrative divisions called *Shum*, which consisted of either one large village or a cluster of small villages in the same general area. Garrisons, or *Ketemaa*, also became important administrative centers in the acquisition of new territories, especially in the Oromo and Somali areas. The delegates of the crown were mostly of Amhara-Tigre descent, who, under the platform of creating an Ethiopian national identity, sometimes forcibly integrated subject peoples into the expanded political system and Coptic Church. Menelik was also the first Ethiopian monarch to introduce the practice of paying taxes to the imperial treasury at all administrative levels.

MODERNIZATION PROJECTS

After the Battle of Adwa, Menelik's Ethiopia was gradually accepted by the European powers as a real political force, and in the last decades of Menelik's

reign he exploited the political environment to embark on modernization reforms that had been delayed for various reasons, including almost a century of internal and external warfare. The unprecedented period of peace that followed the Battle of Adwa led to an increase in foreign contacts. The advent of increasing numbers of foreign craftsmen created an entirely new climate for economic and technological development. A new administrative headquarters, Addis Ababa, was established in 1886 and five years later became Ethiopia's new capital. The city became the site of many of the country's principal innovations, and, because of its large population, enabled a degree of specialization of labor scarcely known elsewhere in the land. Modern bridges were erected in Addis Ababa, Awash, and Gojjam. This era also featured revolutionary developments in education. The first modern school, the Menelik II School, was founded in 1908, and the opening of institutions in Hara and Dire Dawa followed this. Students learned Amharic, various European languages, reading, writing, mathematics, science, and other subjects. In order to consolidate his rule, Menelik encouraged the development of a newly educated elite steeped in Western values and progressive in outlook. As early as 1890, young Abyssinians were sent abroad to Europe, Russia, and Sudan. Together with the home-groomed graduates, new elites emerged to become the cornerstone of the modernizing autocracy. The functioning of the state bureaucracy, the diplomatic corps, and the economy owed a lot to the modernization of Ethiopian education and the nascent secularization of administrative institutions.

Having to contend with the church's frequent opposition to new Western ideas, Menelik entrusted this school and three others in the provinces at Hara, Ankobar, and Dase to Egyptian Coptic teachers and priests. Other innovations in nineteenth-century Ethiopia included the construction of telephone and telegraph systems, water pipes, and modern hospitals and the introduction of new vaccines to help deal with the underserviced health sector of a rapidly expanding population. The continual threat posed by the Italians had led Menelik to reorganize the system of taxation in 1892 and issue the country's first national currency two years later. The currency was based on a silver dollar of the same weight and value as the old Austrian Maria Theresa dollar, which had circulated throughout Ethiopia, as well as much of the Middle East, since the mid-eighteenth century.

In 1894 Ethiopia's first postage stamps, produced in Paris, were inaugurated and the approval received for the construction of Ethiopia's first railroad, which was to link Addis Ababa with the French Somaliland port of Djibouti. Menelik wanted the railroad to provide a means for the transportation of low-price commodities such as coffee, skins, and wax, the main Ethiopian exports. Although the project encountered technical, financial, and political difficulties, the coming of the railway marked the country's greatest technological achievement of the period. Backed by French finance, the railroad project helped turn Addis Ababa into a major city. These developments together with

the construction of modern roads and a new shipping line all led to substantial expansion of the import-export trade. In 1905, the Bank of Abyssinia was established, and two years later the first government hotel was established. Hotels, restaurants, and tailoring establishments all sprang up as symbols of urbanization and modernization.

The host of foreign advisors, ambassadors, emissaries, and adventurers brought problems as well as opportunities. Menelik sought to modernize his realm and thus listened to the advice of foreigners. Each foreign adviser invariably sought to promote the influence and advantage of his own government. Many also suggested impressive if not always economically sound military and commercial schemes. European financiers also tried to impose new forms of control over Ethiopia by exploiting its modernization schemes. Menelik was angered by the terms of European financial involvement and accused many of seeking to compromise Ethiopia's independence by economic means. In spite of the laudable modernization schemes and projects, development was still too slow and limited to greatly change the pattern of traditional Ethiopian society. Local conservative elements wary of modernization schemes encouraged opposition from Empress Taytu and Ras Makonnen against the railroad schemes.

Between 1897 and 1908, Menelik was able to obtain international recognition for the evolving Ethiopia's frontiers, although the country was never safe from imperial intrigues from neighboring Italian Somaliland and from British interests on the Upper Nile. Short of definitive military victories, France, Britain, and Italy continued jostled for influence in the Horn of Africa and Eritrea.

In reaction to the demand by European powers for Ethiopia to honor a 1906 treaty guaranteeing the protection of European citizens, Menelik argued that this invocation was aimed at increasing the colonial spheres of influence in this region. In a speech to his domain, he stated, "We have received the arrangement made by the three powers. We thank them for their communication and their desire to keep and maintain the independence of our government. But let it be understood that this arrangement in no way limits what we consider our sovereign rights."[2]

Menelik won respect both at home and abroad. He had, with the exception of Eritrea, managed to preserve and extend the territories of ancient Ethiopia; he had restored order and held down dissident feudal lords; and he had laid the foundations for further development and modernization reforms. In 1908, Menelik suffered a major stroke that almost completely paralyzed him, although he lingered on until 1913. His death was followed by a series of political struggles. A settlement agreed to by the various feudal lords led to the emergence of a division of power mainly between the empress Zauditu and the regent and heir to the throne, Ras Tafari, later known as Emperor Haile Selassie. Selassie's rule would feature major historical events that brought Ethiopia in confrontation with twentieth-century developments including fascism, colo-

nial wars, and a test of the theory and practice of domestic and internationalist liberal reforms.

NOTES

1. H. G. Marcus, "The Black Men Who Turned White: European Attitudes Towards Ethiopians, 1850–1900," *Archiv Orientalni* 39 (1971): 160.

2. Richard Greenfield, *Ethiopia: A New Political History* (New York: Frederick A. Praeger Publishers, 1965), 126–28.

3

"Afromodern" Aspirations: Political Expansion and Social Reform in Local and Global Contexts, 1884–1935

Princes shall come out of Egypt; Ethiopia shall soon stretch out her hands unto God.

Psalm 68:31

By the mid-nineteenth century, the project of modernity acquired a new momentum in African history. Although the level of external forces on domestic political and economic dynamics varied from one community to another, the identity of social units was evolving as local elites embarked on renewing political and economic administrations and new modes of self- and national definitions. This "metanarrative of modernity" for anthropologist Donald L. Donham also included the spread of the idea that nations acquire modernity status in linear fashion relative to the acquisition of wealth and knowledge. In this regard, both domestic and transnational geopolitics and economic relations also influenced modern Ethiopian history. From the mid-fifteenth century onward, social and political hierarchies between the continent of Africa and the rest of the world and within Africa itself were directly or indirectly influenced by differential access to modern technology and institutions. Inequality in access to international markets, modern weaponry, communications, and education resulted in hegemonic reconfigurations in individual wealth and societal hierarchies and also evolving definitions of ethnicity, the nation, and modernity. Between the domestic agitations and resistance by regional governors who opposed the political efforts aimed at modernizing the legal and administrative structure of the kingdom on the one hand, and the implications of European explorations and colonial activities on the other, the Ethiopian state experienced new complexities, ambiguities, and pluralities in local and regional identities as well as social and political relations. This chapter explores some of the intellectual and cultural dynamics that helped shape Ethiopia's relations with the rest of the African continent and the rest of the world between the late eighteenth and the early nineteenth centuries. This new historical phase began in 1884 when Africa was partitioned by European powers and ended in 1935 when Ethiopia was invaded by Italy under the leadership of the fascist administration of Benito Mussolini.

Historical events of the nineteenth century, such as the abolition of the trans-Atlantic and Indian Ocean slave trades, the development of a "legitimate" trade, and the search for new markets and sources of raw materials by Europe on the African continent drew the continent into new cultural, political, and economic relationships with the rest of the world. The multiple histories of migration that emerged out of the interlocking systems of international capital and political expansion had not only helped create the African Diaspora, but also entrenched a global "color line" of unequal exchange and a Janus-faced "gift" of modernity. The era also gave Ethiopian modernism a distinct and particular edge with two major characteristics. First, with the incursion of the European colonial elite into the Ethiopian sphere of strategic interest, the empire became more concerned with firming up the boundaries of an evolving modern state, especially in the consolidation and expansion of bureaucratic authority in its purview. Second, foreign skilled professionals and advisors were welcomed in Ethiopia as long as they did not seek to impose undue influence on domestic affairs. The rejection of political and economic domination from abroad and the attempt to strike a balance between transformative and conservative forces at home proved to be a daunting and complex task.

In nineteenth-century Ethiopia and before, the dynamic of imperial political economy had continued to encourage a slow conversion of worshipers of polytheistic religions into Orthodox Christian identity. This other metanarrative of modernity, according to Marina Ottaway, was channeled into Ethiopia through the political center controlled by Amhara, and the notion of progress was mapped onto ethnic differences. Becoming modern, "of the times" (zemanawi), "civilized" (siltane), or "educated" (yetamare), required one, to some considerable degree, to adopt Orthodox Christian customs. Modernization also became increasingly identified with the concentration of power in institutions that required literacy, a fact that greatly increased the duress on non-Amharic folks derisively labeled as "pagans," or backward hwalakeri, ripe for political conquest or religious conversion.

Based on the above equations, understanding late nineteenth-century Ethiopian history requires an iconoclastic reading of the multiple narratives of intellectual and political economic paradigms. On the one hand, the Orthodox Church contributed to the consolidation of ethnic hierarchies and its corollary in the form of hegemonic conflicts. It also ensured that the definition of what it means to be Ethiopian was in a constant state of flux. On the other hand, and of equal significance, the impact of emergent or evolving modern theories that validates racial and regional hierarchies also further complicated the history of Ethiopian modernism.

Afromodernity has been described as a particular understanding of modernity and modern subjectivity among people of African descent as they attempt to create a form of relatively autonomous modernity distinct from their counterparts in Western Europe and North America. Afromodernity, according to political scientist Michael Hanchard, was inextricably intertwined with global historical events, particularly the impact of the combination of international slavery and colonialism on people of African descent. The ascendancy of the myth of Africa as the "dark continent" and Africans as the antithesis of Western modernity and modern subjectivity made the modernist project more imperative for Africans. At its broadest parameters, Afromodern projects in the Horn of Africa thus consist of the selective incorporation of technologies, discourses, and institutions of the modern West within the cultural and political practices of African-derived peoples. Ethiopia's (Abyssinian) cultural and political history also played a significant role in the construction and advancement of Afromodernity.

As European ideas and economic interests became the pivotal driving force in the modern international political economy, there was a proliferation of narratives that trumped or remained ambivalent to the idea that European values and interests are invariably superior. For Africans who were configured as the antithesis of Western modernity, Ethiopia's oral and written historical narratives as an ancient civilization that combines indigenous and Orthodox Christian heritage presented a major tool of evaluative criticism of modern global events. Ethiopian history automatically became a defining core of a modern epistemology of racial advancement or at least a counterhegemonic narrative among Africans and African-descended people. European chancelleries and official statements often portrayed Ethiopia as either the anomaly or the paradox of African history. Many European sources described Ethiopians as "black Caucasians" or as a "Hamitic" race of Christians distinct from other Africans. Ethiopia's lack of economic development, however, situated it within most of the narratives that asserted Western hegemony, and more importantly provided a rationale for colonial capital penetration of Ethiopia. Ethiopia's strategic location in the Horn of Africa, a major traffic passage for international trade and resources, also made it a prime target for

European powers. Ethiopia began to face increased opposition to what many described as antimodernist practices, especially in the practice of domestic slavery. As a result, the country encountered opposition to its desire for superior armament from Europe, as select European states placed limitations or total embargo on the traffic of arms to the Solomonic dynasty. In spite of such limitations, the Ethiopian empire was defended by a standing army of virtually all adult male members of the peasantry, who were often well armed and led by able, ambitious, and determined regional leaders. Although there was a lot of division among the Ethiopian regional elites, the hegemony of Orthodox Christianity also engendered "national" unity at crucial moments in history, conducive to massive mobilization of troops.

The concept of "Ethiopianism" had also emerged in the diaspora as an eschatology that combined Christian and secular nationalist traditions as a vehicle to reinforce African identity and proto-citizenship in the absence of protection from the modern nation-state. With the partition of the African continent between 1884 and 1885, Ethiopia's history assumed even greater significance, as it was mythicized as the singular epitome of African independence and national self-determination. Significantly, the Ethiopian state itself also embarked on a series of modernization projects for which the state often trumped her membership in international Christendom, which she claimed was under threat from hostile territories. By the late nineteenth century, this phenomenon, however, gradually acquired less significance until the eve of the Second World War, when global hegemonic forces again came together to undermine Ethiopian independence. At this time, Ethiopia's Afromodern credentials were once again affirmed with the globalizing conceptions of human rights, black nationalism, and various modes of representation of collective identity.

By the dawn of the twentieth century Ethiopia's history had been through nearly five hundred years of relationship with Europe. These engagements were largely characterized by mutual intellectual and cultural exchanges and selective incorporation of modern technologies on the part of Ethiopia with its underdeveloped economy. Instead of European capital, material, or luxury goods, Ethiopian rulers were more interested in military assistance for the project of political centralization and expansion of control over economic production and land holdings in northeast Africa. In this period of momentous change, the Ethiopian state, however, suffered from a lack of national unity, a secular bureaucratic administration, and urban development. These emerged as the greatest obstacle to the state's primary project of modernity. This fact was compounded by the fact that between 1769 and 1855, provincial attitudes of some of the elites in the territory had reached crisis proportions. As political power gradually became decentralized, the state regressed into feudal, regional compartments, and local warlords and traditional nobility competed for supremacy.

Ethiopia also had an extremely complex land-tenure system. In the northern Tigre Amharic provinces, the power base of the imperial authorities, land ownership was vested with the kinship group. Peasant ownership of land was protected by the *rist* system, in which subjects are expected to pay tribute. In addition, imperial land grants to the nobility, or *gult*, and the church lands, which is permanently granted to the Ethiopian Church, together combined to extract surpluses from the peasantry in tribute, produce, rents, and services. This has been described as "a classic feudal trinity of nobleman, priest, and peasant." The southern provinces, which emerged as a political center primarily in the last quarter of the nineteenth century as a result of the military exploits of Emperor Menelik, were characterized by the imposition of alien landlords, or *neftagna*. The imperial authorities allocated gult rights to Amharic and other northern nobility, or in many other cases transformed local chiefs or *balabbat* to landlord status. The imposition of Amhara hegemony over the southern cultural communities meant that identifying with the former's cultural attributes became the measure of one's inclusion into the emergent Ethiopian modern state and its apparatus. Beside coercion and the law, religion provided the major political and ideological institutions that helped reproduce these conditions.

As a result of the above developments, more than its potential as the harbinger of social change, a second imperative for the acquisition of modern knowledge and technology was thus tied to the maintenance of the state's sovereignty and its divine political heritage of Orthodox Christianity. While other parts of Africa experienced the expansion of colonial rule and the decline of the functional power of traditional rulers, Ethiopian leaders exploited the ideological connotations of the Solomonic line to consolidate their hegemonic influence on disparate communities in the empire. Ethiopia's Orthodox Christianity also allowed her to challenge the credibility of the material superiority of the West and its proposed corollary of a civilizing mission.

As Ethiopian society evolved, its elites were interested in transforming their societies; but as high priests of modernity, they were unable to resolve the contradictions involved in the project. The state also could not strike the necessary balance between the adoption of modern secular political institutions and adhering to the historical and cultural essence of Ethiopian nationalism. Faced by opposition from conservative elites who detested the reconstruction of the past, the modernists tried to secure a favored position to help bring social change. They also sought political change to positively transform the infrastructures that impeded development and access to goods and services.

Ethiopia's independence, heritage and civilization allowed African intellectuals to dissociate themselves from the concept of European mission or burden of guiding "lesser races" on the path of modernity. Another common feature in the ethico-political traditions that equate global African and Ethiopian history is discernible in the former's embrace of the scriptural referent to biblical Ethiopia as a divine providential point of reference for the future. The biblical phrase "Ethiopia stretches her hands towards God" became a mantra repeated often in times of individual and community trial and ordeal. The implication is that the Ethiopian is the direct instrument of God, and their righteous cause would ultimately triumph.

With the termination or reconstruction of hereditary political power, citizenship rights, and territorial sovereignty, many of the colonized African intellectuals had also temporarily resolved the problem of alienation by embracing independent Ethiopia. Ethiopia's rich and textured history also presented a perfect rebuttal to the derogation of Africa as historically and constitutionally inferior. Similarly, a growing separatist movement by African Christians also embraced Ethiopia, the site of a historic black Christian nation that had defeated the Italians while maintaining its independence as the rest of Africa was colonized. Africa, they argued, should be evangelized by Africans and not by Europeans.

Between 1884 and 1935, Ethiopia expanded its network of far-reaching tentacles beyond its traditional Western European allies into Eastern Europe as well as select Asian countries in search of development and modernization assistance. Ethiopian history was thus about to be elevated to the modern international stage, foretelling a twentieth century filled with political intrigues, and a yardstick for highlighting the gap between international theories and the practice of political and economic liberalism. The contradictions inherent in Ethiopian modernization reforms, as well as the tendentious penetration of foreign capital and its accompanying long-term concessions on the social and economic fabric of the ancient civilization, ultimately contributed to the dispersal of Ethiopians citizens and their incorporation into the orbit of Western modernity, including that of the politics of the modern African Diaspora.

BETWEEN DIVINE FAITH AND TEMPORAL GEOPOLITICS: ETHIOPIAN LATE TRANSITION TO MODERNITY

Ethiopia's approach to the modern era was defined by a cultural pride and a historically grounded defensive attitude towards external stimuli for change. The Aksumite Empire, the lineal ancestor of modern Ethiopia, was recognized across the world as a land of achievers since classical antiquity. Diodorus Siculus, a Sicilian Greek historian who lived from 90 to 21 B.C., stated that:

> The Ethiopians conceived themselves to be of greater antiquity than any other nation, and it is probable, that, born under the sun's path, its warmth may have ripened them earlier than other men. They supposed themselves to be the inventors of worship, of festivals, of solemn assemblies, of sacrifice, and every religious practice.[1]

In spite of the above definition, Ethiopians had also hosted Venetians who had facilitated the introduction of the territory to European chancelleries and intellectual and commercial circles. Later the *Fra Mauro* map commissioned by King Alphonso V of Portugal had also recognized Ethiopian civilization, as witnessed in the legend of Prester John, a richly endowed African (Ethiopian) Christian king under threat of Islamic invasion. Having rebuffed the encroachment of Somali Ahmad Gran's Islamic jihad with the aid of the Portuguese in the sixteenth century and rejecting the subsequent attempt by the Jesuits' Portuguese mission to convert the country into Catholicism, Ethiopian lessons from the medieval era onwards were best reflected in the reign of emperor Tewodros. It was the emperor who began to dream of modernity under Ethiopia's independently defined and stated terms. Tewodros had reunited the fragmented Abyssinian polities and restored the power and majesty of the medieval empire. He had also sought the support of the European states, particularly England, to assist his modernist project, but was ultimately rebuffed by the English crown. His effort to modernize through the use of force ultimately led to a rebellion on the part of the people and a fateful collision with the superior military forces of the British Empire.

Menelik II (1899–1913) had imposed his stamp on the Ethiopian royal pedigree of political centralization and nation building by introducing a new and improved project of modernity. A major distinction of his reign was borne of a policy of manipulating the varying interests of Ethiopia's European allies as a bulwark to the political milieu in which the promise of modernity revolved around the unbridled expansion of European capital in Africa. In Ethiopia, commerce with the West was perceived less in terms of grand profitable ventures than in conditional concessions and other mutually acceptable terms for the acquisition of modern facilities and military weapons. Thus, unlike most African societies during the era of the scramble for and partition of the continent, the Ethiopian state did not accede to the whim of European powers, nor were they overwhelmed by Western economic exigencies. Under Menelik, Ethiopia developed a modern bureaucracy and embarked on limited social reforms including the introduction of new health and educational infrastructures. As earlier indicated, other accoutrements of modernity introduced to Ethiopia during his reign included the telephone, telegraph, electricity, modern hospital services to major urban areas, the establishment of the Bank of Abyssinia, and the construction of a joint project, the Franco-Ethiopian railroad. Menelik's reforms were, however, tethered to the maintenance of feudal political and social relations that were dependent on the collection of or tributaries from regional governors and the peasantry.

MENELIK II AND THE POLITICS OF ETHIOPIAN MODERNITY

In the second half of the nineteenth century, European political and economic influence in Africa was gradually being consolidated, including the northeastern region, where Ethiopia was at this time consolidating its regional territorial and political spheres of influence. European political rule was ultimately formalized at the Berlin Conference of 1884–1885. Although Ethiopia was spared at the map-making summit, Italy's colonial presence in neighboring Eritrea and later Somaliland proved to be a harbinger of future hostilities and bitter struggles in the region between Ethiopia, Somalia, and Eritrea. The boundaries of modern Eritrea had been established during the period of Italian colonization that began in the late 1800s. An Italian shipping company, Rubatinno Shipping, had purchased the port of Assab from a local ruler, and the Italian government subsequently gained ascendancy over the port in 1882, hoping to use Eritrea as a launching point for its colonization project in the region. The Italian presence in the Horn of Africa was formalized in 1889 with the signing of the controversial Treaty of Wichale by then King Menelik of Showa, later the emperor of Ethiopia, with Count Pietro Antonelli of Italy. While the Amharic version of the treaty suggested that Abyssinia could use Italy as an agent in foreign relations if it desired, the Italian version claimed that Abyssinia was obliged to go through Italy in its foreign relations. Ethiopia had been duped into becoming a protectorate of the Italian nation. For the next half-century, relations between Ethiopia and Italy, despite intermittent diplomatic agreements, were strained by repeated Italian efforts to expand their colonial base into Somali territory and Ethiopia.

British colonial spheres of influence in east Africa also expanded from the Sudan and Egypt and into Somaliland, infringing on Ethiopian border-territories. French control of Djibouti and its important ports also deprived Ethiopia of a main outlet to the outside world, leading to the decline of ancient economic and political sites such as Massawa and Assab. The treaty of Addis Ababa between Ethiopia and Italy had abrogated the much-maligned Treaty of Wichale, thus marking Italy's recognition of the absolute independence of Ethiopia. By stemming this tide of colonialism, Ethiopia's military victory and national pride was also a model of African resistance against colonial rule; if only in theory.

Ethiopia's territorial expansion and political consolidation efforts in the defense of her sovereignty have engendered accusations of Ethiopian or Amhara imperialism against the various smaller nationalities and on either side of the Great Rift Valley. Ethiopia's centralization of power in the region, however, enabled her to avoid the atomization of African political authorities and their subsequent marginalization by colonial forces. Ethiopia expanded her territory as it incorporated part of the Somali territory (previously known as the Ogaden). However, it lost the historic maritime province of the Marab Mellash to the Italians, which the latter rechristened Eritrea. The significance of these geopolitical realignments was to be fateful for the post–World War II history of the Horn of Africa.

Political independence for Ethiopia was hardly adequate to compensate for the lack of paved roads, modern communications networks, and an outlet to sea. The history of Ethiopia and the contentious interpretation of events in the Horn of Africa bordered on the north by Eritrea, on the east by Djibouti and Somalia, on the south by Kenya, and on the west by Sudan continue to date to reproduce transformations of individual and community relations. Within Ethiopian territories, those interested in modern reforms operated alongside conservatives, reactionaries, and ambitious political and military leaders. Another development in Ethiopian history at the dawn of the twentieth century featured the ruling class, who sought to consolidate their political and economic power through tributes, land tax, rent, and surplus labor. The emperor in turn demanded and received fixed annual tributes from the provincial governors. Between the autocratic political control over land and the church imperatives for expansion, peasants were often deprived of inherited lands and control over their labor. Powerful elites also appropriated from the tithes and provisions of the lower class, many of whom were forced to remain in near slavery status. This expansion of frontiers and domination over trade routes and custom duties allowed for the emergence of new domestic power relations with major ethnic and identity implications that portended future conflicts over political control and resource distribution.

Between 1855 and 1889, Ethiopia's vast territories had been consolidated into a cohesive state through considerable reformation of its administrative bureaucracy, and the implementation of reforms that imposed some limitation on the influence of the church. However, the modernizers who felt that Ethiopia needed to open itself to the world in order to survive faced opposition from the conservatives who believed in the preservation of Ethiopian Orthodox Christian traditions. Ethiopian evolution into the modern era also occurred against the background of European nationalist geostrategic conflicts over control of economic highways, resources, and markets. The presence of major European powers that now surrounded Ethiopia also imposed limitations on the march towards modernity. The relative control Ethiopia had over its political future, however, continued to guarantee its status as an African powerhouse. This was especially true since Africa had, with the slave trade, witnessed varying levels of political instability and a complex shifting of political and economic alliances. There were also new political configurations as old relationships based on clan and lineage were altered or replaced by the colonial presence. The threat of external forces also reduced the autonomy required for iconoclastic domestic reformers interested in fundamental changes. The stage was set for the first test in the modern era of the clash between the imperial ambitions of Europe and Ethiopia's modernist aspirations.

The opening of the Suez Canal in 1869 had given the Red Sea region a more prominent, albeit contentious, stature among the powers involved in geopolitical strategic and commercial competitions. As European powers clamored for territories along the Red Sea's coastal area, the combination of Egypt's economic misfortune under Khedive Ismail and the rise of Islamic nationalism in the country led to formal British occupation of Egypt in 1882. This step was a major precursor to the scramble and partition of the African continent. As the British and the French competed for political and economic spheres of influence in the region, the former guarded the White Nile region and found in the Italian presence a buffer power to protect the Blue Nile and its Ethiopian source and tributaries from the latter power.

The historical relationship between European powers, Egypt, and Ethiopia had been characterized by a mutual, albeit complex and unequal, political and economic imperative that was always in a state of flux. With the partition of Africa between 1884 and 1885, a new Manichean relationship of the colonizer and the colonized threatened this balance, and by extension the technological superiority of Europe also foreboded a threat to the sovereignty of Ethiopia. Ethiopian foreign policy had at its fulcrum the search for an outlet to the sea, modern armaments to defend and consolidate its power, and the infrequent reference to the consolidation of the brotherhood of transnational Christendom with Europe. This last feature, however, hinged on an anachronism, since Europe was more dedicated to the expansion of its laissez faire economic interests and the protection of her political spheres of influence. In addition, the new Colonialism enterprise was also an extension of the metropolitan social, cultural, and political system and the goals and franchise of its commercial and entrepreneurial class. Modernity was in essence now constructed as primarily the accession to a European-centered Western foreign policy.

ETHIOPIA'S CULTURAL AND INTELLECTUAL ENGAGEMENT WITH WESTERN MODERNITY IN HISTORICAL PERSPECTIVE

In spite of the proliferation of a modern European intellectual project that described Africa as a land without history, devoid of culture and civilization, a phenomenon rooted in the predilections of colonial encounter, an alternative scheme could be found in earlier collaborations between European and African scholarship. Ethiopian secular and Christian relationships between the sixteenth century and the first decade of the nineteenth century accommodated global intellectual enterprise. A combination of factors, which included the political turmoil as a result of Ottoman Turk occupation of Syria and Palestine in 1516 and Egypt in 1517 and the threat to Ethiopia from Islamic jihad fighters during the first half of the sixteenth century, transformed Ethiopian-European relations. As a result, many Ethiopian monks escaped to Jerusalem and various locations in Europe, and many converted to Catholicism and developed new temporal and spiritual traditions. Some of these monks were eminent scholars well versed in Ethiopian languages, history, and culture as well as theology and philosophy. Many were able to continue their religious and intellectual activities within Catholic orders such as the Franciscans and the Benedictines. Ethiopian missionaries had also migrated to southern Europe,

Austria, Spain, and most of all Italy, where many collaborated with local scholars in their new place of abode. Some of the vibrant Ethiopian intellectual community established in this era could also be found in the Vatican and other parts of Italy, where a convent known as San Stefano degli Abissini emerged as an important center for the study of Ethiopian history and languages. It was here where Ethiopian intellectuals such as Antonio d'Andrade produced several works.

Another exiled Ethiopian Catholic priest, Abba Gorgoryos from Mekane Sillasé in Amhara, traveled to Erfurt, Germany, in 1652 and stayed with scholar Hiob Ludolf. With Gorgoyos' help, the latter emerged as one the most prominent Ethiopian specialists. The relationship produced foundational modern ethnological research and Amharic and Geez literatures. Ludof's *Grammatica Aethiopica* (1661) and *Historia Aethiopica* (1681) were later translated into English, French, and Dutch. His works *Commentary on the History* (1691), *Grammatica Linguae Amharicae* (1698), and *Lexicon Aethiopico-Latinum* (1661) also became standard authoritative texts for teaching Ethiopian studies in European universities and centers of learning. During the nineteenth century, another Ethiopian scholar, Dabtera Kefla Giyorgis, played a crucial role as the teacher of Ignazio Guidi who has been described as the father of Ethiopian studies in Italy.

With the emergence of formal European imperialism in Africa, Ethiopia's intellectual and diplomatic engagement took a turn, for the worse. At the dawn of Italian colonization scheme in Ethiopia, the emissaries from Rome not only to gathered and published scientific, ethnogeographic, historical, and economic data on to Ethiopia but many also offered their services they pursued their political goals to the imperial project.

By 1884, colonial mapmaking in Africa and the expansion of European cultural, academic, and economic influence around the world were accompanied by the belief that most societies were on an evolutionary path towards modernity—when local identities and sociologically backward organizations would eventually give way to a superior cosmopolitan industrial civilization. Ethiopia on the other hand was led by political elites who had embarked on political centralization and thus were able to retain their independence, creating a highly textured indigenous narrative of modernity in African history.

As the twentieth century approached, competing interpretations of Ethiopia's history, intellectual traditions, and modernist aspirations emerged against the background of changing global power relations. The description of Ethiopia also evolved from the romantic fascination in the annals of Christian Europe as the land of Prester John. As the sovereignty and national will of African communities became gradually subsumed into a Europe's orbit, Ethiopia emerged as the romantic beacon of independence and dignity for those who aspire for change in these African societies. Ethiopian defeat of Italy at Adowa in 1896 had also helped redefine the modern Euro-African relationship with the West. Based on the fact that the United States and Europe were extending the reach of "white authority" around the globe, this first modern military defeat of Europeans by non-Europeans preserved Ethiopian independence, and out of Africa came hope for blacks around the world, especially in areas where racial discrimination and inequality was most extreme. Amidst the violence, the racist portrayal of Africa and African-descended people prevalent at the turn of the twentieth century led both African and African American cultural elites to articulate a positive black identity. The transnational ideology of racial uplift believed that material and moral progress on the part of Africans could diminish racism. Leading black scholars and writers adopted propagandist affirmations of Ethiopia's political history in defense of what some described as the "African Personality." In their effort to present an African history that preceded slavery and colonialism, Afro-Diaspora or pan-Africanist writings combined their appreciation for the temporality of African historical experience with the spiritual biblical narratives to forge a new nationalist discourse.

By the early twentieth century, Ethiopia assumed a new significance as the subject of European travel writers, syndicated journalists, explorers, and colonial scholarship. In the spirit of the era dominated by the consolidation of colonial rule, Ethiopia's claims to civilization, national economic independence, or modernist aspirations were often undermined. The English novelist Evelyn Waugh summed up the justification of the colonization of Ethiopia:

> Abyssinia could not claim recognition on equal terms by the civilized nations and at the same time maintain her barbarous isolation; she must put her natural resources at the disposal of the world; since she was obviously unable to develop them herself, it must be done for her, to their mutual benefit, by a more advanced power.[2]

Ethiopia, however, continued to pursue technological and material assistance from Europe, although the diplomatic efforts of its emperors in this regard were often described as "tricking" rather than credentials of statesmanship.

Another example of the evolving relationship between the world and Ethiopia was visible in the exoticism of the land as "savage" or a destination rife with oddities. A popular example was the book *Savage Abyssinia*, first published in 1927. The author James E. Baum had led a field museum expedition to Ethiopia, and the proceedings of their activities received global circulation through regular reports in a syndicated media. Underwritten by the *Chicago Daily News*, Baum had sought protection and guidance from future emperor Ras Tafari, who was already aware and impressed with the "vehicular modernism" associated with such a visit. These included the impact of modern print media, photography, illustration, painting, taxidermy, and film. The primary goal of the future emperor was to appropriate the modern tools associated with the expedition to positively represent both himself and Ethiopia to the global community. He was also of the idea that such positive exposure would not only serve as a harbinger of modernity but would also stave off colonial aggression. Beside its emphasis on African otherness and the supposed Ethiopian suspicion of technology, the publication described the coronation of Haile Selassie, which was witnessed by the visitors, as "a magnificent barbaric spectacle" and a mere ploy designed to preserve the freedom of the nation. Although Baum's writings also reveal an astute observation of the political intrigues and social realities of the land, he was also rather cavalier in the description of Ethiopia as a land that suffers from inherent psychic factors rather than focusing on the structural weakness arising out of hegemonic conflicts in the land. Due to Emperor Haile Selassie's objection, the 1935 reprint of *Savage Abyssinia* was given a new title: *Unknown Ethiopia: New Light on Darkest Abyssinia*.

In a development that later emerged as the pioneer lobbyist platform for articulating modern social, political, and economic necessities of African communities, Ethiopia became an anchor for African modernist narratives. These writings not only highlighted African agency in a modern world but also protested the inequalities inherent in new free trade ventures in Africa. They also called for the political and economic development of African states. In this context, in 1911, J. E. Casely Hayford of Ghana published *Ethiopia Unbound: Studies in Race Emancipation*, and W.E.B. DuBois, the noted African American scholar, wrote an historical pageant called *The Star of Ethiopia*. DuBois' play, which opened in New York City in October 1913, mythologized a modern civilization founded on black culture and endowed with seven essential gifts to the world: iron, faith, humility, sorrow, freedom, laughter, and hope. In each of these examples, an African persona not only fills the central role, but also places "the race" in a positive and culturally inspiring light. In a similar fashion, DuBois also sought to promote Ethiopian history as part of the narratives of development and civil rights in the book *The World and Africa: Inquiry into the Part Which Africa Has Played in World History*.

In spite of the grand evocations, treaties between European powers and Ethiopia were, however, laden with new and unequal caveats. In 1905, Germany concluded a Treaty of Friendship and Commerce with Ethiopia as a result of the diplomatic mission of Friedrich Rosen, followed by the establishment of a permanent German Legation at Addis Ababa. The Tripartite Agreement of 1906 between Britain, France, and Italy attempted to divide the country into three spheres of economic interest without any input from Ethiopia's leader, Emperor Menelik II. In February 1907, John Harrington, British representative in Addis Ababa, secretly urged the Foreign Office and his French and Italian counterparts to abide closely by the agreement on the grounds of maintaining the interests of "whites against blacks."

As a result of this shift in European attitude, Ethiopia was compelled to make numerous compromises to maintain its independence and modernist aspirations. Such concessions to European economic and trading interests also restricted its diplomatic sovereignty and its social and economic aspirations. For example, in spite of Emperor Menelik's displeasure with the Tripartite Agreement, he entered into another "Treaty of Friendship and Commerce" with France on January 10, 1908. Although Article 5 of this agreement guaranteed Ethiopia's right to import firearms through Djibouti and the Protectorate of French Somaliland, the French in return demanded and obtained simultaneous extraterritorial privileges. Article 7 of the agreement specified that French subjects in Ethiopia involved in legal cases must be tried according to French law and, if detained, placed in the custody of the French consul. In a similar vein, the Klobukowski Treaty of 1908 gave European residents in Ethiopia similar extraterritorial rights and fiscal privileges.

Another example of the shifting radical divergence of interests in modern international relations between Europe and Africa was discernible in the former's rejection of Ethiopia's application for membership in the League of Nations at the end of World War I. Ethiopia's independence, according to Europe's representatives, could not obscure the fact that it lacked the "civilization" expected of the community of free nations. Rather Ethiopia was threatened with partition by the victorious Allies along the lines foreshadowed by the Tripartite Treaty of 1906. Ras Tafari, who was an advocate of a single unitary Ethiopian state, succeeded, however, in staving off the design to partition the empire. Shortly afterwards, he was able to officially secure an acknowledgment of Ethiopia's independence by engineering his country's entry into the League of Nations in 1923.

The realignment of European imperial alliance also undermined Ethiopia's modernization scheme. In 1924, Tafari embarked on an important state visit to Europe, the first ever carried out by an Ethiopian ruler. During the visit, Tafari was advised to recognize the 1902 Ethio-Sudanese boundary agreement and the 1906 Tripartite Convention, which declared "that the Ethiopian Government should grant permission to the British Government to construct a Lake Tana dam." The dam's primary design was for the benefit the England's colonial holdings in Sudan and Egypt, with little consideration for Ethiopia's sovereignty and national interests. The project would control the outflow of water and meet the downstream needs of the colonial powers while denying the strategic imperatives of Ethiopia's modernist projects. Believing that this formula would imply his acceptance of British extraterritorial rights in the area, Tafari replied that Ethiopia would build the dam herself, after which she would subsequently "lease the water" to the government of the Anglo-Egyptian Sudan. The British however refused such a proposal. The Italians, on learning of Tafari's rejection, reverted to their earlier proposal for a coordinated Anglo-Italian policy towards Ethiopia. The powers "requested" that

Britain "assist" the Italians in building a railway from the border of Eritrea, cutting through the middle of Ethiopia, up to Italian Somaliland. This plan gained momentum as new discussions emerged about the partition of Ethiopia into spheres of influence for the Italians and the British. In spite of these external challenges, Ras Tafari upon his enthronement as Emperor Haile Selassie would seek to exploit the opportunity to further this unfinished project of modernity began by Emperor Menelik II. However, he had to contend with Ethiopia's domestic endemic hegemonic civil strife and balance of power crises.

MODERNIZING ETHIOPIA: THE ERA OF HAILE SELASSIE

With the demise of Emperor Menelik in 1913, the Ethiopian political terrain experienced extensive religious and political intrigues. In the process of incorporating the periphery of the empire, Menelik had engaged and subdued heterogeneous communities with varying degrees of military resistance. As a result, the system of governance put emphasis on centralization of authorities, an anomaly in a society with real or imagined modernist aspirations. Resistance to paramount rule and economic domination from the center was strongest in Arussi, Gibe, Sidamo, Bale, Ogaden, Kaffa, Wolamo, and Borana. Menelik's achievements as a modernizer had been undermined by the deleterious impact of the military activities in these areas. The incorporation of Sidamo and Arussi was described as one particularly characterized by a high level of brutalism and depopulation. This was followed by resettlement of conquered lands by individuals who wielded Amharist-sanctioned rights and availed themselves of local land and resources. The above activities were also a precursor to latter-day claims of "Ethiopian colonialism" by irredentist nationalists and scholars.

The late emperor's chosen heir was his largely ineffectual grandson, Lij Yasu, who was ultimately deposed in September 1916 by a group of conservative nobles. The nobles frowned upon the young leader's flirtation with Islam combined with his intransigence toward the veterans and nobility. Although Menelik's daughter, who was also Yasu's aunt, was subsequently proclaimed the empress Zauditu, the Ethiopian Church, which had been threatened, withheld its total support and sought to reform itself from within by consolidating its ideological basis of relevance, the empire. Under the rubric of a renaissance project for the Ethiopian Church and Ethiopian traditions, conservatives such as Fitawrari Hapte Giorgis Denagde also endowed Ras Tafari with their support as the heir apparent. This deft political act not only acknowledged the wishes of the old order but also represented the progressive temperament of a growing number of nobles who clamored for change. The church was, however, only interested in modulating its overwhelming influence in the Ethiopian body politic. It indeed was opposed to revolutionary changes in individual adherence to orthodoxy and consent regarding indigenous traditions on the one hand and any effort by the political elites to impose rational bureaucratic reforms on the other. These shortcomings ultimately invalidated the empire's modernist aspirations in spite of the efforts of Ras Tafari in his status both as regent and later as Emperor Haile Selassie.

Tafari Makonnen was born on July 23, 1892, in the village of Ejersa Goro in the Harar province of Ethiopia. His father was Ras Makonnen Woldemikael Gudessa, the governor of Harar, and his mother was Woyzero Yeshimebet Ali Abajifar. Tafari's imperial lineage and claim of hegemonic pedigree was primarily from his paternal grandmother, who was an aunt of Emperor Menelik II. The family also claimed direct descent to Makeda, the Queen of Sheba, and King Solomon of ancient Israel. Tafari received his first educational lessons from priests, notably Aba Walda Kidan, but he was also taught the ways of the Ethiopian aristocracy that included mastering the psalms in Geez through language lessons from orthodox priests. Many of the religious scholars were based at St. Michael's Church in Harrar. Tafari's father, Ras Makonnen, also invited French Catholic Capuchin monks from Harrar to teach his children diverse subjects including French geography, philosophy, Latin, and world history. Tafari learned to speak the Ethiopian languages of Amharic, Tigrinya, and Oromigna as well as international languages including English and German. Upon his appointment as governor of his native province of Harar in 1904, the future emperor was elevated to the rank of *Ras*, or governor, and made heir apparent. As a member of the nobility, he was introduced to the craft of statesmanship at an early age, including such exceptional opportunities as representing Emperor Menelik II at the coronation of King Edward VII of Britain in 1902.

With Regent Yasu forced out of contention, Tafari assumed his position and became the de facto ruler of the empire. At home, the emperor in waiting operated with the major imperative of completing the modernization project initiated by Menelik II. As parts of his duties abroad, Tafari served as ambassador for 14 years, and his diplomatic achievements included the facilitation of Ethiopia's ultimate acceptance as a member of the League of Nations in 1923. He had imagined that membership in the league would ensure his country a period of peace in which to develop free of the danger of the colonial ambitions of other global powers. Ethiopia's membership was of global diplomatic significance as the sole African or African-descended representative in a European-dominated forum. This sentiment was duly appreciated by the scholar W.E.B. DuBois, who had described Ethiopia's admission not only as an important historical achievement but also a significant phase in the world movement to "obtain freedom for the colored races."

In 1924, Tafari undertook an extensive foreign tour that took him to Palestine, Egypt, France, Holland, Belgium, Sweden, Britain, Italy, Switzerland, and

Greece. He approached his tour as a modernist monarch with a progressive outlook as he inspected new inventions and innovations presented in hospitals, factories, schools, and churches. He also made a lasting impression at every port of call, creating a cult of personality at home and an international goodwill abroad. This was a rare feat for an African leader in an era characterized by a narrow discourse limited to the charitable causes on behalf of non-European populations, especially those who reside in Africa. At the end of his visit, Tafari stated that the tour convinced him that Ethiopia needed major innovation and development reforms. He was also said to have taken delight in dissembling and reassembling machinery and equipment imported from overseas.

In 1926, Tafari consolidated his power, taking advantage of the death of two major conservative figures, the old warlord Habta Giorgis and the archbishop Mattheos. He also isolated *rases* who resisted his political influence or modernist initiatives. One of those individuals was Dejazmatch Balcha, the governor general of Sidamo, who had refused to outlaw slavery or embark on any form of development for the province as part of nation building. Some of the older and more conservative nobles saw the writing of change on the wall and tried to convince Empress Zauditu to eliminate Tafari. Unlike the empress, who had only a minimum of modern education, Tafari was at this stage widely read and equipped with a more sophisticated understanding of the nuances of local and global politics. More importantly, backed by his military generals and with an imperial guard composed largely of Ethiopians who had served with the British in Kenya or the Italians in Libya, he forced the hand of the nobles for a coronation and was crowned *Negus* (king) in 1928. The title was validated by a public proclamation that the new king would also have complete control of public affairs.

Opposition to Negus Tafari, however, materialized from other conservatives such as Dejazmatch Balcha Saffo, a general from Adowa, and Ras Hailu Tekle Haimanot, prince of Gojjam, both of whom rebelled on behalf of the princess Zauditu. The princess's husband, Ras Gugsa Wele, the governor of Gondar, also joined in this rebellion; his march from his base towards Addis Ababa led to his defeat and ultimate demise at the Battle of Anchiem in March 1930. News of his wife Zauditu's death followed in the same year, leading to the immediate crowning of the Negus Ras Tafari as His Imperial Majesty, Haile Selassie I, Conquering Lion of the Tribe of Judah, Elect of God, and King of the Kings of Ethiopia. The various rases and ministers of Ethiopia came from all over the empire to pay homage. The official coronation of Haile Selassie took place on November 2, 1930.

International representatives to the Emperor's coronation came from Britain, Italy, France, Sweden, Holland, Belgium, Germany, Poland, Greece, Turkey, Egypt, the United States, and Japan. Emissaries from around the world at the coronation also included Prince Henry, Duke of Gloucester—son of British king George V—Marshal Franchet d'Esperey from France, and Prince of Udine from Italy. The United States was represented by Special Ambassador Herman Murray Jacoby, who brought coronation gifts that were said to have included an electric refrigerator, a red typewriter emblazoned with the royal coat of arms, a radio-phonograph console, 100 records of "distinctly American music," 500 rosebushes, including several dozen of the so-called President Hoover variety, a new strain of amaryllis developed by the U.S. Department of Agriculture, a bound set of the *National Geographic*, a bound report of the Chicago Field Museum's expedition to Abyssinia, and prints of three motion pictures: *Ben Hur, King of Kings*, and *With Byrd at the South Pole*. The celebrations attracted considerable international media coverage, both of the monarch and of the country. The worldwide publicity accorded to the coronation had both positive and negative international ramifications. Through the popular media of the era, Ethiopia became far better known than ever before, above all in Africa and Africa-Diaspora communities, where many regarded the country as an island of independence and old glory in a sea of global imperialism. Observers of the ceremony also included international journalists and writers. Some could only satirize both the ceremony and Ethiopia's Solomonic heritage on the ground that Ethiopia's underdevelopment undermined any significant claim to being a potential player in modern global politics.

The years 1930 to 1935 were a significant period in the consolidation of political authority and development reforms in the empire. Upon his ascendancy, Selassie began a program of political reform by introducing a constitution that shifted the consolidation of the bureaucratic empire away from the calculated balance of disunited regional leaders towards one of decentralized authoritarianism. On July 16, 1931, Ethiopia's first written constitution was formally introduced. Described by some as the "people's constitution," the document aided the new emperor's desire to fracture the power of the feudal lords through the development of the authority of the central government or bureaucracy. He also established a parliament whose function was to discuss matters placed before it by the emperor. In reforming Ethiopia's political structure, the 1931 constitution provided for an appointed bicameral legislature and was the first time that non-noble subjects had any role in official government policy. This house was, however, predominated by members of the noble class who had already served the empire as ministers, judges, or high-ranking military officers. Selassie's control of central power was visible in the fact that he was the one who convened and dissolved parliament, appointed ministers, and had the full power to issue decrees when the chambers were not sitting. He also laid down the organization and regulations for all administrative departments.

It has been suggested that Selassie operated with the support of the educated intelligentsia, many of whom had critically observed various modern constitutions of European states as a model for the newly established bureaucratic culture, its administrative regulations and legal codebooks. The most important influence, it is argued, came particularly from scholars and reformists who not only articulated the need for local reforms but also attempted to mold the form of Ethiopia's external relations. One of the most influential groups was the "Japanizers," who had acquired this moniker because for this very project they had studied the Japanese Meiji Constitution. Impressed by Japan's metamorphosis at the end of the nineteenth century from a feudal society like Ethiopia into an industrial power, scholars like Heruy Welde Selassie, Bajerond Takle-Hawaryat Takla-Maryam, and Araya Abeba identified similarities between the Japanese Tokugawa Shogunate and the Ethiopian Zamana Masafent, the latter being a brief but turbulent period of political history, also called the Era of Prince, that lasted from 1769 to 1855. More importantly, they admired Japan for its administrative reforms that had been a potential tool for resolving the problem of underdevelopment.

Although the constitution created a senate and a chamber of deputies like the Japanese constitution, it was intended as a foundation for strong monarchical government rather than for popular representation. The emperor controlled the Council of Ministers, titles, and personal estates and treaties and had the power to pardon or commute penalties and to declare peace or war. The nobility and the local *Shums*, meaning appoint-demote, existed at the whim of the emperor-nominated members of the chamber of deputies. Of more relevance to Emperor Haile Selassie's hegemonic designs was the declaration in the constitution that his progenitors be declared from the moment onwards as the only legitimate line. According to the new document, Selassie and his sires descended "without interruption from the dynasty of Menelik I, son of King Solomon of Jerusalem and of the Queen of Ethiopia, known as the queen of Sheba." In addition, the emperor's office was described as sacred, his dignity inviolable and his power indisputable. The significance of the references to the nature of the empire and the procedure for imperial succession in the new constitution was that these steps effectively removed the legitimizing function from the church and transferred it into the hands of the monarch who promulgated the document. Nevertheless, the church's conservative presence was maintained, as little effort was made to functionally separate the power of the church from that of state, a prerequisite for modern governance. The church's immense wealth expanded at the detriment of the citizenry, and resources were extracted from national coffers and the peasantry in particular.

Haile Selassie maintained Ethiopia's allegiances to the Egyptian Coptic Church by allowing the latter to appoint a new archbishop to the country. He also appointed five new Ethiopian bishops, and the consecration of these spiritual ambassadors has been interpreted as the harbinger of the Ethiopian Christian Church as a fully functional national institution. The 1931 constitution did little to further modernization initiatives. Although it helped establish a parliament, there was no legal or administrative machinery to implement its programs. There was little judicial interpretation for most people whose fate and fortune were being dictated and shaped by the state. In spite of these shortcomings, Ethiopia as a modern state continues to relate to the world with a false sense of self-sufficiency.

Haile Selassie, however, achieved some success breaking the power of feudal barons by strengthening the authority of the central government and making the positions of the nobles dependent on legal and rational criteria instead of religious and traditional ones. His reform measures included a ban on soldiers' requisitioning or looting supplies from the peasantry, as the crime murder was confirmed as punishable regardless of political rank or economic class. The practice of unpaid feudal lords, most of whom lived off the country land, was an historic tradition designed to maintain balance of power and redistribute tributes to the central coffers. The emperor instead attempted to move the provincial administration closer to his concept of a salaried civil service responsible to the central government. Although the emergent political structure was described as modernist, mainly because rules were laid out for more professional bureaucracy, judiciary, and budgetary institutions, economic roles remained largely based on status as opposed to standards of achievement. In spite of a ban on domestic slavery and the establishment of a new state bank, Ethiopian clientelism guaranteed that political authority and economic transactions remain personalized and in the hands of old and new nobilities. Regardless of the stated commitment to the improvement in the capabilities and delivery of public services, the lack of economic development hindered the introduction of objective, impartial broad-based criteria that could aid professionalism and upward social mobility.

Haile Selassie achieved some success in education reform. He invested in state-sponsored educational projects and scholarship prompted by the desire to groom a future generation that, he expected, would help ease Ethiopia's transition into modern governance. Other aspects of educational reform included the amalgamation and codification of disparate educational administrative units into a singular ministry in 1930. By 1935, 10 new government-subsidized primary schools had been established in various provinces. Although Selassie's government expanded the pre-existing Menelik II school, the first modern Ethiopian school dedicated to grooming the sires of the nobility, he also established a new institution, the Tafari Makonnen School, in 1925. The latter school emerged as an alternative to the Coptic-dominated antecedent. Historian Bahru Zewde argues that the emperor was determined to outdo his predecessor and thus pushed the modernization process much further and faster than Menelik had ever envisioned. At the launching of a school for women in 1931, the emperor and his wife, Empress Menen, encouraged other Ethiopians to provide endowments to help fund new schools.

Education helped forge some level of gender gap, interethnic, and interfaith relations as groups from disparate social and economic classes began to live together with the growth of urbanization. By 1936, there were around 200 foreign-educated Ethiopians engaging in state issues at home and abroad. Communication across the territory was also aided by the importation of cars for private use and for public transportation. The introduction of telegraph lines and the proliferation of radio communication and the establishment of printing presses in Addis Ababa also contributed to the cultivation of modern nationalism. Model provinces were established where administration was controlled by Western-educated elites on the basis of responsibility to the ministry of the interior in Addis Ababa. Modern systems of taxation were introduced, with local salaries generated in the regions and the surpluses remitted to Addis Ababa. Many of the traditional dues popular in the feudal-based regions, usually in the form of food and produce levies, were abolished in favor of controlled taxation.

Although modern education helped eradicate some of the claims of tradition and authority, the attempt to embrace and apply new truths authenticated by the centrality of reason to the society often did not translate into a general improvement of social relations. Gender imbalance and a de facto system of occupational caste meant that the number of educated people remained limited within the imperial system. In addition, education was mainly available to individuals who came from families of the nobility and gentry, many of whom ultimately appended themselves to government's projects or employment. More importantly, Amhara and Tigre were disproportionately represented among this group. In addition, like Menelik, his predecessor, Tafari was uncomfortable with Ethiopian intellectuals who were not steeped in conservative, values, practices and obligations. The emperor, it was popularly acknowledged, also preferred to seek the advice of intellectuals who openly demonstrated their loyalty and deference to him. As a result, social mobility was not adequately connected to distinctive achievements or individual initiatives.

In spite of the above insufficiencies, Haile Selassie–led reforms helped create the foundational building block for the gradual metamorphosis of Ethiopia from a feudal or tributary state to a cash-nexus economic structure and a participant in the modern world economic order. Reform in land holding and land sales and a new form of land measurement and land-tenure reform helped a segment of the community participate in cash-crop production, especially in coffee. The emperor's modernist political reforms were, however, also tempered by a failure to dismantle the indigenous land-tenure system that remained entrenched within the church and state hegemonic order. Hence, social status remained dependent on landholdings, as this provided the basis for class formation and social stratification. The system of *gult* rights granted by the emperor or his designated representative either to members of the ruling group as a reward for service or to Ethiopian Orthodox churches or monasteries as endowments continued to influence social and economic interactions. The holder of *gult* rights, often but not always an official, was entitled to collect tribute and demand labor from those on the land over which he held rights. While some of the tribute was kept, the remainder was passed to the nobility and the emperor, while soldier settlers and older provincial rulers controlled and exploited land and labor in "conquered territories." One's genealogy and status remained the pivotal determinant factors in the allocation of goods, services, and recognition. With the emperor at the very top, the nobility and landlords occupied the highest rung of social and political hierarchy. In the next category were smallholding farmers, controlling small plot of land with low rental value, used to grow crops followed by millions of landless peasants who cultivated rented land.

Ethiopia's infrastructural vulnerability in what was arose out of a dependence on the warrior class of noblemen, who had dual responsibility as administrators in the service of the state. By the twentieth century, most of the southern landlord class consisted of Christian settlers from the north. The tenants, on the other hand, were mostly non-Christians and indigenes of the area. This development points to gradual transformation in ethnic and cultural differences anchored on the old social economic order. It complicated the process of class formations and social relations while laying the foundations for future individual and communal disputes. In spite of the above limitations, the Ethiopian state unified the domestic market with increasingly centralized control over custom revenues. There was also progress in the areas of the organization of the police force and the delivery of public health. Some of Ethiopia's leading notables abandoned careers based on the display of military prowess for ones that stressed the acquisition of capital, especially through the production of cash crops. The modern educational and military institutions, however, emerge as an important outlet for a large segment of the younger generation.

Protecting Ethiopian Sovereignty: The Role of the Military and Academic Sectors

Haile Selassie had begun reforming the military since when, as regent in 1919, he appointed a small group of Ethiopians and Russian officers with many in the former group having served in the British-led King's African Rifles and training exercise. He continued the process through a heavy project of recruitment, armament purchase, and extensive use of foreign military advisors from diverse backgrounds including English, French, and Belgian. The Swedish missions were, however, favored in the training of the Imperial Guard, which helped maintained the emperor's hegemony in the capital while protecting him from regional opposition such as that posed by Ras Gugsa, the governor of Gondar and Begemder, who was soundly defeated in the 1930 conflict. In 1934, a military college was opened at Holeta under the guidance of Belgian instructors, and soldiers of promise were sent to the French military academy at St. Cyr for further training. Ethiopia under Selassie also purchased airplanes that were initially manned by French pilots, many of whom also helped with the establishment of communication and military reconnaissance missions. As part of the building up of Ethiopia's national development, new fleets of airplanes were imported both for state and for military use, and the Ethiopian Air Force was established in 1929. By 1935, of the close to 200,000 to 300,000 men who were mobilized, about 7,000 had received some form of modern military training. By 1933, there were also between 100 and 150 African Americans in Ethiopia, many of whom were motivated to contribute to the only truly independent African state. Two out of the three planes that composed the Ethiopian Air Force were flown by Black Americans: John Robinson and Hubert Julian. Julian had flown to Ethiopia in 1930, where his exploits impressed Emperor Haile Selassie, who awarded him honorary Abyssinian citizenship and the rank of colonel.

Between the end of the nineteenth century and the outbreak of World War II, generations of Ethiopians received secular education in a variety of fields from various academies around the world. Based on their travels, marks were made aware of the technological backwardness of their societies and became progressive advocates of modernizing the Ethiopian polity. In their varied and expansive writings, they hoped that the appeal for social, economic, and technological progress would convince the traditional authorities to be less xenophobic and more importantly embrace change. Historian Bahru Zewde divides these reformist intellectuals into two groups. The first generation received their education at home and abroad during the reign of Emperor Menelik II (1889–1913). With the support of the royal family, foreign benefactors, and Catholic and Protestant missionaries, these reformist intellectuals included Gabra-Heywat Baykedan, Warqenah Eshate, Gabru Dasta, Afawarq Gabra-Iyyasus,Takla-Hawaryat Takla-Maryam, Atsme-Giorgis Gabra-Masih, Heruy Walda-Selassie, Gabra-Egziabher Gila-Maryam, and Deressa Amante. While calling for social, cultural, educational, and administrative reforms, their writings came in the form of ethnography, historiography, and political economy. They wrote on issues of social justice, gender, religious persecution, slavery, famine, poverty, and the question of nationalities. Notable among this group are Gabra Heywat and Afawarq, both of whom condemned the Ethiopian state for the exploitative activities of the military in the countryside toward the peasantry and a policy lacking both *serat*, or ordered governance, and the building of national espirit de corps. According to historian Bahru Zewde, Gabra Heywat Baykadan underscored the importance of this premise with a statement that, "An ignorant people does not have ser'at. And a people without ser'at has no stable power. The source of power is ser'at, not the multitude of an army. A small town governed by law is much better than a big state withoutser'at."

A second group of the intellectuals emerged between the early 1920s and 1934. Most were educated abroad, in the Middle East, Italy, Britain, the United

States, and especially France. They also enjoyed state and royal patronage, and like the first generation of modern intellectuals also wrote with conviction, albeit in less quantity. Examples include Aklilu Habta Wald, who was educated in Egypt and France, Ashaba Gabra-Heywat, educated in Switzerland, Faqada-Selassie and Sirak Heruy, educated in England, and Efrem Tawalda-Madhen, Dawit Ogbazgy, Getahun Tasamma, Engeda Yohannes, Makonnen Hayle, and Makonnen Dasta, all of whom spent some time in Lebanon before shipping out to the United States in search of modern education. Tedla Haile went to Belgium, and Fallaqa Walda-Hanna, Hayla-Maryam Takle, Makurya Walda-Selassie, and Mikael Tasamma were among the group sent to Italy. The group educated in the United States included Bashahwerad Habta-Wald, Malaku Bayyan, and Warqu Gobana, who all attended the Presbyterian college in central Ohio, with the first two doing graduate school work at Ohio State University. Most of these emergent elites saw their education as an extension of Ethiopian national independence and development. Out of this particular group however, Malaku Bayyan emerged as the individual most concerned with bridging the gap between Ethiopia and the larger African American community. As part of his modernist-inspired politics, the Ethiopian scholar had invited a number of African American professionals, including the celebrated pilot Hubert Julian to Ethiopia. Bayyan later exploited his contact with the larger black world during the period of Italian invasion of Ethiopia. While in exile with Emperor Selassie, he was able to galvanize support for the Ethiopian cause through an organization he helped found, the Ethiopian World Federation, whose activities are further explored in this narrative.

Conservative groups in Ethiopia resisted what they considered radical reforms. One such conservative was Menelik II's former minister of war, the aged Fitwrary Habta Giorgis. Fitwrary, like other conservative elements in modernizing societies, was opposed to Haile Selassie's interest in external, mostly European ideas and innovations. Fitwrary led a formidable group of nobles whose vested interests in feudalism largely influenced their opposition to reform. Feudalism varied from province to province in Ethiopia, but was predominant in the Galla region. In other regions the governors and their officials often looked upon the provinces as conquered fiefs. However, they wanted to hold onto them only long enough to take advantage of the resources they might have to offer. There was also a major clash between old ministers and young directors general of institutions stipulated for reforms. In the words of one observer:

> Older men of rank, who still wore baggy white jodhpurs with bandages round their heads and straggly beards round their chins disliked the civil service and the young directors and "to keep them in their place they made these young men with moustaches and European clothes bow down to the ground in the presence of age" and if the young whipper-snappers still wore

shemmas, they had to tie them across their chests out of respect for the old men's blood and rank. Meanwhile, the old men would sit heavily in their chairs exchanging words of primeval wisdom, supporting their policy by proverbs, and pretending not to notice the callow youth around them.[3]

Opposition to foreign influence also came from a small but significant group of Ethiopian intellectuals known as the Young Ethiopian Movement. Led by Kiade Mariam Aberra, a Tigrean from the Italian colony of Eritrea, members also included Wolde Giorgis, Makonnen Hapte Wolde, Ayela Gabre, and Bashawarad Hapte Wolde. Although this group was educated abroad or in the foreign Christian missions, they bridled at the arrival of foreign advisers who were paid very large remunerations. Arising largely out of families of lower and even peasant status, this group also resented the fact that influential government positions were usually reserved for persons of high family rank. They highlighted and discussed the social, economic, and political problems of the industrialized societies while also taking exception to the racial discrimination they faced while abroad. The ultimate goal of this group was greater opportunities to apply their knowledge and skills in their own country. They encouraged Emperor Selassie to recruit more African American technicians and pilots. The planes were used only for transportation of materials and medical supplies. Of more significance to this cadre of reformers was the contribution by black American nurses and doctors from New York's Harlem Hospital. They organized medical-supply drives in support of the Red Cross doctors that assisted the Ethiopian Army. The doctors for these missions also came from America, Austria, Britain, Egypt, the Netherlands, Finland, Greece, Norway, Poland, Sweden, and Switzerland.

The contradiction between Ethiopia's modernist aspiration and the emperor's insistence on it being an absolutist state was further compounded by the brewing international crisis between Ethiopia and her old nemesis, Italy. The vastness of the country and lack of adequate transportation and communication meant that Ethiopia with its defeat by Italy paid the price for the failure to modernize.

Although it was not formerly colonized, Ethiopia did not escape the colonial era, and Ethiopian leaders also endured colonial racial antagonism and repression. The impact of colonialism on Ethiopia was, however, more complex and filled with contradictions. Ethiopia for many centuries resisted integration into the world capitalist system by adhering to a tributary mode of production and by granting only select concession rights to foreign entrepreneurs and investors. The emperor also embarked on the expansion of social, economic, and political modernization reforms. In reality, the above modernization efforts were often superficial and merely paintings of the social fabric with accoutrements of modernity without refashioning the totality of the governmental institutions with the "ether of modernity." This would include the concept of individualism, the centrality of reason, and governance by consent. In contrast to Protestant Reformation, which many adherents often expanded to fulfill secular modernist aspirations, the extrabiblical political tradition of Orthodox Christianity inhibited radical reconstruction of Ethiopian traditions. It should be acknowledged that the threats posed by external forces also engendered the construction of ideological bulwarks against the clamor for radical change. Ethiopia was able to protect its sovereignty through the panoplies of Orthodox Christianity as an ideological bulwark and the firewall for a strong military tradition that honored and rewarded martial activities.

By the end of the nineteenth century Ethiopia had embarked on the selective Westernization of infrastructures and the transition from a tributary or feudal structure into a modernizing autocracy. Although these reforms had been in full swing by the first half of twentieth century, the Solomonic crown could only redefine the divine obligations of the citizenry to the state, and this allegiance was hardly reciprocated by the political elites to the citizenry of the state. Free from the pressures and restraints associated with a mass franchise, the elites expressed the determination to define the course and nature of modernization, but instead the consolidation of royal absolutism limited the opportunities for social mobility for Ethiopian elites and citizenry. The Ethiopian intelligentsia also often found true patronage only through the indigenous royal family, who occupied a strategic post between the encroaching influence of global capital and local public politics. There also emerged a chasm amongst those educated elites who undertook the mission of guiding the state towards reform and others who wanted to protect the absolute rights of the monarchy. As a result, the potential for the foundation for modern political parties and social movement was further undermined.

By the twentieth century, Ethiopian Orthodox Christianity, which found in biblical-inspired narratives the elucidation and predictions of state affairs, gradually found it expedient to fully reconfigure such spiritual foundations with a more sophisticated appreciation of temporal exigencies. With the impetus provided by Haile Selassie, national constitutions and secular memoranda increasingly complemented the Holy Scriptures as the guiding light for Ethiopian national aspirations. Modern reforms were also instigated by a demand for recognition by Ethiopia before the international community and its corollary organizations. The progressive impulse in Ethiopia was in this instance fueled by the promise held in the modern articles of trade and the protective charters of collective security. The expectation in Ethiopia was that these modern institutions would protect its sovereignty even as it provided "good government." In most cases, however effective governance was marked by improved security for select denizens, especially the residents of the capital or those in close proximity to the center of the empire. In spite of the above factors, Ethiopia's lack of "industrial revolution," according to historian Teshale Tibebu, must not be blamed on its "feudal" relations of production. Instead, he argues, Ethiopia's political independence does not separate it from the experience of other colonized African countries. The common denominator is that high fiscal investment on modernist infrastructure was often inadequate for those societies who wanted to frame a reconstruction project that could wean them from the peripheral status in the era of industrial capitalism. Since the modern state in Ethiopia, like the rest of colonial Africa, arose not as an agency of socioeconomic change but as a method and apparatus for garnering resources and maintenance of security, its emergent national bourgeoisies could not possibly replicate the accomplishments of their Western or Japanese counterparts, Tibebu concluded. The future of Ethiopian modernization goals after the Italian invasion, however, proved even more complicated as both domestic and international politics were redefined with major complex and contradictory implications for elites and peasantry alike.

In twentieth-century Ethiopia, a centralized system of governance gained ascendancy as Haile Selassie paid more attention to preserving the throne he had inherited relying mostly on foreign advisors to navigate the global system. Led by a benevolent autocrat, the Ethiopian state condemned or jailed educated elites who operated outside of the bounds of the modernizing autocracy. Many were accused of being heretics and apostates, while others were forced into exile or restricted under the watchful eye of the royal guards and security units. In spite of these developments, educated elites were also able to exploit a combination of unique professional skills and sometimes their familial pedigree to demonstrate their commitment to transforming the status quo when operating in royal circles. Thus with the support of imperial patronage, this group enjoyed relative professional success even if their reformist aspirations were always being truncated. The greatest damage, however, was to be meted upon these educated elites during the Italian invasion when hundreds were summarily executed by the fascist army for spearheading the resistance against the hegemony of colonial invaders.

Although Ethiopia was mythicized as the epitome of African independence, the state also experienced European colonialism, albeit, one filled with complexities, ambiguities, and pluralities. Marina Ottaway argues that Ethiopia did not experience colonialism like other African states, and as a result, the idea of a modern Ethiopian nation did not crystallize around the notion of a common African struggle against a European colonial power. The pressure of foreign capital, however, was equally imprinted on Ethiopian social and political relations, an experience it shared with the rest of colonized Africa. This latter factor, according to Edmund J. Keller, is most visible in the crystallization of new ethnicities and social classes as a result of colonial pressures in the Horn of Africa. In addition, like the rest of Africa, the region also witnessed the formalization of old and new unequal relations as access to capital and resources became racialized on one level—the global—descending into a hierarchy of ethnicities on the other—the local.

The metanarrative of modernity was channeled into Ethiopia through the political center controlled by Amhara, and the notion of progress was mapped onto ethnic differences. As a result, the non-Semitic speaking population was compelled to transform or reconfigure its ethnic and religious identity in order to become modern or adopt Amhara customs to acquire a modern education. This is thus a powerful example of what Michael Hanchard describe as the link between *racial time* and *public time* i.e. the structural inequality that racial differences have imposed on transnational or national political relations. The implication of racial time is manifested in unequal access to the opportunities made available by modernity such as goods, social services, state resources, political power, and cultural hegemony over local epistemologies. Modern inequalities were primarily reproduced in Africa based on differential access to the expansion of a cash-nexus economy and modern education, two dominant signifiers of modernity and ethnic hierarchies. In this regard, the "intellectuals," a category that often included the nobility, military and civilian aspirants to governmental office, invariably all worked with old and new ideas that helped entrench various forms of asymmetrical relationships. As Ethiopia defended its territorial integrity from European encroachment, the militarily superior Amhara-Tigre peoples simultaneously dominated its subject peoples who resided in the margins. In dealing with their subjects, the dominant group manipulated the condition in which politics is played out through the unequal access to institutional goods, services, resources, and power. Ethiopians who harbored radical modernist aspirations were thus trapped between the limitations imposed by the Orthodox Christian demarcation of the nation and the Amhara feudal chauvinism on the one hand and threat of external (European) hegemony via military or economic contraptions on the other. As a result, both Amhara and non-Amhara peasants and intellectuals could not easily translate the domestic political and economic grievances into a viable social and political movement. If modernist reforms and progress could be described as the emergence of a rational basis for revolutionizing the mode of production, commercialization of knowledge, and the devolution of power and fiscal and material resources, especially in tax- and landed-revenue appropriations, and the consent of the governed over those who rule over them, the need for progressive change could not have been more imperative for Ethiopia. Against this background, many Ethiopian political elites at the end of the nineteenth century and the beginning of the twentieth have been described as antimodernist, since power and influence in the state remained entrenched in central bureaucrats such as the *balabats* (local chiefs) or landlords and *neftegnyas*. The most important prerogative of these officials was however limited to the imposition of taxation and security boundaries as opposed to spreading the idea of progress across class and regional boundaries.

Some of the contradictions and ambivalences inherent in Ethiopian modernism were temporarily resolved at the end of the nineteenth and the beginning of the twentieth century. The cultural definition of the nation acquired more relevance as European colonial activities increased in the Horn region. The Italian invasion of Ethiopia in 1935 and events surrounding the breakout of World War II also gave new impetus to Ethiopian narrative of Afromodernity. According to historian Ruth Ben-Ghiat, the Italians, like other imperialist powers, billed their colonial war in Ethiopia as a modernizing mission that would deliver Africans from backwardness, slavery, and chaos. Fascist propaganda, she argued, depicted the Italians as an army of tireless altruists who built roads and bridges, transformed deserts into gardens, and brought peace and prosperity to the indigenous peoples. Ethiopia, on the other hand, also became the anchor upon which the idea of the common African struggle against European colonial powers was drafted within Africa and across the African Diaspora. The significance of Ethiopian civilization and independence led to its description in the twentieth century as "the black man's last citadel," which must be protected at all costs from European colonial designs.

NOTES

1. Bernard Makhosezwe Magubane, "The Significance of Ethiopia in Afro-American Consciousness," in *The Ties That Bind: African-American Consciousness of Africa*, ed. Magubane (Africa World Press, Inc., 1987), 163.

2. Evelyn Waugh, *Waugh Abroad: Collected Travel Writing/Evelyn Waugh* (New York: Everyman's Library, 2003).

3. Richard Greenfield, *Ethiopia: A New Political History* (New York: Frederick A. Praeger, 1965), 174–75.

4

World War II and Aftermath: Reconstruction and Other Contradictions, 1935–1960

There is little evidence that Ethiopia and the dominant Amhara political ruling class considered itself a pioneer "black nation" until the beginning of the European imperial wars, when the linkage between Ethiopian history and antiracist and anticolonial African nationalism became part of the modern lore. Yet, for scholars of African and global political, economic, and intellectual relations the history of Ethiopia was about to acquire an even greater significance when it was invaded by Italy in 1935. This chapter explores how Ethiopia's modernization reforms were interrupted by the historical episode described by historian Ruth Ben-Ghiat as a watershed in the history of the fascist project of Italian modernity. The development in the complex widespread ramifications had tremendous impact on both domestic reform and international diplomacy. Ethiopia also experienced important national achievements as well as national calamities including the loss of a great segment of its population across age, class, and gender. The chapter also highlights the connection between these events and the birth of modern civil rights and decolonization projects in Africa. It critically analyzes the intellectual and political history that occurred between the era of Italian invasion of Ethiopia and the emergence of a new politics of the African Diaspora.

The end of the nineteenth century witnessed the refashioning of "race" and racial relationships on a global scale. This was revealed most clearly in what scholar David Theo Goldberg described as "the spectacle of racial contrast of

Europeaness and Africanity, of civilization and presumptive primitivity." This concept, he continues, was subsequently recirculated between world fairs and international expositions in "European spaces." Even though it had escaped formal colonization in the nineteenth century, Ethiopia's experience in the first half of the twentieth century would be influenced by the shifting matrices of power, culture, and knowledge buoyed by an entwined complicity between geographical definitions and European imperialisms. The idea of Ethiopia as a black nation in colonial discourse was shaped not only by the combination of European military and economic superiority, but also by an equally effective label that reflected broader political ends in the shape of ideas, forms, images, and imaginings about "otherness" and hierarchies of civilization.

The notion of prestige occupies a central place in all colonial discourse, but according to Ruth Ben-Ghiat, it may have held a special meaning for Italians who viewed empire in the Horn of Africa as an escape route from a subordinate international position. Italy sponsored and was in turn legitimated by professional associations such as the Italian Academy and the National Council of Research, ethnographers and scientists who had earlier mapped Italian ethnicity as part of the regime's "revival of tradition" but who now began to investigate the inhabitants of East Africa. Ben-Ghiat concluded that, as demographers compiled a massive "ethnographic atlas" of Italian East Africa and colonial experts displayed their classification of East Africa's "racial types" in periodicals such as *Ethiopia* and *Africa Italiana,* these taxonomies of colonial knowledge drew on technologies of social control and population management that had informed official blueprints for a fascist modernity. One school of thought held that the Pope Pius XI also gave his pontifical blessing to Mussolini's conquest while another suggested that the Pope was either ambivalent or lacked the ability to influence any decisions about the Italian foreign excursions. While the invasion of Ethiopia provided Italian political and popular discourse a temporary tool for the validation of their European identity, the international incident also had the unforeseen result of contributing to the launch of what historian Kevin K. Gaines described as "the short African century of decolonization movements." According to Gaines, the latter activities as part of a new wave of Afromodernity, were advanced by the social transformations wrought by mass labor migrations, military service in world wars, intellectual attacks against Western white supremacy and the spread of antiracist consciousness, and literary and expressive cultures that articulated black peoples' aspirations for cultural and political freedom. By the second half of the twentieth century, the intersection of domestic and international geopolitics ensued that there was hardly any debate about Ethiopia's "blackness" or Africaness as its political and economic fortunes had guaranteed its embeddedness in the new naturalizing and legitimating geopolitical spatial theory of the marginalized—"sub-Sahara Africa."

The foundation for Ethiopia's achievements in modern global political and international relations, especially as it affects race and imperialism, was laid by Emperor Menelik II, who was celebrated around the black world at the dawn of the twentieth century. It is of symbolic significance that Menelik was once approached by Benito Sylvain, a Haitian intellectual and pan-Africanist, who later became the Emperor's aide, to not only embrace his endowed role as "the greatest black man in the world," but also to embark on a program "for the general amelioration of the negro race." Sylvain and African American political activist William H. Ellis were on one hand trying to establish an Ethiopian refuge for black Americans along with business and development plans, while on the other hand they were also of the hope that Ethiopia's endorsement was a requisite for the establishment of a "colored lobby." One perspective held by historian Alberto Sbacchi held that Sylvain failed to receive this endorsement; others such as Olisanwuche Esedebe painted a more rosy picture. Emperor Menelik and the presidents of Haiti and Liberia were subsequently made honorary presidents of subsequent Pan-African congresses because they represented the only independent black nations in an era of European imperialism. In spite of the above developments, Menelik retained his counsel with select European advisers and allies. In a similar vein, his succesor Selassie continued the largely defensive, survivalist foreign policy begun by the late emperor. At the end of World War I, Selassie had courted the friendship of Western powers by dispatching diplomatic missions to the victorious allies in Europe and to the United States, congratulating them on their military triumph. He achieved a great diplomatic success when his country was accepted as a member of the League of Nations in 1923. The expectation was that membership would ensure Ethiopia a period of peace in which to develop free of any threat from the colonial ambitions of other powers.

The reign of Haile Selassie was marked by an increased recognition of the interconnected significance between race, imperialism, and modern African nationalism. As highlighted above, with the exception of Liberia, an isolated nation-state weakened by colonial exploits in West Africa, and Haiti, which was equally undermined by the legacy of slavery and imperialism, the only other historically independent black nation by the twentieth century was Ethiopia. In another modernist twist to African Diaspora movement, "Rastafari," movement emerged in Jamaica among working-class and peasant black people in the early 1930s who declared Haile Selassie the earthly representative of Jah, the Rastafari name for God. The group saw the coronation of Selassie as no less than the realization of the biblical prophecy that "Kings would come out of Africa." The Jamaicans who identified themselves with this monarch of an independent African state accorded the emperor the status of divinity, as the Messiah of African redemption. In essence, the Rastafari movement combined an interpretation of biblical prophecy, black social and political aspirations, and nationalism to help inspire a new progressive and countercultural worldview.

Ethiopia, however, continued to pursue its modernist aspirations and although it had looked toward Europe, it was now exploring the trappings of unique Asian modernism in the first few decades of the twentieth century. Europe was however desirous of stifling a relationship between the Africans and the Asians and more specifically preventing Japan from expanding its cultural, economic, and political influence in the Horn of Africa. This goal coincided with a new social imperialist theory which holds that expansion abroad could remedy social ills at home and that the propagation of one's own culture among the "lesser races" was the noblest act one could perform. The above idiosyncracies were very visible in the colonial activities of the Italians in Africa. According to its minister of the colonies, Aleassandro Lessona, "To draw the Dark Continent into Japan's orbit would deprive Europe the possibility of using Africa for the defense of her civilization." Italy had been unhappy with the 1919 post–World War I treaty that had overlooked its desire for "a place in the sun," in the form of an African colony. As a late participant in the scramble for Africa, Italy had secured Eritrea, which consisted of the natural coastal region and the peripheral foothills of the Ethiopian Highlands, with a capital at Asmara. The African colony was thus for many Italians another symbol of its modern achievements, and a validation of its identity as a dominator in colonial Africa.

Britain and Italy had in 1925 signed and publicized an agreement that not only recognized each other's spheres of economic interest in the Horn region but also affirmed that such interests expanded beyond and into the Ethiopian boundaries. In 1926, Selassie was able to exploit Ethiopia's membership in the League of Nations, and obtained an agreement that guaranteed the state's sovereignty. His dignified insistence that the league's "Treaty Series" should publish his protest against the Anglo-Italian agreement had been described as a major diplomatic initiative in modern African history.

In the early 1930s, as the fascist regime of Benito Mussolini of Italy embarked upon a new period of expansion in northeast Africa, he sought to exploit the fact that Ethiopia's peripheral areas were not effectively controlled from Addis Ababa, the capital. The combination of factors including frequent nomadic raids, migration, and a very fluid social and economic relationship threatened Ethiopian autonomy. Beside the attempt to exploit Ethiopia's feudal structure, the Italians also infiltrated the correspondences and communications of Ethiopian consuls with the aid of its commercial agents, medical personnel, and missionaries. Of more importance, however, was a sense of foreboding in Ethiopia regarding the impending conflict with Italy because of the decline of the united and efficient political and military front nurtured by Emperor Menelik. Unlike Menelik, whose policy was based on the "Amharization" or "Ethiopianization" of conquered chiefs whose power and status no longer depended on lineage rights but rather on military and political services to the state, Selassie's political strategy was based on a policy of centralization. The latter's policy had major negative ramifications for the state, as it engendered ever-present separatist tendencies combined with troubled notions of the relationship between the state, the subjects, and the citizenry. Unlike Menelik, who was able to raise a force of more than 600,000 riflemen combined with a standing army of more than 200,000 and innumerable traditionally armed warriors capable of guerilla warfare as part of national defense, Selassie's modernization scheme had led to more concentration of absolute power in the hands of the emperor. In addition, an emergent class of professional civilian administrators had also pushed the traditional warrior class to the margins. Of most importance, however, was the fact that by twentieth century standards the Ethiopian standing army was overwhelmingly underequipped. It should be added that the colonial presence in the Horn region of major European players placed some limits on the quantities of firearms entering Ethiopia, thus making it very difficult for the government to sustain the policing of its peripheral boundaries. The state's sovereignty continued to rely on the unifying role of Orthodox Christianity and the monarchy, and its legitimating features also served to ideologically unify the population. The Italian invasion was to put the sustainability of Ethiopian unity and modernist project to its ultimate test.

BACKGROUND TO WORLD WAR II: ITALY INVADES "THE BLACK MAN'S LAST CITADEL"

Italy, operating from its colonial base in Somaliland, had considered the Horn of Africa a vast territory of untapped mineral wealth and decided to embark on territorial expansion into Ethiopia. The Wal Wal incident at the unmarked border between Ethiopia and Italian-controlled Somaliland provided the excuse the Italians needed. Wal Wal was an outpost in the Ogaden desert containing wells frequented by Somali nomads who, before European partition, crossed between territories now occupied by the British, French, and Italians. The infamous Wal Wal pretext was not only a deliberate provocation but also emerged as a test of endurance for the fluid nature of African physical and social mobility, the viabilities of transnational treaties, the exercise of power in colonial expansion, and competition over national rights.

Egged on by a nationalist press, Italy proceeded to consolidate its presence in the Horn with the construction of a new military fort towards the end of 1934. This action ended the bulwark provided by the framework of the Anglo-Ethiopian Boundary Commission, which had maintained a competitive albeit precarious balance of interests. The Boundary Commission had challenged the Italians, but withdrew its presence when it encountered hostilities in the form of a low-flying military plane over an Anglo-Ethiopian military force garrisoned in the area. The British chief of the mission, Lieutenant Clifford, declared the reason for withdrawal as the need to "avoid a diplomatic incident." The commission subsequently stationed an Ethiopian military unit which invariably found itself engaged in military skirmishes with the Italian garrison. Two weeks later, Ethiopian and Italian forces consequently clashed at Wal Wal, thus beginning the series of events leading to the formal Italian invasion of Ethiopia and a precursor to World War II.

In January 1935, Ethiopia lodged a formal complaint with the League of Nations, demanding that both the spirit and letter pertaining to collective security agreements embodied in its charter be invoked and applied. Ethiopia's grievance was that the body was not adhering to its operating maxim that an attack on one member of the league was to be considered an attack on all the members. The British government made some tentative efforts at mediation, with minimal positive effect. European states had generally come to terms with each other's political interests via "bilateral partition treaties" that drew boundaries between their respective spheres of influence in Africa. Others had imposed direct control over African states and societies by force, a process that was often long and bloody. The United States abstained from partaking in the dialogue by taking refuge in an isolationist policy, while the French, wary of pushing Italy towards an alliance with Germany and thus upsetting the balance of power, instead forbade the export of arms into Ethiopia. As an extra measure, France also supported territorial adjustments in favor of Italy at Ethiopia's expense.

The Hoare-Laval Pact of 1935—named after the British secretary of state for foreign affairs, Samuel Hoare, and the French prime minister, Pierre Laval— sought to partition Ethiopia as a last means of ending the Italo-Ethiopian war. The document in question was written to satisfy the demands of Benito Mussolini, who had insisted on making Ethiopia the newest Italian colony. In 1894 Emperor Menelik had struck a deal with France to assist in the construction of the Ethiopian railroad. Upon completion in 1917, the Djibouti to Addis Ababa road carried 75 percent of Ethiopia's foreign trade and in 1933 returned a profit of 200 francs per transported ton to its French investors, who subsequently owned 20,000 out of 34,000 shares. Part of Pierre Laval's deal with Benito Mussolini included the sale of 2,500 French shares of railroad stock to the Italian government. The Hoare-Laval Pact also stipulated that while the mountainous south of the Ethiopian empire was to remain independent, most of the rich and fertile north was to be delivered to Italy. Mussolini was ready to concur and append his signature until the plan was leaked and subsequently denounced by many international observers as a betrayal of the Ethiopian sovereignty and national interest. When the League of Nations finally lifted its arms embargo against Ethiopia, the Franco-Italian agreement ensured that guns and ammunition could not reach the African state by way of the railroad from Djibouti but only by motor truck to Harar 125 miles from the British Somaliland border. Based on the above developments, many observers condemned the vulnerable position from which the Ethiopians were forced to operate. The loudest and most consistent forms of protest came from the African Diaspora communities.

African associations like the Nigerian Prominent Lagos Women's Society and the Ethiopia Relief Fund Committee of Enugu passed resolutions of protest, with the former group drafting a message that was forwarded to the League of Nations. In Africa, the West African pilot under the editorial command of Nnamdi Azikiwe also campaigned on behalf of Ethiopia. An Abyssinian Relief Fund was established in Trinidad, which called for colored people in England, America, Africa, and the West Indies to support its mission. Black protest organizations also exploited a burgeoning pan-African media and propaganda tools of the Marcus and Amy Jacques Garvey–led Universal Negro Improvement Association. Examples of such groups in the Caribbean included the Friends of Ethiopia, the Afro-West Indian League, and the Negro Welfare Social and Cultural Association, all from Trinidad. Anti-Italian colonialist sentiment was also expressed in the British Guyana, Grenada, Saint Vincent, and among the black population in Venezuela. A Diaspora organization, the Ethiopian World Federation founded by Dr. Malaku Bayen, Emperor Selassie's representative in the United States, also launched a new publication, titled the Voice of Ethiopia (VOE), which had global subscription and distribution coming across the globe. As a result of the international campaigns, the British government dissociated itself from the much-maligned pact that would have partitioned Ethiopia, and diplomats Hoare and Laval were both forced to resign their appointments. The Italo-Ethiopian crisis was, however, just about to reverberate around the world.

On October 3, 1935, without a formal declaration of war, Mussolini ordered an attack on Ethiopia from Eritrea and Somalia. Ethiopian forces had been ordered to withdraw from the lines of confrontation so as to expose Italian aggression to the world and to stretch the enemy's line of supplies. On October 7, the League of Nations unanimously declared Italy an aggressor, yet it failed to follow up with any meaningful action. The general mood of the greater European populace seem to be on the side of Ethiopia. Emperor Haile Selassie had become the embodiment of African nationalism at home and in the black world and a symbol of interwar liberal humanitarianism and international misgivings about the warped notion of balance of power in Europe and the rest of the world. In any case, the growing sense of another global hegemonic conflict loomed large.

The above events were highly significant in the build-up to World War II because they demonstrated the weakness of Europe and the unwillingness of the League of Nations to aggressively combat the growing threat of fascism. In Ethiopia, the national army experienced some defections among its ranks especially in the peripheries of the empire including Tigre and Oromo. Across the land, however, the nobility and their subjects did not wait for Emperor Selassie to formally declare war before the consensus was reached that the citizenry must rise and defend the territorial integrity of their land and the pride of their ancient civilization. When Mussolini's army finally made its foray into Ethiopian territory, Ethiopia mobilized its armies by beating the *negarit* (war-drums of Menelik) at the palace in Addis Ababa.

Although its armies put up a great resistance to the invasion, Italian success against the Ethiopian army was almost superior to the former's military technology. Most of the Ethiopian troops were armed with swords, shields, and outdated weaponry and were indeed no match for the modern artillery of the Italians, which included tanks, machine guns, and airplanes. In addition, the Italians received a numerical boost from its *Askaris,* or colonial troops made up mostly of Africans conscripted into the army, especially from Eritrea. The invading army also used poison gas not only against Ethiopian soldiers but against civilians, including women and children.

EARLY ETHIOPIAN RESISTANCE

Some historians contend that the five-year Italian occupation of Ethiopia was the understated marker of the start of World War II. In so doing, they also underscore a lack of acknowledgement of Africa's contribution to the military and political successes of World War II. The scholars were particularly concerned with the war crimes committed against African patriots, many of whom sacrificed their lives as part of the Ethiopian and Allied forces who resisted and ultimately defeated fascist ideology and military aggression. As part of its effort to revive "national interest" and resistance against the colonial invasion, Ethiopia made efforts to press recalcitrant *rases*, that is, governors, into the service of the state. As subjects, many of the administrators had real grievances against the state, and thus their support could not always be relied on. Some of the political leaders in the vassal territories, such as Ras Hailu Tekle Haimanot, prince of Gojjam, had been humbled and imprisoned by Emperor Selassie. Others, like Ras Haimanot, had also been neutralized and restricted, but upon his liberation chose to collaborate with the Italian invaders. Another former prisoner of the emperor, Deajazmatch Balcha, however, followed a very different course and later emerged as an iconoclastic figure of the Ethiopian resistance movements. This Oromo noble in defense of Ethiopia resorted to the traditional stratagem of guerilla warfare as part of an insurgency against the Italian occupation. A popular narrative of resistance chronicled how Balcha's life ended in the battlefield. At the end of his military wits and lacking adequate replenishment, the noble warrior had conveyed a message to the local Italian commander near Harrar to arrange a surrender. Wrapped in his traditional white shawl and sitting under a tree, he beckoned to the commander and his guards, and as they approached him let out a loud cry invoking the spirit of "Menelik, my master" as he pulled out a machine gun. Balcha succeeded in dispatching all of the senior Italian officers before the latter's accompanying orderlies summarily gunned him down. As part of their resistance effort, many Ethiopians often invoked the biblical phrase popularized under the reign of the late Emperor Menelik, "Ethiopia stretches her hands towards God." This spiritual invocation not only formed the basis of Ethiopian rejection of the offer of Italian "protection" prior to being victorious over the invaders in the first Italo-Ethiopian war of 1890, it was also now the vocalization of the temporal military and political victory.

During the war, Emperor Selassie was active in the defense of his territory as he joined his troops at the warfront, even manning antiaircraft guns during the battle of Maichew. He was also proclaimed to have embarked on several trips to the ancient church of Lalibella to pray without his usual large, protective royal entourage and cavalry. His diplomatic representatives on the other hand were busy building international diplomatic support to shore up military supplies and seek redress against Italian aggression. In spite of a valiant effort of the Ethiopian troops, they were pushed back on the northern front and all the way to Harerge. With this development, Emperor Selassie and the royal family were advised to escape to Jerusalem.

By March 1936, Europe's interest as well as that of other international diplomatic communities had shifted away from Africa as Hitler's army moved into the Rhineland, and the war cloud threatened to spread beyond the Horn of Africa. In May 1936, the Ethiopian royal family fled just days before Addis Ababa, the capital was occupied. From Jerusalem, the emperor prepared a presentation of Ethiopia's case before the League of Nations. In June 1936 in Geneva, Switzerland, Emperor Selassie read a speech, described by U.S. *Time* magazine as one of the noblest, most factual, irrefutable, and moving ever made before the League of Nations. In spite of the bellowing jeers and curses of the Italian press gallery that went on for more than 10 minutes, Selassie's speech, titled "Appeal to the League of Nations," provided the disparate antiimperialist and antifascist platforms a most articulate, yet civil indictment of the modernist notion of collective security and international morality. Selassie was subsequently named *Time* magazine's "Man of the Year" for being an icon for antifascist movements around the world. The fact that the emperor's speech was read in Amharic as opposed to the traditional "diplomatic languages" also placed Ethiopia and Africa in the annals of modern global political and international relations. Among the issues raised in the emperor's speech was the prediction that fascism would boomerang upon the rest of Europe if left unchecked. The emperor's final statement, "It is us today. It will be you tomorrow," has been described as the final epitaph for the impotent League of Nations. Ethiopia's appeal and request for a loan to help defray the cost of war, however, fell on deaf ears at the summit as the world's great powers seemed ambivalent about its travails. Ethiopia won a moral victory and some modicum of international support from transnational progressive movements and especially Afro-Diaspora political organizations. The Italo-Ethiopian war set the stage for domestic and international political realignments in Ethiopia, Africa, Europe, the Caribbean, and the Americas.

In the United States, thousands of black Americans expressed a desire to fight for Ethiopia in a spirit of a modern pan-Africanist impulse, but the U.S. State Department refused to issue the required travel passports. On the other hand, hundreds of Italian Americans, including New York mayor La Guardia, rallied and raised volunteer troops on behalf of Italy, and many Americans of Italian descent obtained the permission to travel and fight for Italy. It must also be noted, however, that some Italian Americans also participated in highlighting the Ethiopian cause. Led by political figures such as Harry A. Maurer, they submitted a petition protesting the policy of the Fascist regime to the Department of State, and a petition to the Italian ambassador in Washington. Some scholars have also argued that only two years after an outburst of enthusiasm for Mussolini following the Duce's conquest of Ethiopia and the establishment of an Italian empire in eastern Africa in 1936, Italian Americans had begun to distance themselves from the fascist regime especially in the wake of the passing of racist, anti-Semitic legislation.

Systematic opposition to Ethiopian interest, however, emerged in the United States from the Federal Bureau of Investigation, wary that the intersection of antifascism and antiracist movements threatened the domestic, social and political order. The bureau actively monitored recruitment of volunteers on behalf of Ethiopia in the African American communities, but such efforts could hardly terminate the sweeping tide of this latter-day "Ethiopianist" intellectual and political project. The crisis in the Horn of Africa also led civil rights organizations like the National Association for the Advancement of Colored People to support the Ethiopian cause. Its official publication, the *Crisis*, regularly educated the larger community and general public about events in Ethiopia and the rest of colonial Africa. Other African American organizations explored the possibility of floating financial loans for Ethiopia with the assistance of the U.S. State Department, but received little encouragement. In New York, Harlem-based associations including the Universal Negro Improvement Association (UNIA), the Young Men's Christian Association (YMCA), the Elks, and the League of Struggle for Negro Rights came together under the platform of the Provisional Committee for the Defense of Ethiopia. Notable speakers at pro-Ethiopian rallies included Adam Clayton Powell, minister of the Abyssinian Baptist Church; Joel A. Rogers, a noted journalist; Willis Huggins, a historian; A. L. King of the UNIA; and James W. Ford of the U.S. Communist Party. In July 1935, the American League against War and Fascism and the Provisional Committee for the Defense of Ethiopia sent Willis Huggins to Geneva to present a petition to the League of Nations.

Huggins had also convened with two Ethiopian diplomats, Azaj Workneh Martin, minister to the court of St. James, and Tecle-Hawariate, minister to France and a delegate to the League of Nations. In London, Ladipo Solanke, leader of the West African Students Union, also helped organize public events to protest the invasion of Ethiopia.

The African Diaspora's public dissatisfaction with mainstream perspectives of Ethiopian history and civilization in the context of the Italian invasion of the African state encouraged the *Pittsburgh Courier,* a leading African American newspaper, to dispatch journalist Joel A. Rogers to cover the war. Rogers's departure on the SS *Normandie* on October 1935 invariably confirmed him as one of the first black war correspondent in the modern era. Rogers published a popular, illustrated pamphlet entitled *The Real Facts About Ethiopia* the following year. In 1934, African American historian William Leo Hansberry had helped launch the Ethiopian Research Council to stimulate American resistance to the Italians in Ethiopia and to disseminate knowledge about the history of Ethiopia. In a similar vein, in 1935, the International Council of Friends of Ethiopia was established to mobilize "Black support." Another association, the Blyden Society (named after the nineteenth century black leader Edward Wilmot Blyden and formerly known as the Harlem History Club), also performed an outstanding role as support group for Ethiopia. One of the movement's able leaders was John G. Jackson, who in 1939 authored the publication, *Ethiopia and the Origin of Civilization.* Other diasporic activities on behalf of Ethiopia in the United States came from the Ethiopian Students Association, the National Negro Congress, and the Council of African Affairs, led by Dr. Max Yergan. The 1930s and 1940s were marked by an internationalism and fellowship among the colonized peoples of the globe. It also witnessed a mobilization of African Diasporic solidarities on the basis of what historian Penny Von Eschen described as the forging of a historical and social "identity of passions." The above individuals and communal associates developed an imagined community that would include all people of African descent. As architects of the politics of the African Diaspora they creatively reshaped the language and ideologies of the 1930s and constructed the politics of the African Diaspora. In doing so, they also benefited from a powerful cross-fertilization of socialist internationalism and the elevation of the struggles of colonial peoples for independence. And these goals were anchored upon resisting the Italian invasion of Ethiopia.

The Ethiopian Resistance to Italian Occupation

In spite of the international outrage against its actions, the Italians consolidated their hold on Ethiopia, a process that began with the occupation of the capital, Addis Ababa. In early June 1936, Rome promulgated a constitution that adjoined the Ethiopian empire to its erstwhile colonies of Eritrea and

Somaliland to form the "Africa Orientale Italiana," or "AOI." This administrative unit was subsequently divided into six provinces that included "Eritrea," which consisted of much of Tigre and was centered on Addis Ababa; "Galla-Sidamo," with its epicenter in Jimma; "Harar," with its focal point being the city itself; and "Somalia," which also enclosed much of the Ethiopian Harar province. Eritrea was expanded to include the northern Ethiopian province of Tigre, and the Ogaden area was merged and redistricted into Italian-controlled Somaliland and designated as part of the new colonial principality. All the above provinces were directed from Addis Ababa, the major political seat of the viceroy.

By December 1936, Italy declared that the whole country was fully pacified and under the effective control of the colonial authorities. The fact was, however, more complicated. The Italians were either mostly confined to their forts or restricted to major towns. Besides the geopolitical restructuring of Ethiopia, colonial administrative units were also established to replace old imperial provinces. A corollary of the military occupation and administration was that the Italian army and officials and members of the Fascist Party often employed brutal force in suppressing local communities. Aided by five different police forces in Addis Ababa—the *carabinieri*, the colonial police, the police of the army, the Blackshirts, and the secret police of the party (the OVRA)—brutal punishment and summary execution were meted out to individuals and communities engaged in counterhegemonic activities. The Italian administration stressed white racial and especially Italian superiority over the local communities, who were in essence segregated based on a public policy that restricted them to the lowest level of public status or employment. Italy also imposed state control over the Ethiopian economy as it appropriated the state's gold reserves and production.

In spite of military and political efforts the Italians began to question the human and material costs of fighting Ethiopian resistance. In addition there was a growing international outrage over some of the most brutal forms of exploitation in the twentieth century.

The Italian administrators had, however, engaged in some capital development such as the expansion of commercial agriculture and improvements in public services tied to road construction, bridges, hospitals, and schools. The above projects and the facilitation of Italian settler communities to help with development initiatives, however, could not alter the primary purpose of Italy's presence in Ethiopia: the Italian "place in the sun," a strategic site for future territorial adventures and hopefully exploitation of available natural resources. In addition to the cost of demographic colonization, the Italians also encountered delays and difficulties in creating unified zones of colonization that were contiguous to another. As a result, most colonial settlements were isolated in enclaves thus creating additional expenses for the metropolitan government. In addition, there was also a lack of employment for many colonists as a sizable number were forced to settle in areas deemed unhealthy and dangerous. According to historian Haile Larebo, the Italian Ministry of Colonies was unprepared to deal with the pressures that came from the unemployed Italians who sought work and land in Ethiopia, nor were they equipped to deal with the demobilized soldiers, and a strong business lobby that wished to expand its commercial enterprise in Ethiopia.

Active resistance, among the restive Ethiopians continued, and in February 1937, after a failed assassination attempt against the Italian viceroy Graziani, the colonial forces unleashed a three-day reign of terror on the local communities. Close to 30,000 Ethiopians, including nearly half of the fraternity of young citizens educated at home and abroad as part of Ethiopian modernization project, were summarily executed. It was later confirmed that the Italian leader Benito Mussolini had in the early phase of the invasion highlighted the need to eliminate the young Western-educated in Ethiopia to thwart the potential of an organized a counterhegemonic intellectual and political project. The Christian Church in Ethiopia also suffered from fascist persecution, as many patriotic monks who resisted the Italian presence were summarily executed. Churches were razed to the ground as priests, deacons, and bishops, including Abune (Bishop) Petros and Abune Mikael, were executed for the crime of providing encouragement to the patriots who had planned to retake Addis Ababa from the occupying force. Following the discovery of weaponry meant for the resistance at the Shewan monastery of Debra Libanus, the Italian forces summarily eliminated 350 monks, and their bodies were disposed of in a nearby gorge. The occupying authority subsequently appointed a new archbishop for the Orthodox Christian Church, thus breaking the centuries-old tradition of spiritual coordinator between Ethiopia and the Egyptian Coptic Church.

Among the celebrated patriots of Ethiopian resistance was a 21-year-old man from Eritrea named Zerai, who had been dispatched to Rome to present some captured Ethiopian trophies, including a sword, at a public function that included fascist leader Benito Mussolini and the king of Italy. Unaware of the grandeur of the occasion and hardly playing the part of a representative of a subjugated people, Zerai knelt in prayer and regret upon noticing the gold Lion of Judah, which the Italians had removed from the Addis Ababa railway station. As the Italian police tried to restrain him, he turned around and killed five fascist officials. Zerai was then brought down in a hail of bullets and later died from injuries, but he was commemorated at the end of the war and has been ever since. To commemorate his contribution to Ethiopian independence, the first military vessel of the Imperial Ethiopian Navy in the postwar era was named after this icon of national resistance.

Another popular war tale involved the military resistance displayed in the fight against the Italians in Shewa by Dejazmatch Fikre Mariam and Gimma Sembete. Although both men were killed in battle, the body of Mariam was never located, giving rise to the lore that his concern for the morale of his troops and followers led the mortally wounded general to crawl into a cave or crevice to bury himself.

Heroic female members of the patriotic front included Woizero Balainesh of Arusi, Lakech Demissew, Woizero Ayalech, Konjit Abinnet, Woizero Likelesh Beyan, Woizero Abedech Cherkose, Likk Yellesh Beyen, Abebech Cherkose, Kelemework Tiruneh, and Kebedech Seyoum. Perhaps the most accomplished of this group was Shawaragad Gedle, who, before joining the patriots, had bestowed her personal resources to the International Red Cross working in Ethiopia. Her active resistance to occupation led to a series of public whipping and imprisonments, including a close shave with death during battles in the Debra Berhan region. Shewaragad, who also lost a son in the Italian reprisals, died during the chaos and general insecurity that ensued at the end of occupation.

In spite of Italian reprisals, the Ethiopian resistance nevertheless continued with the church providing both the inspiration and a unifying umbrella. In an attempt to create a bulwark against the church, the Italians displayed a favoritism towards the Muslim community as it aggressively promoted Islamic influences. The Italians sponsored Islam as the alternative ideological underpinning as a means of creating new fissures in the Ethiopian body politic. This policy was particularly observable in the colonial establishment of higher schools of Islamic instructions in Harar and Jimma.

The Italian invasion and occupation of Ethiopia was accompanied by numerous atrocities including the summary execution of captured prisoners without trial and the elimination of Christian Orthodox Bishops and non-Christian notables labeled as "witch doctors." Punitive expeditions were sent to regions like the Ankober area, and large tracts of occupied territories were depopulated. After the Graziani assassination attempt, the fascist Blackshirts were let loose in Addis Ababa and surrounding towns and many historic structures including the St. George's Cathedral, built during the reign of Menelik II, were destroyed.

About 300 of the young Ethiopians educated and groomed by Selassie as part of the new generation of intelligentsia were summarily executed. Some have argued that this missing generation was a broken thread in modern Ethiopian intellectual and political history. Historians wonder if the lost generation could have interceded to help resolve some of the modernist project contradictions of Ethiopian modernity. The clash between the proud and influential older generation and the revolutionary counterpart was fully consummated in the post–World War II era. The total number of civilian Ethiopian deaths resulting from Italian punitive actions was placed by some sources at approximately a quarter of a million but postwar estimation of casualties was considerably higher.

FASCIST MODERNIZATION PROJECTS

During their five-year occupation, the Italians did much to dismantle Ethiopia's national institutions, which were then replaced with what the colonial authorities considered to be more modern substitutes. In reality, the new formulation was more conducive to exploiting the country's rich yet untapped economic potential. One of Mussolini's primary goals was the settlement of the Ethiopian heartlands with a crop of Italian middle class and a sizable peasant class, who he believed could help transform the extractive industry for mineral resources in Ethiopia and hopefully help turn the agricultural sector into the "granary" of Italy. The Italian administration also curbed the power of the traditional elites, abolished the *gabber* peasantry labor tied to the local system of land tenure, and infused massive amounts of capital and developmental infrastructure into Ethiopia's underdeveloped economy.

In spite of the overwhelming effort, it became evident by November 1937 that the Italian policy of occupation and pacification was a failure. One of the banes of the colonial administration was corruption in its bureaucratic ranks. General Badoglio, the commander-in-chief of Italian forces, was reputed to have taken close to half of the 1,700,000 Maria Theresa thalers (Ethiopian currency) that had been confiscated from the Bank of Ethiopia in the immediate aftermath of Ethiopia's defeat.

As a result of the above and other shortcomings, the Italian viceroy of Ethiopia, Marshall Graziani, was recalled and new policies were enacted. Many of the concentration camps filled with Ethiopian prisoners were shut down, and a general policy of appeasement was launched. As part of the new order, a new program of economic development was established in the ministries of industry, commerce, and agriculture. The Italian settler families were expected to participate in agricultural programs, overseeing local and migrant laborers to achieve the goal of expanding cash-crop production for export. Local investments including oil mills, flour mills, saw mills, and textiles and cement producing factories emerged as part of the accoutrements of the Italian project of colonial modernity. Other colonial modern endowments in Ethiopia included newly paved roads, imported Italian cars and trucks, and the proliferation of new skills related to the maintenance and service of modern transportation in the country. Some of Ethiopia's architectural landscape also bore the mark of the Italian presence in places such as Harar, Jimma, Gondar, and Addis Ababa. The Italian Ministry of Colonies helped construct low-cost housing structures in some major Ethiopian cities and Addis Ababa, the capital, which also at this time received its first major-scale urban supply of electricity. Although there were several forms of professional and personal liaisons between the Italian colonial personnel and Ethiopian citizens, the policy of racial segregation enforced a separation of public facilities and a ban on interracial marriage. The

Italian colonial project proved to be an overambitious scheme. The agricultural resettlement plan ultimately produced insufficient returns and the administration was forced to resort to the importation of grains. The invasion and occupation of Ethiopia had required the drafting of close to 500,000 Italian troops, out of which some 15,000 were killed and 200,000 wounded. At the end of the day, Ethiopian officials estimated that it had lost close to 760,000 members of its citizenry during the occupation.

Many of the old guards of the indigenous Ethiopian policy in the south continued to resist Italian control from the epicenter of the empire. Rasta Desta Damtew in Sidamo, Bejorond Fikre Selassie in Arusi, and Dejazmatch Beyenna Merid in Bali all remained in control of their governorates for a long time. Patriot bands also flocked to join individuals like Balambaras Abebe Aregai, Gimma Sembete in Gala, Fitwrary Baide in Harrar, and Blatta Takele at Sabata. The most organized intellectual opposition to Italian occupation, however, came from a patriot group called the Black Lion organization. The leadership, both political and military, was drawn from the educated elite, many of whom not only expressed dissatisfaction with the lack of access to basic modern material necessities in Ethiopia but also sought to overhaul the state's military defense infrastructures. Led by the British-educated veterinary surgeon, Dr. Alamawarq Bayyana, another Anglophile, Faqada-Sellase Heruy, and Benyam and Yosef Warqenah, sons of Ethiopia's minister to London, the Black Lion set out a 10-point manifesto for a nationwide resistance cum renewal of the society. The constitution of the "Black Lion" included the following: an affirmation of the supremacy of the political over the military command; provisions for the humane treatment of prisoners and the non-molestation of the peasantry; the prohibition of exile; and the injunction of suicide rather than capture by the enemy. Members had expressed to Emperor Selassie's beleaguered viceroy, Ras Imru, the need to evolve a more modern and democratic concept of organization and leadership while bestowing on the latter the leadership role in carrying out their mission. Imru was, however, forced to surrender to the Italians in December 1936, after which he was kept in captivity until his demise. Subsequently Kefle Nasibu and Balay Hayla-Ab provided military leadership among the Black Lions. After having been recruited amongst several others from the Tafari Makonnen School to become cadet-officers at the Holata Military School. In spite of their ambitious program, both the political and military wings of the Black Lion organization enjoyed limited success. Nevertheless, they left a remarkable imprint on the spatial and theoretical scope of Ethiopian resistance against Italian fascism. Many leaders of the organization, including Bashahwerad Habta-Wald, Faqada-Selassie, Benyam, Yosef, Kefle, and Balay, were arrested and summarily executed following the attempted assassination of the Italian viceroy, Marshall Rodolfo Graziani.

In spite of the heavy casualties suffered by their homeland, some Ethiopian elites such as Afawarq Gabra-Iyyasus, an intellectual and diplomatic representative to Rome, helped the fascist cause and gave glowing accounts of the overall mission of the Italian regime, especially in agricultural production and development initiatives. Other Ethiopian notables including Blatta Walda-Giyorgis and Walda-Yohannes also offered their allegiance to the Italians. Others individuals who gave their service to the Italian administration included Qagnazmatch Takla-Marqos Walda-Gabrel, a former secretary to the emperor, Blatten Geta Walda-Maryam and Berhana Marqos, both ex-diplomats, and Blatta Ayyala Gabre and Balachaw Jamanah, who were also notable bureaucrats in the state. One school of thought described the defectors as opportunists who embraced the Italian pretense to a civilizing mission in Ethiopia in order to pursue self-centered goals of upward mobility. Others argue that these individuals were misguided by the progressive veneer of fascist ideology, and once they realized the true mission of the colonial authorities, they ultimately emerged as tragic figures and paradoxical entities who in their desperation for progress and modernization reforms embarked on a trip down the wrong and treacherous path.

Most of the patriots in Ethiopia and loyalists to the imperial family, however, continued to resist the idea of permanent Italian occupation. A continuous guerilla warfare by the patriots, who numbered close to 300,000, forcibly transformed the occupation into more or less a garrison presence. Ethiopian novelists, poets, and dramatists also drew extensively on their country's fascist experience in many of their postwar writings. Germachew Tekla-Hawaryat, Ato Welde-Giyorgis Welde-Yohannes, Senedu Gebru, and Aseffa Gebre-Mariam, among others, provided a written dimension to the popular oral traditions and songs of Ethiopian resistance. The Ethiopian prime minister, Bitwodded Mekonnen Endalkatchew, also published a novel specifically addressing some of the historical events surrounding the invasion and occupation.

Although the traditional military and political class of Ethiopia had been less than successful in the major battles of Tembien and Maichew, a new group emerged towards the end of the war. This consisted of *balabat*, or low-level indigenous administrative personnel, drawn from the surrounding countryside. This rank also included several members of the noble family. Another group of elites also came forth motivated by the desire to deconstruct and overhaul what they considered to be some evidence of atavism of the Ethiopian political system. In the latter group were mostly graduates of the new Holeta Military College and St. Cyr in France. The desire for domestic reforms was highly tempered by a new definition of national interest anchored upon a postwar effort to obtain redress and recognition for Ethiopian sovereignty. It has been argued that the nationwide resistance to Italian occupation ultimately made the invasion more of an interlude in the course of modern Ethiopian

history. However, this qualification does not mitigate the negative psychological and structural impact of Italian aggression upon the Ethiopian body politic and national interests.

Whereas many Italian and European media outlets and publications un-
derreported the Italian atrocities in northeast Africa, there were also other international publications that expressed serious concern about the plight of the
Ethiopians. A good example was the *New Times and Ethiopian News*, founded
and edited by the English suffragette and activist Sylvia Pankhurst. An out-
spoken enemy of fascism and a critic of Britain's political project aimed at
postwar deconstruction of a united Ethiopian state, Pankhurst devoted the
last 40 years of her life to Ethiopian and other antifascist causes. She was
consistent in her support for Ethiopia, which was able to remain as Africa's
principal independent state. Ethiopia also garnered support in the international media from European liberal circles, especially from metropolitan
progressives and socialists. These included Mauden Royden, a pioneer suffragette, and Wilfred Roberts, a British member of Parliament. Yet, none stood
out more than Sylvia Pankhurst. In addition to the 1935 publication, *Ethiopia,
A Cultural History,* in 1936 Pankhurst launched the first edition of the *New
Times and Ethiopia News,* a weekly paper that was in circulation for 20 years.
The paper, which at its highest level of popularity sold 40,000 copies weekly,
was circulated extensively throughout West Africa and the West Indies. Africans on the continent and in the Diaspora warmly appreciated Sylvia Pankhurst's relentless campaign for the restoration of Ethiopian independence, first
against the Italians and then against the British postwar designs. The scholar
W.E.B. DuBois surmised that Ms. Pankhurst single-handedly introduced
"black Ethiopia to white England, to give the martyred emperor of Ethiopia
a place of refuge during his exile and to make the British people realize that
black folks had more and more to be recognized as human beings with the
rights of women and men."[1]

While in exile in Britain, Haile Selassie continued to appeal for the support
of the Western democracies to embrace his cause. He, however, achieved limited success until Italy entered World War II on the side of Germany in June
1940. With the emergence of the fascist Axis, Britain launched a new military
program that combined the resources of the Allied powers and that of African
forces, which included soldiers from Ethiopia, Nigeria, Ghana, the Sudan, and
southern Africa. Other soldiers also came from the Indian subcontinent. The
first stages of the military campaigns were primarily designed to dislodge the
Italians from Ethiopia and British Somaliland which the Italians had annexed
in August 1940. A second mission was to repulse the Italian threat to another
British colony, Sudan. The task of commanding this diverse campaign fell on
the leader of the Anglo-Ethiopian military mission, Colonel Orde Wingate. As
part of the military equation, Ethiopian patriot fronts were also able to secure
entry into Ethiopia through the British colonies of Kenya and Sudan.

Haile Selassie had nurtured the image of a warring emperor, albeit one with a modernist inflection. To consolidate his reign and political image, while in exile, he was able to broadcast and arrange for propaganda leaflets to be dropped into Ethiopia. With the aid of pamphlets and newspapers and the proliferation of oral traditions, hagiographies, patriotic songs, and poetry, Ethiopia not only resurrected its past histories on behalf of the new cause for victory but also launched a new clarion call for national unity and development.

On January 20, 1941, Haile Selassie arrived in Gojam and immediately undertook the task of harnessing the disparate local resistance groups under his military and political control. By the end of the year, Ethiopian troops successfully engaged in and won several territorial battles waged against Italian forces. However, they continued to face a domestic threat due to isolated pockets of resistance from local irredentist forces. Many of the indigenous rebels had exploited the chaotic atmosphere and the reconstruction of political alliances and balance of power to carry out raids and pursue parochial ambitions. The emperor reentered Addis Ababa in May 1941 backed by the Anglo-Ethiopian troops. He also sought and received limited help from the British to suppress domestic political intrigues in the far-flung Ethiopian empire. As part of the new arrangment Selassie signed an agreement with London in January 1942, which later proved to be controversial based on language that suggested a new and unequal power relation. Britain's role in liberating Ethiopia from Italian rule gave it heavy influence over postwar reforms. Selassie, however, expressed concern that Ethiopia not become a de facto protectorate of Britain. Nevertheless, Ethiopia signed the 1942 agreement, which gave Britain extensive control over her finances, administration, and territorial integrity. The British government also obtained a measure of control over diplomatic prerogatives in the new role as "advisors" and judges in key Ethiopian administrative networks. As part of the new equation, the commander in chief of the British Forces in east Africa also superseded the command of Emperor Selassie in determining air traffic rights, the declaration of war and state of emergency.

Emperor Selassie was able to make amends and regain most of his power in 1944 upon the signing of the second Anglo-Ethiopia Agreement. The new political arrangement also granted Ethiopia the right to appoint its foreign representatives. Of high relevance, a section of the Addis Ababa–Djibouti railway was conditionally restored to Ethiopia, guaranteeing access to external trade as well as arms supplies for the defense of the country. Within the scope of the new agreement the Ethiopian Ministry of War placed the army under the guardianship of the British Military Mission to Ethiopia (BMME) for organization, training, and administration. The British government also proceeded to take control of the Ethiopian territories of Eritrea and Ogaden. The former was to be divided so that the lowlands were united with the Sudan, with which they shared geographical, ethnic, and religious affinities, and the predominantly Christian highlands were to be allowed to form a separate state. As for the latter territory of Ogaden, it was to be added to British Somaliland and the former Italian Somaliland to create what was described as Greater Somalia. These decisions not only perpetuated the administrative divisions set up during Italian occupation, but ultimately denied Ethiopia access to the coast while sowing the seeds of political irredentism and ethnic conflicts for the future.

Critics of the Anglo-Ethiopian Agreement stressed that although the British helped remove the yoke of Italian colonial power from Ethiopia's back, but that the British sought to replace the Italians with a more sophisticated colonial relationship. The historical events that occurred in northeast Africa between 1885 and 1939, and particularly in Ethiopia, merit recognition as an example of the challenges and dilemma faced by modern African states during a period some have described as the "high noon" of European colonialism.

Due to World War II events, a renewed role for Ethiopia's military emerged. The antiquated hierarchical structure of the military supported by provincial levies was jettisoned followed by the establishment of new military doctrine and a professional modern army. The creation of a strong national territorial army also had as a secondary motive the disarming of various guerilla bands, many of whom took advantage of the social and political instability to engage in personal enrichment and territorial aggrandizement. Many of the men in these rebellious ranks were incorporated into the national army. Ethiopia also signed a convention with London that guaranteed military assistance to assist with the training and organization of a professional corp that would carry out postwar social and political reconstruction.

Some historians described the end of Italian occupation in 1941 as one filled with missed opportunities for both de facto and de jure reconstruction of Ethiopian society. World War II had elevated the discourse of Ethiopian modernity as defined by the possibility of improving the lives of a population that was rapidly increasing in number and had both conventional and unique needs. The major contradiction that has always been part of Ethiopia's modernization process, however, reemerged at the end of the war. There was wide chasm among the elites between those of a critical and independent spirit and a commitment to revolutionary transformation of the human condition on the one hand and another group of "educated nobility" on the other. While the former group was largely made up of individuals whose middle class position and status were largely independent of landownership, the latter group swore allegiance primarily to Emperor Selassie, who seemed bent on a minimalist approach to reforming the absolutist state governed by a centralized monarchy. The Western-educated elites were later accused of jettisoning their reformist responsibilities. The fascist invasion of 1935 had put an end to the experiment of collaboration between the reformers and the benevolent autocratic modernization of the royal leadership. Due to the Italian invasion, many of the Ethiopian intelligentsia were killed or went into exile. For those who stayed, instead of social and political critique, survival often meant acquiring a new imprimatur of the loyal and dedicated servant of the state. These domestic turn of events were, however, also being dictated by the evolution of international politics and diplomatic relations.

POSTWAR ETHIOPIA: RECONSTRUCTION, REDRESS, AND RENEWAL

Although fascist atrocities during the war were widely condemned by a select number of individual organizations, the subjugation of Ethiopian citizenry went officially unacknowledged by the League of Nations. The atrocities only became the subject of international judicial consideration after Italy's entry into World War II in 1940. In Europe, many who supported Ethiopia in Europe during the war later capitulated to the politics of the day, which placed more emphasis on the transcontinental strategic and, according to some, a racialized alliance amongst fellow European states including Italy. An often-cited example was that of Philip Noel-Baker, a minister in the Foreign Office in Clement Attlee's post–World War II government. A future Nobel Peace Prize winner, Noel-Baker summarily ended his campaigns for Ethiopian rights in his status as a Labor MP in favor of the UK Foreign Office dictates which had always evaded any specific questions of Italian war crimes.

As earlier stated, Italy's invasion of Ethiopia became the catalyst for the intersection of the internationalist anticolonial activities and the domestic civil rights and antiracial movement in Africa, Europe, and the Americas. According to historian Joseph E. Harris, the invasion led to the development of an international constituency spanning the United States, the Caribbean, Europe, and Africa in an affirmation of a shared identity and racial and colonial burden among people of African descent towards the establishment of postwar antiracist, anticolonial, and civil rights movements. The events that followed the invasion of Ethiopia also led many in the black intelligentsia to question the commitment of European liberals, and particularly that of European Communists, when it was revealed that the Soviet Union had contravened a latter-day League of Nations' sanction that barred nations from trading with fascist Italy in war materials. Pan-Africanists and black activists including Marcus Garvey, the leader of the Universal Negro Improvement Association (UNIA), described Europe's part of the indifference to Ethiopia's plight as a legacy of modern racism. Scholar activists such as George Padmore, C.L.R. James, Ras Makonnen, Jomo Kenyatta, and I.T.A Wallace Johnson, all of whom had helped established the International African Service Bureau in 1937, also drew up the link between anticolonialism and antiracism. This union, they argued, was the necessary prerequisite for global democracy. Other anticolonial groups such as the International Committee on African Affairs under Max Yergan and aided by the social activists, artists, and scholars Paul and Eslanda Robeson also fueled the free Ethiopia campaign. The National Association for the Advancement of Colored People (NAACP) not only implored the U.S. government to be more proactive on the Ethiopian cause but also underscored the Soviet Union's hypocrisy for supporting the vision of collective security except when it applies to modern black nations. As part of the implication of Ethiopian history on African Diaspora intellectual traditions, a segment of an emergent radical black scholarship described fascism not as some aberration from the march of human progress, but as a logical development of Western Civilization itself. Their group viewed fascism as a blood relative of slavery, imperialism, and the racist ideologies that were already in place at the dawn of modernity. They in turn, called for a transnational, interracial alliance to help resolve some of these not so positive contradictions of modern civilizations.

Haile Selassie's return as a power player in the Horn of Africa after his time in exile hinged on the support of British Prime Minister Winston Churchill and Foreign Secretary Anthony Eden, who saw him as a strategic albeit unequal partner in the Horn of Africa region. After the surrender of Italy, the demise of Mussolini, and the collapse of fascist reign in Europe, the Allied powers led by Britain accepted Italy back into their fold but chose to ignore Ethiopia's claim for redress. Towards the end of the war, the newly established United Nations created a War Crimes Commission, but Ethiopia was the only major ally of the Western powers that was excluded from its fold. In July 1946, the Ethiopian government embarked on a diplomatic initiative to seek redress for Italian war crimes. This process began with a major diplomatic correspondence that drew attention to Europe's failure to acknowledge the spirit and principles of diplomatic charters. Article 37 of the draft treaty presented by the Ethiopians also demanded that: "Italy will restore all Ethiopian works of art, religious objects, and objects of historical value removed from Ethiopia since October 3, 1935." The treaty accepted by the international body, however, only dealt with war crimes in a general sense without any specific reference to Ethiopia's request. In addition, the deliberations over the postwar treaties were restricted to four ambassadors from Rome, the Soviet Union, the United Kingdom, and the United States.

Ethiopia listed its grievances and subsequently forwarded them to the U.N. secretary general in New York, the International Military Tribunal in Berlin, and the British Legation in Addis Ababa. With the help of an American advisor, Professor John H. Spencer, Ethiopia pressed the council to include two important points in the document negotiating an Italian peace treaty in 1946: 1) that World War II began for Ethiopia on October 3, 1935, the date of the Italian invasion; and 2) that the powers accept the principle of *postlimitium*, that is, the agreement that the Ethiopian government had continuously exercised jurisdiction over its affairs for the period after the 1935 invasion as well as before it. According to the principle, once an enemy occupation is terminated, a state may treat its existence as having survived without interruption. With the second request, Ethiopia sought freedom from the confiscations of her property, including the regulations and controls imposed on it by the Italians and later carried over by the British and Allied powers. As a result of the dialogue and international discourse generated by the Ethiopian government's lobbying efforts, she was able to include two provisions regarding Italian atrocities. However, other obstacles were on the horizon for Ethiopia.

As plans were being finalized to sign the treaty in 1947, Ethiopia faced continual obstacles from the UK and the United States and many other international powers that either opposed or were ambivalent about its requests. Ethiopia had a select number of European allies on the war crimes issue, including Australia, Norway, and Czechoslovakia, but was given only five months to prepare its case for review. In addition, the review committee rejected the label of genocide in favor of a crime of mass murder. The distinction provided various forms of safety net for Italy on the one hand while increasing the threshold for Ethiopian diplomatic and judicial representatives on the other hand. Hindered by a lack of time, a large body of qualified juried personnel, and the cooperation from the Allied powers in the preparatory phase for adjudication, the Ethiopian government was forced to submit only a limited number of charges. Ethiopia directed its advocate, General Baron Eric Leijonhufvud, a Swede, to present only 10 charges. As part of a compromise, an agreement was drawn up that, if those accused of crime against Ethiopian citizenry were surrendered by Italy, a court made up of a majority of European judges must try the accused. Out of 50 suspected war criminals, 10 individuals were officially accused of "systematic terrorism." They included:

1. Marshall Pietro Badoglio, commander-in chief of Italian forces at the time of the invasion
2. Marshall Rodolfo Graziani, commander of the Italian forces in Somalia and later governor-general of Italian east Africa and viceroy of Ethiopia
3. Alessandro Lessona, Italian secretary of state for the colonies for much of the occupation period
4. Guidi Cortese, federal secretary of the National Fascist Party in Addis Ababa at the time of the Graziani massacre
5. General Guglielmo Nasi, Italian governor of Harar
6. General Alessandro Pirzio Biroli, sometime Italian governor of Amhara
7. General Carlo Geloso, Italian governor of Galla-Sidamo
8. General Sebastiano Gallina
9. General Ruggero Tracchia

10. Enrico Cerulli, chief of the political office for east Africa in the Italian Ministry of Foreign Affairs, director-general of Political Affairs, and vice-governor-general of Italian east Africa.

The Ethiopian Government also published a two-volume compilation, *La civilization de l'italie Fasciste,* which contained texts and French translations of fascist telegrams ordering "war crimes": the use of poison gas, the mass execution of prisoners of war, the shooting of "witch doctors" and "soothsayers," and the killing of the monks of Dabra Libanos. The publications also contained certified affidavits from war victims including photographs of Ethiopians as the Italians selected them for execution.

The Allied powers led by Britain, however, questioned the veracity of Ethiopia's case against Italy on the grounds that it was nearly impossible to identify the hierarchy of authority within the fascist colonial authorities regarding who gave the orders to engage in mass killings of Ethiopians and the military attacks on the International Red Cross stations in the country. Meanwhile, the United States pursued a policy largely characterized by ambivalence towards Italian aggression. Ethiopia was faced with mounting pressure to outline the procedural structure for what was at that time a novel platform, especially as it affected the acknowledgement of obligatory rights for non-European peoples in modern international treaties. The Ethiopians were also hampered by opposition from Great Britain, the only member of the four great powers with which it had signed a war treaty. Ethiopia finally decided to cut its losses and called on the four powers who had representatives in Rome to act on its behalf, but this was promptly rejected on technical grounds. Left with only one option, a direct approach to the Italian government, Ethiopia not only encountered ambivalence from Western fora, but also a stiff opposition from the Italian press. Although it failed to achieve its total objective, as a result of the Ethiopian campaign, Italy became the first nation ever cited for crimes against humanity by the U.N. War Crimes Commission. It has been argued that by their actions the Allied forces did not want to alienate a fellow European state and as a result argued that the Italian atrocities in Ethiopia which began in 1935, had "no relation" to the European war, that began in September 1939. Political activist Sylvia Pankhurst, however, blamed Ethiopia's failure on Britain's limited interest in war crimes committed against non-Europeans.

Ethiopia came out of World War II and particularly, the Italian occupation in a very weakened structural condition, although the opportunity for consolidation of Imperial political authority was quite high. As noted earlier, some Ethiopians, including Ras Gugsa of Tigre and Ras Hailu of Gojjam, had collaborated with the fascists. Gugsa became disgruntled at not having been made king of Tigre. Both leaders were victims of Haile Selassie's divisive policies, which had favored other groups like the Raya and Azebo cattle raiders, and thus they chose to attack the emperor's retreating forces at Mai Chew.

In spite of these recalcitrant forces, other citizens maintained a dogged guerrilla campaign against alien rule in both urban and rural areas. The resistance force was comprised of the armies of Ras Imru, Ras Desta, Abebe Arregai, Belai Zelleke in Gojjam, and Amoraw Wubineh in Beghemidir. Others included Dejazmatch Wondwossen Kassa, Dejaazmatch Asfaw Wossen Kassa, the Bishop of Wello, Abune Petros, and a large portion of the peasant intelligentsia. As a result of this heavy opposition to foreign occupation, the Italians never gained complete control over the more than 350,000 square miles of the territorial country.

Many of the Ethiopians who died during the occupation period were young, educated people who had been groomed as the pillars of Haile Selassie's modernizing autocracy. Selassie had, however, preserved his political image as the living symbol of Ethiopia with his initial active participation in the war effort before his strategic retreat into exile. He had also helped consolidate his international reputation through campaigns against Italian aggression during the Italo-Ethiopian war and, afterwards, against the efforts of European powers to partition his country. The latter achievement was remarkable since most European colonial and military officials in Africa were suspicious of an independent African voice in an era that later emerged as the highpoint of formal imperialism on the continent. As Europe's influence began to wane, the United States emerged as the dominant power at the end of World War II.

When the U.S. forces liberated southern Italy in 1943, they also helped establish a government that was led by Field Marshall Badoglio, the former Italian viceroy of Ethiopia. The articulation of the Truman Doctrine and the Marshall Plan, both of which asserted U.S. guardianship of the "free world" against Communist threats, also contributed to the demise of the politics of the African Diaspora. The latter group had exploited the Ethiopian crisis to jettison real and imagined notions of provincialism and disempowerment, but with the Truman Doctrine, domestic voices of dissent against U.S. policy were restrained or silenced. In addition, the U.S. Marshall Plan, which was extended primarily to European colonial powers, also marginalized African national and transnational interests. In spite of these shortcomings, the cross-fertilization of ideas and emotions that emanated out of the invasion of Ethiopia later influenced the character of the pivotal 1945 Pan-African Congress in Manchester, England. At the summit, the African Diaspora associations argued for the end of racial discrimination and colonialism. They also called for a project of economic reconstruction for Ethiopia and the rest of the African continent. The ensuing politics of the Cold War, however, engendered new fissures and realignments in domestic and international relations with major ramifications for Ethiopia, Africa, and the rest of the world.

The end of Italian rule in Eritrea in 1941 gave rise to an even more strident separatist movement spearheaded by Eritrean Unionists and vigorously supported by the Ethiopian government. Conversely, an equally strong movement for independence developed, particularly among the Muslim section of the population. The U.N. resolution of 1952 to federate Eritrea with Ethiopia was essentially a compromise formulated to accommodate these antithetical positions. Ethiopia's experience in World War II appeared to have further convinced Emperor Haile Selassie of the reality of facing a global political arena in which there were no permanent friends or foes, but only permanent interests. Unhappy with British administrative and fiscal control over his territory during the war, the emperor subsequently looked towards the United States as a countervailing power to help with Ethiopia's domestic and international aspirations. The British were in turn also relinquishing the burden of the empire, as America became the new dominant political and economic hegemonic force.

Haile Selassie signed lend-lease agreements with the United States in 1941 and 1943, which brought the first transport aircraft to Addis Ababa in 1944. The following year, another agreement between Ethiopia and Transcontinental and Western Airlines (TWA) led to the establishment of Ethiopian Air Lines (EAL). In this arrangement, TWA agreed to provide managerial and supervisory personnel for three decades, but Ethiopia was more interested in nationalizing its airline for part of the life of the deal. An Ethiopian general manager for the airline was appointed in 1971, as a domestic network emerged to help facilitate national integration and transportation of agricultural commodities.

In 1953, a mutual defense pact guaranteed U.S. military assistance totaling more than $200 million over a 20-year period. Ethiopia also received aid from India, Sweden, Israel, and the Soviet Union. The military aid enabled Ethiopia to retain its independence while also suppressing domestic rebellions. After his restoration to the throne, Emperor Haile Selassie continued the earlier policy of state centralization and curtailing the power of the aristocracy. His early modernization efforts, however, proved to be disruptive rather than having a cohesive effect. Postwar reform, on the other hand, allowed the bureaucratic empire a potential larger measure of control and defense capability. The regional notables, the telek sawach ("big men"), with military, political, and economic power, were reduced in significance, with economic power being the only major concession retained by this group if members wanted to perpetuate their relevance. Many were forced to give up huge gult holdings, their personal army, and regional autonomy.

Selassie introduced three major structural reforms in the imperial administration. First, he established a British-trained standing army that was completely under his control, thus making regional armies and their commanders obsolete. Second, he arranged for a new fiscal system under the Ministry of Finance, ending many of the taxes and labor that the church had imposed on the peasant class, especially the gabber. For the first time, taxes paid in the form of a new currency were collected on a large scale by salaried civil servants in the Ministry of Finance and forwarded directly to the state treasury. This step professionalized the bureaucracy and theoretically deprived district administrators of the right to command arbitrary amounts of goods and services from subjects in their jurisdictions. Administrators could also rely on their monthly salaries and rents they collected from tenants on privately held land.

Between 1941 and 1961, the Ethiopian government revised tax laws on numerous occasions in an effort to increase the amount of state revenues garnered from agriculture and to increase productivity. It has been argued, however, that Selassie's attempts to enact land reforms were weakened significantly by his initial failure to curtail the privileges of the royal class; taxes were levied on the land being cultivated by peasants, but not on land owned by the nobility. As a result, emphasis was placed on improving the extractive capabilities of the state rather than on development. Under the new land-tenure system, tenants became expendable and eviction was commonplace. The heaviest tax burden fell on the peasantry in both the north and the south, though the most severe effect was felt in the latter region where the majority of tenants were peasants. In 1945, an order made it possible for landless and unemployed people to claim at least 20 hectares of government land for private cultivation; however, the traditional nobility continued to dominate discourses on land reform, and the peasants were either effectively denied any compensation or were forced to give up their claims due to lack of capital. With the commercialization of agriculture and the infusion of foreign capital, and foreign technical assistance, some local entrepreneurs—mostly young and educated members of landholding families and merchants—were able to invest limited amounts of money made through commerce on new ventures.

The third level of reform was visible in the reorganization of provincial administrators guided by a decision to reduce the power of the aristocrats and limit many of the discretionary powers of local governors. Administrators at all levels were also reconfigured as employees of the Ministry of the Interior, and most state officials were provided with supporting staffs including clerks and secretaries on the payroll of the state.

During the events leading to World War II, Haile Selassie had excessively relied on the League of Nations and European armies for political survival. The emperor had allied himself with the Western Powers, but in the ensuing era of the Cold War he also sought a level of autonomy by embracing the Nonaligned movement. Selassie made the first of seven visits to Washington, D.C., in 1954 when he met with President Dwight Eisenhower. During this visit, he privately expressed his disappointment at the small amount of material assistance, mostly in military aid that Ethiopia was receiving from the United States. When the United States reneged on an earlier promise to help construct the Nile-fed Aswan Dam of Egypt, Ethiopia reached out to the

Soviet Union, Yugoslavia, and Czechoslovakia, and in the process declared tentative support for a policy of state socialism.

Some scholars have divided Ethiopia's educated elites into two broad categories from the pre- and post-Italian invasion periods. While the earlier group viewed Emperors Menelik and Selassie as patrons and allies, the latter group of elites had looked towards Emperor Tewodros the pioneer radical modernist for inspiration. Historian Bahru Zewde identified three major forces that guided the twentieth-century intellectuals. They wanted: (1) to institute ordered governance or ser'at—justice and equality through the rule of law and a meaningful constitution; (2) to eradicate poverty in Ethiopia by making the peasants owners of their own products and controllers of their means of production (Demanding an equitable system of taxation and suggesting that the land be returned to the tiller, they identified a slogan that was later exploited by generations of would-be revolutionaries and argued that the gabber, the tribute-paying peasant, was a major obstacle to progress.); and (3) to ensure justice and equality among religious and national communities. Selassie's modernization project was as a result invariably anchored upon the cultivation of an educated elite found predominantly in Amhara and Tigre.

At the end of World War II, there was a consolidation of modern town and city projects, although only Addis Ababa and some coastal Red Sea ports witnessed major development initiatives. Agriculture, which was historically the major economic activity in Ethiopia, received the most attention as decisions were made to improve the nation's extractive capability and encourage commercialization. Indigenous entrepreneurs, however, lacked the necessary capital to partake in this process. The few Ethiopians who were able to make investments came from the wealthy aristocracy and the royal family. Foreign investors were also invited to participate in the development of an urban industrial sector.

By the 1950s, there was a notable growth in the number of Ethiopians with degrees in higher education. The hopes and aspirations for this group often included the benefits of modernity such as democracy and higher living standards. In spite of its limited size, this group was more ethnically varied than their predecessors, although Amhara and Tigre were still disproportionably represented. In 1957, Emperor Haile Selassie summed up his 27-year reign with a list of achievements that included the adoption of the nation's first constitution, the first popular elections, and the inauguration of public welfare and health and education programs. Lower-level traders and craftsmen, however, not only occupied a space below the educated government workers in income and status, but also remained in the majority. Both groups also had limited influence on the government, which at this stage was more interested in development programs focused on the expansion of large-scale capital-intensive ventures, with emphasis on foreign investment. It was also difficult to shed the legacy of the imperial social order. A majority of the skilled craftsmen often belonged to minority ethnic groups. Workers of varied ethnic backgrounds and the general populace of unskilled labor dominated the very bottom of the urban social scale.

During this era, Emperor Selassie was accused of ignoring "the national question" in his reformist policies. The empire consisted of culturally subordinated ethnic groups, which were not politically integrated into the nation as it expanded between the early nineteenth century and the mid-twentieth century. Although there was a proliferation of rhetoric and for a united Ethiopia, the dominance of the Amhara cultural group was also reflected in the delivery of social services and opportunities for social mobility.

On December 13, 1960, while the emperor was abroad, a coup d'etat took place led by the commander of the Imperial Bodyguard, Mengistu Neway. Other participants in the plot included the police chief, state security officials, and a handful of radical intellectuals, many of whom had familial ties to the military. The coup was initially a qualified success as the rebels seized the crown prince and more than 20 cabinet ministers, along with other government leaders. They declared a manifesto that included the establishment of a government that promised improved economic, social, and political conditions for the general population. The plotters approached Crown Prince Asfa Wassan, who was reputed to have a strained relationship with his father, the emperor. Support from the Crown Prince was also necessary in order to receive the sanction of the church. The Imperial Guard, led by rebel leaders, seized strategic points in Addis Ababa, including all communication centers. The Crown Prince appointed a new premier and declared via a radio announcement that the coup was a means to end 3,000 years of injustice, poverty, and ignorance. He also promised to set up a true constitutional monarchy and ultimately allow the creation of political parties. The plot was, however, poorly organized and the rebels failed to secure strategic posts across the country or the total expanse of the capital. Frustrated by its failure and realizing an impending doom, the rebels shot a few government officials and fled into the mountains. Emperor Selassie was greeted with wild cheers when he landed in Asmara, Eritrea, which had been reclaimed under the command of a loyalist general. However, the political events foretold the great challenges which awaited both the educated elites and the rapidly expanding population of poor masses.

Some scholars have argued that Ethiopian intelligentsia suffered as a result of the Italo-Ethiopian war, when a sizable corp was liquidated by the fascists and in the postwar era the surviving elites were marginalized as a result of political instability and social malaise. According to scholar Messay Kebede, by the time Haile Selassie came back from exile and was returned to the throne by the British, Ethiopia had already lost its freedom and sovereignty despite the open misgivings of the patriots. The Ethiopian state, it is argued, had become a link in the global imperialist chain, and the faster its incorporation into this structure the fewer the opportunities for real modernization reforms. Unlike Ethiopia, critics argue, the capitalist societies upon which Selassie would now depend were characterized by a flexibility that allowed for progressive reforms and a renewal of elites, endowing those societies with the power to survive. In spite of the yearnings of his citizenry for modern government and development initiatives, the emperor instead embarked on duplicitous reforms embodied by a continued portrayal of his regime as a paternal and modernizing autocracy. As a result of Ethiopia's acquiescence to externally oriented capitalist initiatives, national development, social mobility, and modernization ultimately became secondary to the consolidation of imperial power, thus further implanting underdevelopment. The Ethiopian Left also argued that the time-tested albeit imperfect indigenous principle of autarchy, or a policy of national self-sufficiency, was replaced by a dependence on imports and economic aid. Hence the postwar era represented a prime but lost moment for large-scale progressive reform. The destruction of the intelligentsia invariably resulted in the loss of a critical, independent spirit and a commitment to revolutionary transformation of the human condition, that ultimately undermined the potential of Ethiopian project of modernity. As long as there was no independent-minded intellectual or political base to support Emperor Selassie, he proceeded to forge reformist initiatives on his own terms. This absence of a critical spirit that could mediate the needs and consent of the governed to higher authorities engendered a high level of administrative complacency. In addition to the expansion of elite and popular resentment, natural disasters and the violence fomented by irredentist movements also threatened the populace and its territorial integrity. The hubris of the royal household and its supporters was reflected in prestige projects and international excursions and all these developments helped lay the foundation for the social, political, and economic tribulations that Ethiopia faced in the decade that began in 1960.

NOTE

1. Mary Davis, *Sylvia Pankhurst, A Life in Radical Politics* (London: Pluto Press, 1999).

5

Conservatives and Liberal Reforms, 1960–1974

By the beginning of the 1960s, a combination of political and economic centralization, diplomatic statecraft, and modernization of its military had allowed Ethiopia to increase and consolidate the scope of its territory. The emperor also embarked on securing his political administration through a balancing act that consisted of gradual integration into the world capitalist system on the one hand while holding onto the conservative trappings of bureaucratic empire on the other. This precarious assumption was going to have important ramifications for the royal authorities and the Ethiopian state. Ethiopia also continued to manifest a new and improved status and significance on the African continent, earned mainly during the military and diplomatic events surrounding World War II and its aftermath. By the middle of the 1960s, however, the inherent contradictions and conflicts that grew out of the political brinkmanship of Emperor Haile Selassie had exacerbated tensions in domestic political affairs. Of more importance was the fact that urbanization, industrialization, and commercialization invariably gave rise to the formation of new restive classes, which juxtaposed sharply against older and more conservative status groups. In addition, the very seeds of urban discontent were being sown in low-level industrialization sites such as Addis Ababa, Asmara, and Dire Dawa. Unequal access to power and modern facilities further raised knotty questions about the meaning of ethnic identity and in turn the relation of ethnicity to nationalism and the nation-state. The various groups were often split along more particularistic lines in their attitude toward the national question. As a result, many of the post–World War II developments further complicated the affairs of the state with the crystallization of new ethnicities and contested debates that ultimately led to a serious of violent conflicts.

In the realm of international diplomacy, the United States emerged as the most favored power in Ethiopia international diplomacy and foreign relations. This course was primarily dictated by the latter's desire for fiscal and technical assistance for its modernization projects as well as the continued survival of the imperial bureaucracy. The United States was also courted by Ethiopia to counterbalance the colonial history and legacies wrought by British and French powers who continued to protect their interests and influence in the Horn of Africa region. At the end of the World War II, the United States also emerged as Ethiopia's biggest external trading partner, importing nearly 40 percent of the latter's export products. Although Ethiopia packaged some incentives to further stimulate mining activities, there was a bias towards the generation of import as opposed to export duties. Ethiopian goods for export included civet musk, hides, and skin, and wax; coffee was, however, the biggest export commodity, 70 percent of which went to the United States. Expatriates dominated the trade, although minor competition came from an emergent class of Ethiopian nationals most of whom were handicapped by lack of resources. Having direct access to the royal family or patronage from the emperor's allies allowed some entrepreneurs to dominate the local economic sectors including the textile mills and brewery industries.

The budding industrial sector was dominated by foreign capital, and the result was one of mixed blessings. Indigenous entrepreneurs lacked the necessary capital to participate in the development of an urban industrial sector, and the government's effort at increasing revenue through agricultural taxes also recorded muted success. Commercial agriculture thus became the favored policy, and projects were concentrated in select regions such as Shoa, Hararge, Chilalo, Wollamo Humera, and the Awash Valley. Agricultural operations in the valley were stimulated by foreign investments. The Dutch HVA were offered large tracts of land for sugar plantations and a sugar factory at Wonji. Activities in the valley, however, reconfigured the social, cultural, and economic lives of several cultural groups in the area. The most negatively affected included the Afar, Gile, Kereyu, and Oromo peoples where peasants and pastoralists were displaced to make way for the expansion of commercial enterprise. The seminomadic inhabitants of the valley surroundings were evicted, thus further complicating the problem of rural poverty. Another by-product of government policies resulted in soil exhaustion and widespread drought and famine that claimed hundreds of thousands of lives as traditional grazing lands and environmental buffer zones were turned over to commercial entrepreneurs.

Ethiopia also a faced another major structural problem in its effort to industrialize its agricultural base. The declining price of export commodities and the rising price of imports both undermined the state's economic foundations for growth. Of most significance, however, was that Ethiopia's agrarian economic base lacked the amount of state-sponsored fiscal subsidies required to effectively compete in the world market. Foreign capital and aid donors had required that Ethiopia dismantle what many described as an antiquated feudal structure and arguably the major obstacle to the integration of the state's rural sector into the global market. Like most post–World War II postcolonial African states political economy characterized by development policies and politics, Ethiopia resorted to foreign loans to narrow the gap between incoming revenue and national expenditure. The era was also marked not only by a dependency on foreign capital but the corollaries of such an unequal relationship. These included overwhelming external influence in domestic programs in the social, economic, and national defense sectors. Ethiopia's debt to the outside world in turn ballooned, with the United States emerging as the major creditor and influential determinant of the country's foreign policy.

There were, however, other obstacles beside the Ethiopian government's failure to embark on a progressive reform of peasant agricultural and social-economic relations. The aristocratic and exclusivist nature of the export commodities trade in Ethiopia also created a major gap between the elites and the rest of the citizenry. Domestic financial loan policies neither encouraged small industries nor enhanced the growth of a sizeable indigenous business class. The country's very high level of illiteracy was also not conducive to the cultivation of a sizeable middle class nor was it substantial enough to carry out ambitious national development initiatives. Although Ethiopia has a long historical tradition of literacy, this was often exclusive to official chroniclers of the Ethiopian court and the church.

While the impact of the structural evolution of agricultural practices was moderate albeit momentous for the elites, the impact on the peasantry was more harsh and urgent. The commercialization of agricultural practices in fact benefited elites like traditional rulers, many of whom in spite of financial benefits not only lost their political autonomy in the process but also found their social relevance in domestic activities eroded. The rapid commercialization of agriculture, according to historian Teshale Tibebu, led to the "depeasantization" of households, as agricultural lands were indiscriminately privatized. As part of the process, he argued, national development plans became avenues for corrupt officials to appropriate resources under the facade of numerous white elephant projects. Some of these officials later emerged as newly minted entrepreneurs.

Agricultural commercialization upended old relationships, and the exhaustion of the soil also led to an accelerated migration of peasants into urban areas. The penetration of traditional economies led to a population expansion visible in new demographic pressures and social dislocations that in turn triggered large-scale urban crime and prostitution. Ethiopia, however, embarked on the creation of new institutions geared towards its development initiatives. Examples include the government's creation of a principal agency for mobilizing and directing capital for agricultural development through the Development Bank of Ethiopia and the Ethiopian Investment Corporation, which later merged to establish the Agricultural and Industrial Development Bank. The bank allowed the nascent Ethiopian bourgeoisie to gain control over some coffee plantations. The beneficiaries, however, consisted largely of the children of aristocratic families or imperial land grantees who were thus was too closely identified with the status quo to forge a democratic capitalist regime.

Ethiopia's First Development Plan (1957–1961) was hinged on developing a strong infrastructure with special emphasis on transportation, construction, and communications. These projects were in theory an integral effort at incorporating Ethiopian regions far and wide, especially those outside of the urban purview of Addis Ababa, the capital. An added benefit would be the reduction of Ethiopian's dependence on foreign expatriates, as emphasis was laid on the establishment of an indigenous cadre of skilled personnel equipped to operate an emergent industrial economy. Development was, however, restricted to the major cities and only commensurable with the exploitation of the economic resources of each region instead of improving the quality of life for people in the disparate peripheral areas. The second Five Year Development Plan (1962–1967) was designed to launch a 20-year program that would change Ethiopia's primarily agricultural economy into an agro-industrial one. Projects were scheduled to include diversification of production, introduction of modern processing methods, and expansion of the economy's productive capacity to increase the country's growth rate. The third Five Year Development Plan (1968–1973) also included the stated goals of increased productivity in the agricultural sector, especially for the benefits of the peasant. This development plan's objective also included the expansion of educational opportunities.

Although Ethiopia's economy underwent some diversification as the manufacturing and service sectors were expanded, commercial farmers and large landowners were often favored and they also had easier access to credit. In addition, the economic programs failed to improve the lives of most Ethiopians. Close to four-fifths of the population were subsistence farmers who lived in poverty. In addition, the peasants were often forced to pay taxes, rents, debts, and bribes. Another area where the peasants could have derived some profit for their effort was in the production of hides and skins for export. Here, the state cultivated the traditional husbandry to make this sector the second-largest export commodity, but benefits were either marginal or inconsistent. Record shows that from 1953–1974, Ethiopia's balance of trade with the outside world registered annual deficits except for the year 1973, when the sales of oilseeds and pulses helped reduce the stress on the economy. As a result of its economic fortunes, the country resorted to foreign grants and loans to finance its balance-of-payment deficits.

There were other unanticipated by-products of the Ethiopian development plans. Although Emperor Haile Selassie had anchored the crux of modernization policy around an educated elite, the major educational institutions and other social amenities were established in the national center and was dominated by the Amhara ruling ethnic group. The general neglect of health care, housing, sanitation, and water development, especially in the small towns and countryside, meant that there was no local safety measure to help deal with the burden of poverty, illiteracy, and poor health. Peasant revolts were common but were often unorganized and lacked durable strategic leadership. There was also sporadic resistance, including notable tax rebellions in Bale in 1964 and Gojjam in 1968.

Foreign expatriates, such as Asian entrepreneurs, and American Peace Corps volunteers tried to fill some of the void in social services helped. Widespread inequalities engendered sobering consequences among groups such as the Oromo, Somali, and Eritreans, most of whom resented some of the implications of the nation-state's policy. Critics of the government argued that the state's course of action was a political strategy of systematic marginalization of its denizens by starving them of economic and political opportunities. Others stressed that the center diplayed little or no concern about the cultural and historical survival of the various subordinate groups. The social impact of the state's development policies gradually undermined rather than bolstered the authority of the regime of Emperor Haile Selassie.

In spite of the social and economic problems highlighted above, Emperor Selassie continued to nurture his image as a modernizing and benevolent autocrat. He also maintained the precarious balancing act of political reformism, philanthropism, and absolutism and became more sophisticated in patronage and punitive efforts aimed at protecting the erosion of his political authority. Employing the critical flexible resources of the military, the bureaucracy, and a pool of educated elites, he was quite successful in cultivating the imperial hegemonic value system until the 1960s. Opposition to the emperor and his policies became most strident among the intellectuals and a growing number of student radicals. It is remarkable that also included among the former group were some younger members of the aristocracy and a new generation educated abroad under the auspices of royal patronage. Elites intellectual communities had become frustrated by the limited opportunities for the expression of diverse or alternative political opinions or as a sizable group began to call for radical social and political reform. One of the notable intellectuals was the American-educated Garmame Neway, whose populist organization skills and innovative and progressive reform in the civil service had endeared him to the intellectuals. The political establishment, on the contrary, considered Neway a threat and tried to make him into an alienated figure, thus further contributing to his political frustration. Neway ultimately turned to his brother, General Mangestu Neway, the commander of the Imperial Body Guard, and the two brothers together embarked on executing a military coup in 1960.

THE MILITARY COUP

On December 13, 1960, while Emperor Haile Selassie was on a state visit to South America, the coup planners struck. The putschists released a manifesto condemning Ethiopia's backwardness, especially in comparison with the postcolonial African states, and promised to expand the industrial and educational base of the country. They also courted the support of the military constituency with the promise of increased salary for the soldiers. The coup recorded initial gains in the capital, with the rebels seizing the crown prince and more than 20 cabinet ministers and other government officials. The prince was ordered to read a statement over the radio which included the statement that, in spite of 3,000 years of Ethiopian history, little or no progress was made in agriculture, commerce, or industry. The speech also laments the "ignorance and standard of living" of the Ethiopian populace. This statement helped to secure the support of the university students, many of whom demonstrated in Addis Ababa to affirm their inclinations.

The proposed revolution was undermined by poor planning. Although the putschists promised to improve the social welfare condition of the peasantry, they also acknowledged the continual relevance of the royal authority. In addition, they promised to honor all preexisting international commitments. What turned out to be the most tragic consequences for the plotters, however, was the lack of support of the Imperial Bodyguard. Although the military served as the backbone of the revolt, the planners failed to inform core members of the enlisted men either in the army officers or air force corp. Due to these short comings, forces loyal to the throne eventually employed the overwhelming force at their disposal and routed the rebel forces. General Germane was killed during a fight with loyalists. His brother Mangestu was wounded, captured, and was later hung after a brief trial.

Although university students demonstrated in favor of the coup, the core of the army and air force units had remained loyal to the emperor. The church also disapproved of the attempted coup. The patriarch of the Ethiopian Church had condemned the rebels as antireligious traitors as he delivered prayers for those who fought as loyalists to the conservative order. The church also called for Ethiopian citizens to honor their traditional duty of devotion and faithfulness to the emperor. Emperor Selassie returned to the capital on December 17 and was restored to the throne as thousands jubilated at the return. It has been argued that Selassie retained his popularity with the general populace for historical and existential reasons. Many Ethiopians saw him as the apotheosis of nationalist courage, a carry-over of the pre–and post–World War II era, and the older generation in particular saw the emperor as the embodiment of both the traditional order and the state's modernist aspiration.

Although the coup failed, it engendered an increased political dissent, especially from those who decried the absence of meaningful political and economic reform. In addition, the Ethiopian middle class and the modern educated class, particularly the technocrats who could not find employment and opportunities appropriate to their unique aspirations of upward mobility, continued to bristle at the perennial influence of traditional nobility and landowning gentry. Many critiqued what was described as the social and economic stagnation in the civil service and other state-run administrative parastatals. Their frustration was more acute when they compared Ethiopian conservative policies with that of more ambitious postcolonial African states led by postwar nationalists. Of equal significance, a new radical movement most conspicuous among the student population resented Ethiopia's formal entry into "the periphery of global markets" dominated by Western economies. This group of intellectuals condemned what was described as the assumptions of colonial-style developmental policies, that cemented Ethiopia's future as that of a perpetual laboring class in global economic relations. Since Ethiopia's economic development was largely dependent on coffee production, the Oromo, who made up the bulk of important denizens of the agricultural region, witnessed a radical reinforcement of landlord-tenant relations. Between 1961 and 1972, Ethiopian coffee in the world market increased from 75,000 tons to more than 111,000 tons, with more than 50 percent of the production coming from two predominantly Oromo provinces, Kaffa and Sidamo.

Tensions between Amhara-Tigre settlers and Oromo tenants often led to violent conflicts as settlers, investors, and speculators reaped the profits of sales while the peasants struggle to feed their families. The acquisition of neighboring coffee-rich territories of the Sidama and Gedeo region also resulted in violent rebellion usually followed by reprisals and retribution on the part of the government. Other forces fueling social dislocations and resentment included the disparity in the status of land ownership between the northern and the southern regions of Ethiopia. In the northern Tigre Amharic provinces, the power base of the imperial authorities, land ownership was vested with the kinship group. Peasant ownership of land was protected by the *rist* system, in which subjects are expected to pay tribute. In addition, imperial land grants to the nobility, or *gult*, and the church lands had combined to extract surpluses from the peasantry in tribute, produce, rents, and services. The south, on the other hand, played host to alien landlords, *neftagna*, or local chiefs or *balabbat* who had also the use of acquired landlord status. Beside the use of coercion and the law, religion provided the major political and ideological institutions that helped reproduce these series of unequal relationships.

The development of the private ownership of land resulted in forcible dispossession of peasant lands who in most cases were forced into tenancy. In other areas the influence of settlers, most of who were Christian, over a predominantly Muslim or animist population further complicated the overwhelming sense of alienation on the part of the peasants. In addition, traditional social cultural relationships were forcibly disrupted by the burden of large-scale mechanized farming. The Land Tax (Amendment) Proclamation of 1966, for example, abolished rist gult land-holding rights, but landowners retained large portions of their landed property in private holdings. The combination of the crown's policy of land gifts, a feature of patron-client relationships and the expansion of the commercialization of agriculture increased the level of social and economic inequalities in the countryside.

The government attempted to alleviate the burden of levy on the peasants by introducing the 1967 Income Tax Amendment Proclamation. The law abolished tithe, replacing it with a graduated tax on agricultural earnings, including rent from land. Landowners, however, decried the move, and conservative elements were mobilized within the parliament into practically disabling the effectiveness of the bill. As a result, there was growing dissatisfaction with Ethiopia's government economic policies, as rebellious opposition grew in the towns and countryside. Although the decades of the 1950s and 1960s witnessed close to 11 percent annual growth in the manufacturing industry, the condition of the workers in the urban industrial economic sector remained dire. The average industrial worker earned the equivalent of between 40 cents and $1.25 daily, and the combination of low payment and urban unemployment threatened the survival of the imperial bureaucracy. In spite of the growing threat, the authorities continued their policies unabated, and instead expanded the state's security and defense capabilities. Government crackdowns often resulted in the death of peasants across the nation. Labor unions were discouraged from embarking on protests, and dissenters were often summarily dealt with through large-scale destruction of property and other forms of state-deployed violence. The above social and political environment sustained and subsequently gave impetus to the emergence of a revolutionary intelligentsia and the radical Ethiopian Student Movement.

It has been argued that the radicalization of Ethiopian students was a combination of domestic and external forces. Students from their respective institutional bases often espoused the "rights of nations to self-determination." Others expressed dissatisfaction with the social and political hierarchy in their homeland and were motivated to build an Ethiopia based on the idea of "equality and consent." Other influences on Ethiopian students came from interaction with scholarship students from other parts of Africa and across the globe. An intellectual historical critique of Ethiopia in transition came from author Bahru Zewde, who stressed that although the pre–Italian invasion intellectuals wanted to ensure the equality of all regions and the separation of church and state, their theories of progress were accompanied by minimal systematic research methodologies. The activities of postinvasion intellectuals, particularly the student movement, on the other hand, were largely dictated by the theoretical desire to eliminate class and ethnic hegemony and oppression. The latter group, however suffered major shortcomings because most of the scholar/activists had minimal practical experience with democratic and critical traditions. As a result, iconoclasm was the order of the day, with minimal allowance for nuances or well-defined boundaries. In spite of these reservations, Zewde concluded that the two intellectual milieu had assumed the burden of opposing the excesses of the bureaucratic empire with dignity and emerged as heroes of Ethiopian history in this phenomenon.

The emergence of student opposition was another example of the historical paradox of post–World War II Ethiopia. A primary factor in this phenomenon was the proliferation of secondary and higher education institutions. The national government under the auspices of the Ministry of Education of Ethiopia had in December 1949 launched a plan for a future university. Christian missionaries and private individuals had also contributed to the growing public and private investment in education. In 1950, at the request of Emperor Selassie, Addis Ababa University was founded with the help of a Canadian Jesuit, Dr. Lucien Matte. The institution began as a two-year college known as the University College of Addis Ababa (UCAA), and expanded to include the Engineering College and the Building College in Addis Ababa. Between, 1951 when it began operations, and 1953 the university became affiliated with the University of London. Also of importance is the Agricultural College established as a result of intellectual engagement with Oklahoma Agriculture and Mechanical College (OAMC). The Jimma Agricultural and Technical School opened in October 1952 to serve mainly as a feeder for the Imperial Ethiopian College of Agriculture and Mechanical Arts (IECAMA), later called Alemaya College of Agriculture (ACA). A public health college was also established in Gondar. By 1961, a select number from the various colleges were integrated into what became known as Haile Selassie I University. Although emphasis was now placed on expanding domestic educational facilities, and the number of enrolled local student population continued to increase, many young Ethiopians continued to travel overseas for higher education, with the United States emerging as a favorite destination. Overseas student bodies such as the Ethiopian Student Union in North America (ESUNA) and the Ethiopian Students Union in Europe (ESUE) later emerged as active participants in their home country's political activities.

Another important program launched in this era was the Ethiopian University Service (EUS). Established in 1964, the EUS required all university students who completed their third-year college studies to serve for one academic year across the country in their respective fields. The program exposed students to the conditions in the countryside, often in the role of secondary school teachers, where they successfully introduced a younger generation to national social and political ideas. More important, however, many volunteer college students who for the first time witnessed the pitiful conditions in which most peasants lived became politically radicalized and increased their oppositional activating to the status quo. There was also the proliferation of political publication, social critique, and satire among the population, and these activities extended into poetry and debating gatherings.

By the middle of the 1960s, Marxist ideas began to be systematically incorporated into student activism. This development coincided with the emergence of a radical core known as the "crocodiles" among the leadership cadre of the student movements. Marxism-Leninism not only provided a principled way to reject the West, which had supported Haile Selassie and what critics described as Ethiopian backwardness since the end of World War II, it also represented a way towards the attainment of modern material comforts outside of the West's economic and political influence. The historical appeals for the Ethiopian Marxist utopian goals were often grounded in the Russian and Chinese revolutions as the sites of alternative historical transformation. A minority yet buoyant group of students, however, expressed the desire for political freedom and self-determination in the language of Western liberalism. Other young intellectuals simply added their voice to that of the postwar generation in other African cosmopolitan sites. They expressed an often-maligned yearning for changes in social and political transformations of revolutionary proportions, an expression of solidarity with the anti-imperialist and anticolonialist fervor in Africa and around the world. Literary renaissance in Amharic literature and abstract art also blossomed in this era featuring personalities such as Mangestu Lamma and Tsagaye Gabra-Madhen in drama; novelists Berhanu Zerihun, Ba'alu Germa, and Haddis Alamayahu; and Garba-Krestos Dasta in abstract art.

The growing popularity of the Marxist antibourgeois battle cry and liberal catch phrases such as "free speech" and "self-determination" became a source of frustration for the government, which was still reeling from the attempted military coup. The formation of an umbrella body, the University Students Union of Addis Ababa (USUAA), signaled the ascendancy of the Left in Ethiopian student politics. The state reacted to student protests with expulsions and school closures.

The year 1965 marks a turning point as the slogan "Land to the tiller," became a popular chant as well as a marker of the transition from the reformist to the revolutionary era in the cognitive and operational scope of oppositional activities. When the parliament began to debate the regulation of tenancy in

1965, the student population voiced their political opinion with an increasingly strident rhetorical condemnation of the Ethiopian regime. Some scholars have accused the students of mistaking the means of the revolution for its end. The "Land to the tiller" revolution in its overwhelming fascination with socialist orthodoxy, according to philosopher Messe Kebede, ultimately stymied the seeds or potential of growth inherent in the Ethiopians body-politic. This was true particularly true in the south where the roots of individual enterprise stood the best chance of survival. As a result of the vulgar revolution, the fight to free the peasants, he concluded, produced the unforeseen result of a blanket distrust for private enterprise and the marketplace. The potential for an alternative route towards progress was later compounded by state aggrandizement of private land for commercial purpose.

While students and intellectuals operated mostly from their bases in the towns and especially in Addis Ababa, the capital sporadic peasant rebellions against the policies of the state emerged in the countryside. The economic unrest and widespread poverty in the rural areas converged with growing political irredentism as ethnic and cultural groups decried the overcentralization of power in the hands of the Ethiopian crown. The failure of the imperial federal administrative structure also helped perpetuate rather than alleviate economic inequalities. The transfer of local powers to state appointees as part of post–World War II reform led to a corresponding loss of control of regional affairs to the central authority figures in Addis Ababa. Although some cultural and religious communities expressed minimal resistance to their marginal role and status in the Ethiopian state, others picked on sore points of contention such as the hegemony of Orthodox Christianity over Muslim and animist faiths and the continued hegemony of Amhara social, cultural, and political practices over other minority groups.

It has been argued that the great emphasis on ethnicity in the twentieth-century Ethiopian state could be blamed on the increasing needs of modern life, individual consumption, and the state's imperfect administrative and redistributive mechanism. In this regard, unlike modern societies where economic activity is dictated by competition in the creation of new resources, Ethiopia experienced a chronic underdevelopment that is often manifested in the violent competition for scarce resources. Increase in population growth and the unequal spread of modern education in Ethiopia accentuated rather than ameliorated scarcity and competition. As a result, the only way of controlling resources was the appropriation of power and the enactment of various forms of exclusionary policies on the part of the state and its allies.

THE NATIONAL QUESTION IN POST–WORLD WAR II ETHIOPIA

As Ethiopia dealt with pressing economic issues, the state also witnessed the explosion of the divergent interests and aspirations that threatened the social fabric of the country. The combination of domestic and external geopolitical forces helped triggered irredentist aspirations. The Ethiopian state made little or no reference to ethnic, linguistic, and religious diversity in official narratives and printed literatures. In addition, there was structural inequality in funding for development projects and support for varied cultures, languages, and religions. The geopolitical expeditiousness that characterize World War II was followed by a series unfulfilled promises such as the British government proposal to support Eritrean nationalist demand if the latter worked against the interest of their Italian colonial masters.

The Horn of Africa has historically been acknowledged as an area rich with a history of communities pursuing intergroup mutually beneficial relations interspersed with periodic conflicts. The late nineteenth and twentieth centuries, however, witnessed the emergence of new obligatory political imperatives, which distorted the mutual geopolitical rationale in the region. In this regard, the Ethiopian crown has been accused of forcibly configuring cultural communities as peripheral "subjects" and "dependents" to be pacified rather than protected. In reaction, many groups became more militant in their opposition to Ethiopian absolutist monarchy, taxation, and land assessments. The dissatisfaction with the hierarchical social, political, and economic structure of the Ethiopian state that was anchored upon Amhara cultural domination also precipitated new projects of reconstructed historical narratives. The latter-day historiographies often described denizens of the ancient Ethiopian state as cultural communities who operated in parallel existence. This was accentuated by the emergence of binary epistemologies and Manichean world views. By the mid-twentieth century, most of these communities emerged in the public sphere and international stage as nationalist movements with increasingly violent expressions and contentious mythologies of past and future glories. The stagnation and underdevelopment of the Ethiopian economy only exacerbated the tensions.

Ethiopia had emerged from World War II with the desire to regain access to its traditional Red Sea coast line in the Eritrean territory. European colonial interests in the Horn, especially in the Italian reign in Eritrea, invariably secured Ethiopia's status as a land-locked modern state. While Ethiopia argued that ties between the ancient state and Eritrea go back to antiquity, Eritrean nationalists contradicted the former's claim by stating that they had always had autonomous historical relations with powers besides those fostered by the Solomonic royal lineage. The Italian-ruled Eritrea, the nationalists argued, had never been firmly under the control of modern Ethiopia.

After the Italian interlude in Ethiopia, Eritrea was administered by Great Britain until 1950, when the United Nations decided to federate the territory with Ethiopia. The U.N. resolution had called for an autonomous Eritrean government consisting of legislative, judicial, and executive branches. As part of the "federal" status within the Ethiopian state, Eritrea was also in theory granted some responsibility over domestic affairs, foreign affairs, external trade, defense, communications, and currency. In addition, an imperial federal council consisting of equal members of Ethiopian and Eritrean representatives was given the responsibility of governance and drawing up a constitution during a transitional period applicable until September 1952. The Federal Act of 1952 had created the Eritrean Legislative Assembly, and political organizations, which had been operating at subterranean levels, emerged in the open. The associations often had to work with a political framework that acknowledged and sought to balance the significance of religious identities with rights associated with place of birth or natal influences. Different groups also parlayed religious and cultural associations into programs for increased autonomy within the Ethiopian state or a declaration of an agenda for a separatist independent state. Only three parties emerged: the Unionist Bloc, comprised mainly of Christian Eritreans; the Democratic Party, which had formally been the Independence Bloc, with mostly Christian and some Muslim members; and the Muslim League of the Western Province. The election results, however, meant that disparate compromises were struck among the dominant political associations, most of whom who were united under the banner of Eritrean autonomy. The Eritrean flag with the "UN blue" field and green emblem was adopted in 1952 and used until the territory was absorbed into Ethiopia in 1959, when it became a "flag of liberation" until 1993 when true independence was won.

By 1952, the Ethiopian government had embarked on a systematic deconstruction of Eritrean autonomy. The process began with the suspension of the constitution, and a year later, the proscription of trade unions. Emperor Selassie pressured Eritrea's elected chief executive to resign, made Amharic the official language in place of Arabic and Tigrinya, terminated the use of the Eritrean flag, imposed censorship, and moved many state businesses out of Eritrea. By 1956, all major political parties had been banned and the National Assembly temporarily suspended. In addition, the Eritrean flag and code of laws were summarily replaced by Ethiopian versions. In 1960, the federal political arrangement was effectively dissolved as the assembly, convinced by the imperial authorities, voted to change the name of the government from the Eritrean "government" to "administration." On November 14, 1962, the assembly completed the transition process through a vote that fully incorporated Eritrea into Ethiopia as its fourteenth province. These activities were much to the dismay of Eritreans who favored a more liberal political order. Radical opposition emerged as early as 1958 with the founding of the Eritrean Liberation Movement (ELM). Operating from a platform that exceeded the political goal of a federated autonomy, this movement, which primarily consisted of intellectuals, students, and urban wage laborers, now demanded the establishment of Eritrea as a separatist entity. The leaders of the movement also began to cultivate the ideas of resistance and national consciousness among average Eritreans. The opposition movements like the ELM were, however, systematically undermined by Ethiopian authorities which unilaterally annexed Eritrea in 1962. By 1964, the ELM had been infiltrated and its activities totally undermined, only to be replaced by other rebellious entities. The Eritrean Liberation Front (ELF) was established in 1961 by the Eritrean Muslim population in exile, particularly those based in the Middle East. Unlike the ELM, the ELF emerged as a liberation army with a platform that proclaimed its readiness for a protracted war of national liberation. A few modern radical Arab states such as Syria also saw Eritrea as part of the *Umma* (community of Muslims) and were ready to support the movement. By 1971, the state of guerilla campaigns by Eritrean groups had reached such crisis proportions that the emperor was forced to declare martial law in the region, and half the Ethiopian army was deployed to contain the nationalist struggle. Three major separatist groups, the Eritrean Liberation Forces based in the Barka region, the People's Liberation Forces located in the Red Sea area, and the Salfi Nasenet Eritrea (Front for Eritrean Independence) established from the Akala Guzay region, all came together in 1972 to form the Eritrean Liberation Front and Popular Liberation Forces (ELF-PLF). The coalition was reconstituted as the Eritrean People's Liberation Forces (EPLF) shortly afterwards. The armed struggle in Eritrea lasted from 1961 to 1991.

The few initiatives that were taken for peaceful resolution of the armed conflict were aborted by half-heartedness on either side. Particularly after the 1974 revolution, the military option increasingly became the choice of both the Ethiopian military regime that had taken the helm and the Eritrean guerrilla movement, which had come to view itself as invincible. Towards the end of the 1980s, the military seesaw tilted decisively in favor of the Eritreans. In May 1991, the Eritrean Popular Liberation Forces (EPLF) triumphantly entered the Eritrean Asmara, heralding the birth of an independent Eritrean state.

Given the alliance that the EPLF had forged with the force that simultaneously seized power in Ethiopia, the Ethiopian Peoples' Revolutionary Democratic Front (EPRDF), and the support that the latter gave to Eritrean independence, the two countries appeared set for an era of peace and cooperation. On the surface, everything appeared peaceful but the potential for trouble remained—particularly on the issues of the boundary, currency, and the hundreds of thousands of Eritreans who continued to reside in Ethiopia. These issues were at the root of the new round of conflicts that flared up in 1998 and remain fully unresolved to date.

Another conflict triggered by modern geostrategic and economic aspirations of Ethiopia emerged with the creation of new boundaries in 1948. A new map placed Somali nomads under formal Ethiopian administration. Ethiopian control of Ogaden emerged as an issue of more significance for political and nationalist figures since critical resources such as water and later oil were to be found in the region. Ethiopian effort towards integrating the Somali as subjects was characterized by a carrot-and-stick approach. The former made overtures on the grounds of historical relations of spiritual and filial significance between the two entities. Resistance on the part of the latter ultimately led to the deployment of military expeditions in the region. Somali resistance to Ethiopian authority in this region dates back to the political and economic events between 1887 and 1955. Having secured recognition of its claim over the Ogaden through a series of treaties with Britain, France, and Italy, Ethiopian hegemony in the region became heightened in the late 1940s and early 1950s. The Somali resistance in return was constructed on the platform of "national" origin traced back into antiquity. Bound together by language, custom, Islamic religion, and sociopolitical organization structures, Somalis in the Republic of Somalia, Djibouti, Kenya's northeastern province, and Ethiopia's Ogaden proclaimed a common heritage. Somali nationalism was also nurtured with the legacy of cultural icons such as Mohammed Abdille Hassan and the legend of Ahmad Gran. The Western Somali Liberation Front based in Mogadishu emerged as one of the more dominant resistance movements. When Somali, which unlike Ethiopia identified more with an Islamic heritage, became independent in 1960, it further complicated the seeds of territorial conflicts sowed through colonial mapmaking in East Africa. The Somalis in frontier districts of Ethiopia such as Dallo, Wabe, El Kere, and Ganale not only constantly rebelled against the state but also resisted the presence of the Ethiopian national army, police, and settler militias.

Another source of national conflict was the Tegre province, where the numerically superior Oromo formed the single largest ethnic group in Ethiopia (between 45 and 50 percent). The Oromo live in Ethiopia's agriculturally rich southern regions. Situated mostly in the southern region, the Oromo had been historically marginalized in cultural, political, and economic relationships within the Ethiopian empire, especially from the mid-nineteenth century onwards. Oromo nationalists have argued that their domination by the northerners has been misunderstood, disregarded, and sustained by foreign allies of the Amhara-led Solomonic crown. They stress that both historic and modern friends of the Ethiopian state were mainly interested in cultivating the powerful state's strategic importance and thus chose to overlook Ethiopia's internal contradictions. Oromo nationalism was also based on a common history, a unique administrative system known as Gadaa, a social stratification partly based on an eight-year cycle of age sets. Generational sets move from one level to another after each cycle for a 40-year period until completion at the Luba level, an adult male suffrage membership. At each stage, Gadaa members are educated in Oromo history, military strategy, law, and governance. Although Gadaa is no longer widely practiced, it remains influential. The Oromo had also been systematically Christianized by the dominant orthodox church as local shrines across the land were destroyed in favor of churches as part of Ethiopian hegemony. Oromo resistance over time included the Azebo-Raya revolt of 1928–1930; the Oromo Independence Movement of 1936; and the Bale rebellion of the southeastern region of 1964–1970. There were also the protests of the Gedero or Darasa in the southern province of Sidamo and the Gojjam area in the northeast. In 1936, a confederation of Oromos from Harage, Shoa, Jimma, and Ilubabor came together under the umbrella of the Western Oromo Confederation. This group had in 1936 sent an appeal based on the basis of self-determination to the League of Nations. Oromo rebels also exploited Islam as a nationalist ideology for their nationalist projects. By the mid-1960s, Oromo nationalism was dominated by the Mecha-Tulema, a self-help association with political and cultural attributes led by the dominant figure Tadesse Biru, whose influence and nationalist activities culminated in his arrest by Haile Selassie's government in 1966. He was sentenced to death, a penalty that was later commuted to life in prison. In the Bale Province, Wako Gutu, a local leader, emerged as the most important foe of what was considered a battle for Oromo's liberation from the Amhara group. His armed resistance began in the 1940s and continued until his death in 2006. Oromo militancy declined in the 1960s but reemerged with the formation of the Oromo Liberation Front (OLF) founded in 1973. Opposition to the state hegemony continued from the Somalis, Eritreans, Oromos, and Afars.

The achievements of Emperors Menelik II and Haile Selassie I helped project Ethiopia's image as the epitome of African independence and self-determination. As political leaders, they presented an image to the world community of an Ethiopia that was a viable and unified nation-state whose origins go back to antiquity. One of the contradictions of Ethiopia's role in the modern world was visible in 1966 when Emperor Selassie visited the Caribbean, making stops at Trinidad-Tobago, Jamaica, and Haiti. In Kingston, Jamaica, he was mobbed by the Rastafarians, who considered him their spiritual leader. Haile Selassie's latter-day modern aspirations were, however, characterized by a series of contradictions: the conscription of the Ethiopians into the periphery of Western capitalism, overcentralization of political power, the imposition of a disciplined production regime to feed the export-oriented economy, and a misguided belief in the inviolability of the nation-state led by the ancient regime. The unforeseen product of modernization reform and its effect on the notorious 1972 drought was aptly described by Edmund J. Keller, who declared that:

Peasants and pastoralists living on the margins of subsistence have had to cope with such phenomena from time immemorial. As a result of the process of modernization and the centralization efforts of the state, however, the lives of poor rural inhabitants had been unalterably changed. More and more of their surplus production has either been demanded by landlords and the state, or been translated into cas in order [sic] to meet tax obligations.

Their freedom of movement and their access to land was also now inhibited by state regulation or by a complex and aggressive burgeoning market economy. Traditional survival mechanisms were either gravely weakened or completely inoperable. Rural people unwittingly had become extremely dependent on the state. For its part, the state was more concerned with economic growth and political survival than it was with meeting its inherited social responsibilities.[1]

In addition, rapid economic expansion had also engendered its own contradictions between the old and emerging new orders further complicating longstanding inequalities based on ethnic and class distinctions.

By the fourth decade of Emperor Haile Selassie's reign, there was large-scale dissatisfaction with the personalization of power and the restriction the monarchy placed on political dissent. Ethiopia's modernization and liberal reforms left the hereditary influential nobility in place, albeit under new bureaucratic institutions and agencies that are totally or partially controlled by the state. As a result, loyalty to the crown often overwhelm contracts and appointments based on merit. This feature of the state contributed to the prevalence of weak institutions and the failure to grow the economy . Although private ownership of land and a rigid social stratification had formed part of Emperor Selassie's modernization reforms, the lack of progress in capitalist-guided development initiatives, the dominance of the principle of heredity, and failure of land and trade reforms and underdevelopment had quashed a generation's aspirations. The ensuing condition helped make socialism appealing as a counterhegemonic strategy. Ethiopian modernization also had the unforeseen result of undermining Emperor Haile Selassie's influence and strategic initiatives. The combination of old age and centralization of power had isolated the emperor from his power base, the nobility, and the countryside. The privatization of land was marked by expropriation and displacement and the erosion of the monarch's hegemony. The breakup of the patron-client relationship between peasants and lords, which in the past had been used in the appeasement of conflicts also undermined social and political stability. For the peasantry, the overemphasis on commercial agriculture combined with the failure of monocultural cash-crop policies meant that social mobility for the ambitious was stagnated.

ETHIOPIA'S FOREIGN POLICY

In 1967, Selassie visited the United States with the goal of requesting military aid to counter the Soviet's support for Somalia. During this extended trip, the emperor also stopped by the Kremlin, where he implored Moscow to withdraw their support for Somalia. The situation in Somalia was characterized by the state vigorously pursuing a policy of uniting all Somalis under one flag. Described by some as "one people under many states," the Somali territory remained divided among former European colonial authorities who struck multilevel alliances with traditional rulers, enforced of course by unequal access to arms and capital. The quest for a reunification of a greater Somalia came to be enshrined in the five-pointed star that the Somalis adopted as their national emblem on independence. Two points of those stars were realized when British and Italian Somaliland united to form Somalia on the morrow of independence. But that still left the Somalis, who found themselves scattered among the neighboring countries—Djibouti, Ethiopia, and Kenya. Of the three regions that were regarded as *terra irredenta,* it was the Ethiopian region of the Ogaden that became the major target of Somali irredentist aspirations. This led to a minor clash between the two neighboring countries in 1963 and a major war in 1977–78. The latter, resulting in the defeat and disintegration of the Somali army, augured the end of the dictatorial Siyad Barre regime.

One year before political independence was achieved in Sudan, a civil war began between northern and southern regions of the country. Southerners were afraid that the new nation would be dominated by the north, reflecting divisions further emphasized by the British colonial policy of ruling Sudan's north and south separately. While the north of Sudan had historically closer ties with Egypt and was predominately Arab and Muslim, the south of Sudan was predominately black, with a mixture of Christianity and animism. A mutiny in 1955 by southern units of the Sudanese army stationed in the Equatoria province snowballed into the first Anya-Nya movement, as the southerners' armed struggle spearheaded by the Sudan Africa National Union (SANU) came to be known. The southerners' quest for autonomous status stood in fundamental collision with the integrationist and assimilationist policies pursued by successive regimes (military as well as civilian) in Khartoum. As the intransigence of the north escalated, the southerners also raised the stakes higher, from autonomy to independence—in somewhat the same manner as the Eritreans shifted their goal from the restoration of the violated federation to unequivocal independence.

The Addis Ababa Agreement of February 1972 ended the first phase of the civil war by recognizing the ethnic plurality of the Sudan. The agreement granted regional autonomy to the south, provided its proportional representation in the national assembly in Khartoum, and recognized English as the principal language of the region. Unfortunately, the agreement was abrogated in 1983 by General Nimeiry, the same northern ruler who had signed it in the first place, with the imposition of the Islamic sharia law throughout the country and the breaking up of the south into three regions. Exacerbating the situation was the conflict over two vital resources: oil and water (the latter triggered by the Jonglei Canal project, which aimed to drain the southern swamps known as the *sudd*).

Thus was initiated the second chapter of the civil war known as Anya-Nya II, led by the Sudan People's Liberation Army (SPLA) and the Sudan People's Liberation Movement (SPLM), as the military and political wings were respectively known. The second chapter of the Sudanese Civil War has lasted two decades with major implications for the Ethiopian state, which has had to play host to Sudanese refugees.

The final unraveling of Ethiopia's imperial order began with a succession of military mutinies, popular demonstrations, and industrial unrest. These events were preceded in 1972 by a major drought in the northeastern areas of the country. In a single year, between 100,000 and 200,000 people died from starvation and malnutrition. The Wollo and Tigre region, which had supplied 40 percent of Ethiopia's total food production, lost about 20 percent of its human population and 90 percent of the animals. As the information about the drought spread across the country, students and other concerned and enlightened citizens established public food donor campaigns. Of more importance to the survival of the political order, however, was that the students at Haile Selassie University also began a series of campus protests in 1973. This development was met by punitive campaigns that led to the arrests and death of many of the protesters. The detention of student leaders and mass deportations by the government also led to an exodus of many activists. Of most importance was dissatisfaction with the condition of the peasantry.

The government's response to the drought itself was pretty tepid and uncoordinated. In addition to the climatic and natural disaster, Ethiopia was also undergoing serious economic problems due to a global increase in oil prices and a decrease in the international price for coffee, Ethiopia's major export crop. Taxi drivers and transporters had gone on strike in February 1974 to protest against government directives that fares should be standardized and not increased, although oil prices had increased threefold.

The ineffectual treatment of these crises, combined with images of officials including the emperor engaged in public displays of state pageantry, helped cement the impression that government officials remained above the fray while the greater population suffered. Accusations of rampant corruption among government officials also became part of the lore beyond the urban areas. The emperor was accused of amassing a stupendous amount of wealth based on an official policy that blurred the line between royal and national coffers. Public officials including teachers, soldiers, students, and intellectuals also demanded constitutional reform. The schoolteachers had gone on strike demanding pay increases and the repeal of a policy of "Education Sector Review," a prescription of the World Bank. As high-school students joined the politicized university students, the teachers were granted an audience with the emperor, who must have been surprised by the inclusion of land reform in the protesters' demands.

On January 12, 1974, soldiers of the Territorial Army's Fourth Brigade at Negele protesting poor food and water conditions rebelled and took their commanding officers hostage. The Ethiopians had over the years been politicized by the monarchy, with factions including the Imperial Bodyguard and the Territorial Army, which was in turn divided into many factions. There were also other groups brought together by virtue of their graduation from either the Harer Military Academy or the Holeta Military Training Center who began to experience mutinies in various garrisons. News about the rebellion spread to other units and throughout the military, including those stationed in Eritrea.

Between February and September 1974, the character of the simmering Ethiopian revolution changed from protest to insurgency. In March 1974, labor unions under the coordination of the Confederation of Ethiopian Labor Unions (CELU) called for industrial action, which threw the country into turmoil. The people responded with strikes, boycotts, and other forms of militant action, which paralyzed the public sector and public utilities and thus added to the pressure of popular movement.

As peasants broke out in open confrontation with landlords and public authorities, other segments of the communities with claims of marginalization also emerged. Such was the April 1974 demonstration by the urban Muslims, when the trader class who numbered close to 100,000 added to the voice of clamor for change. They called for an end to discrimination against Muslims and the right to own land like Ethiopian Christians. In coffee-rich Jimma, the southwestern province, the unpopular governor Dajjazmach Tsahayu Enqwa-Sellase was deposed.

The emperor attempted to make concessions to the various groups, and on February 28, 1974, obtained the resignation of his prime minister, Aklilu Habte-Wolde. A new cabinet was established under the leadership of the incumbent minister of communications, Lej Endalkatchew, who promptly promised to embark on land and constitutional reforms. Demonstrations, however, continued as people became increasingly aware of the erosion of the myth of unity and viability constructed by Emperor Selassie and his imperial bureaucracy. It must be highlighted that political resistance was mostly urban and lacked central coordination, a fact that emboldened individual actors while militating against government suppression of the activities. As the protest spread from Addis Ababa into the provincial cities, the administration combined its conciliatory overtures with use of blunt force. Police actions became severe especially in Jimma (Kefa), Metu (Ilubabor), Asela (Arusi), and Arba Minch (Gemu Gofa). On September 12, 1974, Haile Selassie, emperor of Ethiopia, was deposed by popular revolt, thus bringing to an end the lineage of the oldest Christian theocracy in the world. According to scholar Marina Ottaway, Selassie was heralded initially as the pioneer modernist and progressive emperor who would guide his country into a new era. By the 1970s, the script had been flipped and he was identified by many, and especially the educated citizenry, as the very cause of Ethiopian backwardness. As if to confirm this point, the earliest signals after the emperor's overthrow point to a liberalized political environment and a public sphere more vibrant and expanded than at any time in Ethiopia's modern history. A new energy was also unleashed among cultural groups such as the Oromo, Somali, Afar, and Eritreans, who became more assertive in challenging the legitimacy of the Ethiopian state.

The emergence of the military as the revolutionary vanguard for the spasmodic resistance to the ancient regime was a very gradual process. The military took advantage of the vacuum created by the lack of a revolutionary organization. The process began with the attempt by the hegemonic elites to cultivate a segment of the military led by Colonel Alamzawd Tasamma, the commander of the Airborne Brigade. The latter's subsequent effort to shore up support for the old order helped trigger the emergence of the reactionary Coordinating Committee of the Armed Forces, the Police, and the Territorial Army. With this action, a section of the military had exploited the mass protest and rebellion and thus hijacked the Ethiopian revolution. The cabal was composed of a body of young military officers, none above the rank of major, drawn from the main units of the army, air force, navy, and police. After September 1974 the body became known as the Provisional Military Administrative Council (PMAC), or simply as the Derg (Amharic for "committee" or "council). The political events in 1974 led to the deconstruction of 16 centuries of royal rule, summarily replaced by a military body known as the Provisional Military Administrative Council. The first challenge faced by the Derg came in the form of the increased permissiveness of civil society, especially in urban centers such as the capital city of Addis Ababa, and the politicization of peasants in the countryside. The Derg was thus saddled with the responsibility of hatching a blueprint for control over government and politics that above all would be counterhegemonic to the legitimacy and principles of the moribund Solomonic dynasty.

NOTE

1. Edmond J. Keller, "Ethiopia: Revolution, Class, and the National Question," *African Affairs* 80 (1981).

6

"Afro-Marxism": Engaging Local and Global Orthodoxies and the Price of Revolution, 1974–1991

The final stage of Ethiopian revolution began in January 1974 with a series of mutinies led by the military in various provinces and demonstrations by restive citizenry in the capital. In what initially started as an urban phenomenon, students, teachers, civil servants, and soldiers embarked on a rebellion against the imperial representatives of Haile Selassie, its supporters of nobility and feudal aristocracy, and the nascent national bourgeoisies. Popular campaigns and uprisings were accompanied by calls for the separation of church and state and equality of religious, regional, occupational, and economic groupings.

On June 21, 1974, the Coordinating Committee of the Armed Forces, Police, and Territorial Army now known as the Derg elected Major Mengistu Haile Mariam as leader and Major Atnafu Abate as deputy. Although the new regime lacked a coherent ideological platform, its members were very conscious of the radical pulse of the civilian population and decided to follow in this track. Of more importance, the Derg began to appropriate the revolutionary ideas of the Ethiopian leftist intelligentsia. The Derg also appropriated the Marxist rhetoric of the intellectuals and students in order to marginalize opposition on the Left. Political scientist John Harbeson identified three distinct phases in the development of Ethiopian socialism during the revolution. In the first phase, which began in December 1974, the Derg declared its commitment to Ethiopian socialism, followed by a declaration of a corollary economic policy. This phase, he argues, was characterized by pragmatic judgments, general formulations, and moderate tone. The second phase featured the promulgation of sweeping reforms designed to root out the socioeconomic underpinning of the old order and to mobilize masses of rural and urban constituents for the revolutionary struggle. The dominant feature of the third phase was the launching of a new Democratic Revolutionary Program and the strengthening of grassroots management committees. This last step was an attempt to invest the masses with significant political power, leading to the creation of a People's Democratic Republic at the national level. The Derg, in desperate need of an ideological posture that would provide it legitimacy among students and the rural and urban masses, adopted populist slogans such as *Ethiopia Tikdem* (Ethiopia first) on the one hand while employing the threat of extreme force on the other. The modern experimental artistic fervor and the entertainment and recording industries that had begun to thrive in the 1950s and 1960s came to a sudden halt as artists were expected to concentrate on revolutionary duties and images.

Core members of the Derg and their allies began to establish a hegemonic project that, like Emperor Selassie, was modernist, but unlike him was less reliant on the United States or the capitalist market-based system. Instead, Ethiopia's political system and economic structure embraced planning in all sectors of the society. The meaning of Marxism in this context, according to scholar Marina Ottaway, was implicit "not so much in its utopian vision of human liberation—a theme familiar to Western Marxism—but in a story of how a weak and backward collection of nationalities, located outside of Western Europe, attained unity, wealth, and international respect. This was in essence, she argues, "the allegory of the Russia, and later, the Chinese revolution."[1] Marxism-Leninism has also been described as a pliable tool in the hands of the Mengistu regime for its vision for social, political, and economic modernity. Mengistu had embraced the maximalist view of the state as the major agent of economic development and social transformation. The government also embarked on the reorganization of the agricultural production system and the relocation of the population from overcrowded and ecologically exhausted areas to more fertile one. Other programs include the acceleration of industrialization and the spread of literacy.

The year 1975 also witnessed the Derg riding on the revolutionary wave to impose a radical land reform that was accompanied by the nationalization of major economic outposts. In what was described as an acknowledgement of the popular slogan "Land to the tiller," the action brought the military leaders an initial substantial amount of goodwill from the general populace. The new leaders promulgated far-reaching urban and rural land-reform programs, as they mobilized more than 40,000 students and teachers to explain and implement their revolution in the countryside under the auspices of *zemecha*, Amharic for "campaign." As part of this initial land reform in 1975, the military government launched the Development through Cooperation Campaign through a forced mobilization of university and secondary school students to explain the socialist revolution, including land reform, to peasants. The program also aimed to improve the traditionally low literacy rate.

The Derg, however, sought to combine its socialist rhetoric with political pragmatism, which critics would later describe as schizophrenic and ineffective. These balancing act included a condemnation of "the limitless idolatry of private gain" and wastefulness of capitalism economic cycles, while tolerating the blend of public and private ownership of the means of production and the rejection of quasi-feudalism under Haile Selassie, while calling for the revival of old Ethiopian traditions. In this regard, although the revolution glorified and redeemed the nation, it also failed to provide a definition of the nation. Another contradiction was the Orthodox Church, an institution that had enjoyed the patronage of the state for more than a millennium and a half and that lost its status and landed property through the radical land nationalization proclamation of March 1975. The Derg, however, remain committed to the old Orthodox Christian demarcation of the nation, which was antithetical to the proclamation of the equality of ethnic groups. The contradictions and ambivalences of the revolution, according to Marina Ottaway, were an attempt to employ Marxist-Leninist doctrines and more importantly the lessons of the Russian revolution to the domestic project of curbing the threat to the nation. Such a threat, she stressed, was most evident in the explosion of ethnicity that occurred between 1975 and 1976. In the same period, the government nationalized private banks and insurance companies. All banks and financial institutions under the National Bank of Ethiopia were placed under government control and supervision. The prevalence of inflation, war expenditures, and budget deficits, however, did little to remove Ethiopia's dependence on foreign aid.

The Derg also established a 50-member civilian advisory council, the *Yememakert Shengo*, to be consulted on selective issues. It issued a statement that highlighted its version of Ethiopian socialism, or *Hebrettesebawinet*. This philosophy stressed equality, self-reliance, and the dignity of labor, the supremacy of the common good, and the indivisibility of the Ethiopian nation. The Derg embarked on building communication links to civilian groups at home and abroad as they sought to cultivate the support of those who had opposed the old regime.

Between 1974 and 1987, the coercive apparatus of the Ethiopian state rapidly expanded. In the meantime, the rank and file members of the Derg arrogated to themselves the responsibility of breaking down the hegemonic power once wielded by the old traditional order. The Derg and its allies confiscated the cars and properties of elites and arrested reactionary elements suspected of entrenched interest in the royal authorities. Based on his pedigree, which included that of a military hero and veteran of several military exploits, General Aman Michael Andom, who was not a core member of the

Derg, became head of state, chairman of the Council of Ministers, and minister of defense. His voice of caution and opposition to ideas popular with members of the Derg, however, sealed his fate. He had recommended that the size of the Derg be reduced from its 120-member governing body and proposed reconciliation with the Eritrean insurgency; he was also opposed to the imposition of a death penalty for former government and military officials. In an environment characterized by political instability and massive rupture in the body politic of the state, some civilians called for a "people's government." The lack of espirit de corp within the Derg itself was even felt in the Derg, where the clamor for a populist people's government found supporters among some members.

The radical wing of the Derg began to move against those it considered dissidents within its rank. Isolated and now viewed as an icon for those opposed to the Derg, Aman withdrew and sought support from a larger cadre of the military. On November 23, 1974, in what later became known as "Bloody Saturday," General Aman Michael Andom and two other Derg members who had supported him were killed, accused of resisting arrest. In the same night, 59 former officials, the majority of whom were Amhara were also executed. Brigadier Teferi Benti, a Shewan, was appointed chairman of the PMAC and head of state. Power, however, lay in the hands of Major Mengistu, the first vice chairman, and Major Atnafu emerged as second vice chairman.

Mengistu continue to consolidate his power base, and Ethiopia began preparation for a new military offensive in Eritrea. A decree promulgating Ethiopia as a socialist state was enacted on December 20, 1974. In the following year, the Derg revoked all royal titles and declared that constitutional monarchy was to be abolished. The traditional fate was sealed when Emperor Haile Selassie died in mysterious circumstances in August 1975 and with the removal of the patriarch of the Ethiopian Orthodox Church, Abuna Tewoflos.

Once the civilian population realized that the revolution had been hijacked by the military, who promptly appropriated the former's reformist language, select members of the civilian population began to operate from a platform of an informal oppositional party. The civilian counternarrative fed on the lack of improvement in the welfare of the masses in spite of the radical land reform and redistribution. Students who had been recruited to partake in grassroots education also became disillusioned, and many began a more critical analysis of Marxism-Leninism. The opposition, however, remained uncoordinated and was continually distracted by conflicting claims of nationalism and socialism.

The Derg in reaction embarked on erecting a façade of representative political practice and popular participation. Although it did not tolerate political parties, it allowed for representation on the Politburo. Among the community of those who returned home to help with the stated reconstruction project were future members of a political organization later known as MEISON

(All-Ethiopian Socialist Movement) and *Wez Ader* (League of the Working Classes). Another group, the Ethiopian People's Revolutionary Party (EPRP) emerged with some link with the Eritrean People's Liberation Front (EPLF) and later with the Tigrean People's Liberation Front (TPLF). Several other political associations emerged to join in the conversations for building the conditions feasible for social reform, a progressive civil society, and the public sphere. The working relationship between MEISON and EPRP led to the establishment of the Provisional Office for Mass Organizational Affairs (POMOA). A rift later emerged between the two dominant political associations, and this schism would be fundamental to the shaping of the postrevolution history of Ethiopia.

MEISON was dominated by older returnees from the Diaspora who were in favor of a "controlled democracy" and were more amenable to working with the Derg in a strategic alliance of convenience. Its leader Haile Fida was the Derg's chief political adviser. The EPRP on the other hand leaned towards the idea of a "people's democracy" and later emerged as a dominant critic of the Derg. Featuring a coalition of intellectuals, students, teachers, merchants, and government bureaucrats, the EPRP began a systematic campaign to discredit the government.

A REIGN OF TERROR

Due to their marginalization, EPRP members resorted to armed struggle in the urban centers in what later became known as the "white terror." This reign of violence was characterized by indiscriminate killings of opponents and their family members. Following the nationalization of urban land and bourgeois properties, The MEISON acquired a monopoly in appointment of cadre throughout the country and in the formation of the urban neighborhood associations, or *kebele*. By employing traditional cultural forms, the Marxist government was imposing its own hegemonic project of socialist programs in a manner it felt could be comprehended and embraced by the people. As tension grew between the EPRP and the MEISON, a schism also emerged within the Derg. A section led by Chairman General Teferi Benti wanted a less entrenched relationship with MEISON and a bit more rapprochement with EPRP. They also called for a moratorium on waves of violence and reconstruction of party alliances based on progressive goals and consolidation of the new order.

Beginning in the year 1976, Colonel Mengistu Haile Mariam unleashed another round of violence as he attempted to reassert his authority. Mengistu had been highly dissatisfied with operational restructuring within the Derg, which saddled him with ceremonial duties as power became more concentrated in the hands of the secretary general, Captain Alalmayahu Hayle. In July 1976, Major Sisay Habte, chairman of the Political and Foreign Affairs

Committee (PMAC) was eliminated. Also killed were Brigadier-General Getachew Nadaw, commander of the Second Division based in Eritrea, and members of the Derg including Lieutenant Bawqatu Kasa and Lieutenant Selashi Bayyana. On February 3, 1977, at a meeting of the Standing Committee of the Derg, Lt. Gen Teferi Benti, the chairman, Captain Alalmayahu, Captain Mogas, and Lt. Colonel Asrat Dasta, chairman of the Derg's Information and Public Relations Committee, were summarily executed. This was later followed by the elimination of Atnafu, Mengistu's last rival within the Derg.

The coup gave Mengistu and his leftist allies the opportunity to pacify those considered to be enemies of their revolution, especially members of the EPRP. Known as the era of "Red Terror," during this time members of EPRP and their friends and families were subjected to indiscriminate attacks and summary executions. By 1978 both MEISON and MEISON parties had lost their relevance for the military leaders. Writing during this troubled era, scholar John Harbeson had observed that:

> In the process of policing the revolution by rooting out opponents of, and conspirators against the revolution the Derg may have begun to assume the political style of the regime it replaced, much against its apparent will. The Derg has felt obliged to use force to secure the revolution and possesses greater capability to execute this task than to mobilize a revolutionary constituency in pursuit of the posited goals. As a consequence, the Derg's working priorities perhaps unavoidably are coming to resemble, at least in appearance, those of the previous regime notwithstanding the reforms augurated.[2]

With virtually all civilian opposition groups either destroyed or forced underground or into exile, the Derg had no option but to embark on its reform programs. It also embarked on a domestic policy that sought to strike a balance between the demands of an unwieldy multiethnic state at home and a foreign policy with the façade of Ethiopia as a unified polity to the outside world.

THE DERG, THE NATIONAL QUESTION, AND ETHIOPIA'S FOREIGN POLICY

The overthrow of Emperor Selassie provided an impetus to the idea of self-determination among the competing cultural groups. There were numerous outbreaks of revolts in most parts of the country, with the most activities centered in Eritrea and Tigre. The Eritrean Liberation Front (ELF) and the Eritrean People's Liberation Front (EPLF) led the most active secessionist rebellion, another reason behind the Derg's decision to expand on its decision for a military settlement in the Eritrean-controlled region. In 1975, the troubled

Eritrean territory erupted as nationalists launched an attack on Asmara, an uprising that was suppressed but opened a Pandora's Box in Ethiopia's domestic and international politics. As a result of this event, the United States signaled a change in the policy that facilitated the sales of arms to Ethiopia under the 1953 Mutual Defense Assistance Agreement. The above conflicts only confirmed the reputation of the Horn of Africa as a region continuously in crisis in spite of being one of the most important and strategic areas of Africa and the global economy. Ethiopia occupies a predominant position in the Horn because of its demographic importance, since about 85 percent of the area's population lives in the country. The Horn has also been described as a bridge between Africa and the Middle East as well as a gateway to the oil fields of the Persian Gulf. The region also play host to diverse ethnicity, languages, and religious practices. Based on the above factors, events in the region were exacerbated to new levels as a result of Cold War political drama and conflicts.

By 1977, all of the country's 14 administrative regions played host to one form of insurgency or another. Rebel-held territories faced a continuous threat of invasion from the Ethiopian army. The Tigrean People's Liberation Front (TPLF) was very active in Tigre, while the Oromo Liberation Front (OLF) was active in the southern regions of Bale, Arsi, and Sidamo. The Western Somali Liberation Front was active in the Ogaden and the Somali Abo Liberation Front (SALF) based their insurgent activities in the countryside. The Afar Liberation Front (ALF) also began cooperating with Eritrean groups.

In the spring of 1977, Somalia invaded Ethiopia. This was so far the most serious external challenge to the revolutionary regime and only helped to consolidate the Derg's hegemony with the Ethiopian people. The Somali government of Siad Barre had tried to annex the Ogaden region by providing supplies and logistical support to a proxy front, the Western Somali Liberation Front (WSLF). The group captured large parts of Ogaden from the Dire Dawa area southward to the Kenya border. The Somali government support for WSLF combined with mutiny by Ethiopian troops particularly in Jijiga culminated in the fall of the town to the insurgents. The Ethiopian government under Mengistu Haile Mariam in desperation turned to the Soviet Union, who subsequently dropped Somalia in favor of the bigger and more strategically significant Ethiopia. In a classic Cold War role reversal and realignment of power, the Soviet Union switched allegiance from supporting the self-described "scientific socialist" Somalian administration. The decade-long alliance ended with the expulsion of Soviet advisors and the abrogation of the Treaty of Friendship and Cooperation between Moscow and Mogadishu. Ethiopia's relationship with the United States was, however, also souring and undergoing transformation. By 1977 and 1978, the Soviet Union military aid to Ethiopia was estimated at one billion U.S. dollars, thus exceeding the total U.S. aid to Ethiopia between 1953 and 1977. The 1953 mutual defense agreement between Ethiopia and the United States was subsequently terminated. The Cold War policy of the United States under President Jimmy Carter had also involved encircling Ethiopia's Marxist-Leninist administration with support provided for bulwark states in the Horn of Africa region. The United States in turn also established strategic military and economic relations with Ethiopia's neighbors, especially Egypt, the Sudan, Kenya, Oman, and of course Somalia.

Beginning in November 1977, the Soviets directed massive military assistance, including into Ethiopia. Between 1977 and 1990, Soviet military assistance to Ethiopia was estimated to be as much as 13 billion U.S. dollars. In addition, close to 17,000 Cubans arrived and together with Ethiopian troops stemmed the expansion of Somali forces, ultimately recapturing Jijiga and driving the latter forces back to the transnational frontier. The victory cemented Ethiopia's new status as the military client of the Soviet Union and Cuba. Military advisers also came from other members of the Soviet bloc. Bulgaria, Czechoslovakia, East Germany, and Poland at one time or another sent advisors to Ethiopia. After routing the Somali invaders, Ethiopia's leader, Mengistu, followed up on his desire for a military solution in Eritrea. The Ethiopian army occupied several Eritrean towns but failed to dislodge the nationalists from an outpost called Nakfa, where guerilla and propaganda activities lasted for years. Annual military campaigns by Ethiopian forces not only failed repeatedly but also proved very costly to the government. Between 1982 and 1985, the EPLF and the Derg held many rounds of talks in an attempt to resolve the Eritrean conflict, but this yielded no meaningful gains. By the end of 1987, insurgents in Eritrea and Tigre were in control of close to 90 percent of both regions. Armed struggle in Eritrea lasted from 1961 to 1991, a period marked not only by tens of thousands of casualties but also by ferocious contestations of identity in the public spheres and through competing historical narratives. While Ethiopians considered Eritrea to have historically been an integral part of Ethiopia, Eritreans took pains to portray the two countries as sharply distinct entities. As Eritreans pushed the stakes higher—shifting from the restoration of the federation to the unequivocal recognition of Eritrea's independence—successive Ethiopian regimes resorted to force as the ultimate solution.

The Oromo also became more militant and in 1973 established the Oromo Liberation Front (OLF), with the clarion call of "total liberation of the entire Oromo nation from Ethiopian colonialism." Led by Oromos from Arussi Province, it claimed broad-based support from other Oromo groups.

The policies and practices of the dictatorial regimes that dominated the Horn have been devastating. International powers also contributed to the instability in the region. Western expansionist national policy, which has often had as its sole principle the advancement of the national interest, also helped fuel the conflicts in the region. The legacy of colonial mapmaking, ineffective political administrations, and implacable competition for power and resources among elites and communities has produced terrible results. Between 1982 and 1992, two million people died in the Horn of Africa due to a combination of war and famine. Many more became refugees, further destabilizing social and political relations in the neighboring countries. The Cold War in essence contributed the denial of civil and political rights to the people of the Horn. The series of wars in the region has also undermined the fundamental rights to freely determine their political status and pursue economic, social, and cultural development.

The Derg in pursuit of its foreign policy goals also sent emissaries to Middle Eastern countries such as Syria, Egypt, Libya, Iraq, and Saudi Arabia. In 1981, a tripartite agreement was struck between Ethiopia, Libya, and South Yemen. A diplomatic relationship was also nurtured with Israel. In 1984, close to 10,000 Beta Israel (Ethiopian Jews; also called Falasha) were secretly airlifted from Ethiopia to Israel. In May 1991, towards the end of the Mengistu regime, an additional 15,000 were taken out after negotiations between Israel, the United States, and Ethiopia.

The impact of the Cold War on Africa added a new dimension to the nationalist fervor, peasant unrest, and upheavals on the part of the citizenry, especially the students and intellectuals. The adoption of the moral and ideological imperatives of Marxist philosophy on the African continent had engendered debates about the gap between the theory and practice of Afro-Marxism. Some scholars have described Afro-Marxism as the precept guiding those African intellectuals and political leaders who rigorously applied the principles of scientific socialism to African conditions. Although it adopted Marxist-Leninist doctrine and analytical terminologies of self-definition and public policy, the Derg was unwilling to share power with non-military personnel or acknowledge the rights of the marginalized ethnic nationalities of Ethiopia. Ethiopian leaders appropriate "Leninism" or "Marxism" without necessarily opposing orthodox features, including religion as a social institution, or encouraging the expansion of a politicized working class as the basis for a vanguard party. Instead emphasis is often placed on charismatic pragmatism and an authoritative state apparatus directed at achieving national development. Other scholars have suggested that Afro-Marxist regimes combined Leninist and populist traits, attracted to the promise of governmental efficiency and authority and the social discipline of the Soviet model. They also embraced the principle of self-determination and solidarity inherent in socialist theory. The most important features in these regimes were the combination of ideological priority and a commitment to a centrally planned economy that guaranteed production, distribution, and exchange. Critics of the above features of Afro-Marxism also suggest that a system in which economic power was concentrated in the hands of the state and ultimately one individual could hardly be described as truly African.

By the 1980s, the government faced numerous challenges, the most important of which was a severe famine that led to the death of over one million of its citizens. Massive drought assistance from abroad could not make up for the decline of the agriculture and manufacturing sectors, lack of foreign exchange, and a crippling defense budget. The government attempted some measures of conservative fiscal management through the reduction of capital expenditures, higher taxes on exports and imports and consumer and luxury goods, a wage freeze for senior government officials, and domestic borrowing, but this proved inadequate. The wind of change in international relations also did not augur well for the Ethiopian regime. By 1985, when Mikhail Gorbachev came to power, Soviet attitude towards Ethiopia underwent a transformation as the fiscal and military aid declined. Mengistu visited the Soviet Union in 1988 but received minimal assurance of support. Instead, Gorbachev was said to have expressed the desire for Ethiopia to embark on Soviet-like glasnost reforms, which included economic liberalization and political decentralization. By 1990, Soviet military advisors were withdrawn, and the number of military supplies continued to dwindle until 1991, when the military assistance agreement formally expired. The Ethiopian regime also encountered problems such as a lack of resources, droughts, the social dislocations of rural communities due to resettlement, problems with land tenure, villagization, and the conscription of young farmers to meet military obligations. Mengistu continues to declare policies aimed at ameliorating the condition of the peasants including passing the decree that guaranteed the free movement of goods, removed price controls, and facilitated secured land tenure. In March 1990, during a speech he gave to the Central Committee of the Workers Party of Ethiopia, President Mengistu declared the failure of the Marxist economic system. He also announced a new policy of political decentralization, but the end of his reign was visible at hand. Between the mid-1980s and the early 1990s, the potential for renewed opportunities for a fiscal and material relationship between Ethiopia, East Germany, and North Korea failed to materialize.

The Derg stayed in power for 17 years and was eventually overthrown in May 1991 by the Ethiopian People's Democratic Front. By the end of its reign, the Derg regime in Ethiopia had lost support at home and became an anathema in a post–Cold War global stage. Critical examination of Ethiopian Afro-Marxism acknowledges the contribution of intellectuals, students, and the peasantry. On the contrary, peasants, workers, and oppressed groups were largely excluded from contributing to party policy. The supposed revolutionary vanguard of Ethiopia also failed to emerge, since the Worker's Party of Ethiopia, which commenced in 1984, was dominated by the military at all levels. Agricultural productivity under the Derg could not match the population growth rate. The Derg-sponsored land reform has been condemned as being antithetical to modern motivations and methods, a development that stifled the social basis for the regeneration of local elites. In addition, the imposed communalism, others argued, stifled the spirit of competitiveness and individual contributions. In spite of its failures, the Derg was credited with the protection of Ethiopian sovereignty. In the tradition of its predecessors, albeit in a much weakened and less significant status, Ethiopian leaders have been successful at playing off foreign interest groups against one another while seeking to advance domestic political goals. Perhaps the best description of the transition from the Derg regime to its successor, the Ethiopian People's Revolutionary Democratic Front (EPRDF), came from historian Bahru Zewde, who concluded that:

> ... the existence of the classic forms of class exploitation in Ethiopia created a fertile bed for the growth of the seeds of Marxism-Leninism. Adumbrated by the students and intellectuals, it was appropriated by the soldiers. The latter outsmarted and out-maneuvered the urban left, only to be ousted unceremoniously in turn by the rural-based left, which has in the meantime adjusted to the "New World Order" by shedding off, at any rate at the formal level, its Marxist-Leninist attributes. International power alignments thus played a significant role in the initial adoption as well as eventual rejection of Marxism-Leninism, and nowhere was this more starkly clear than in the case of Somalia. In the end, therefore, both African socialism and Marxism-Leninism failed to have enduring impact anywhere in Africa. Yet, this is not to say that the concerns and aspirations that led to their temporary appeal and ascendancy are no longer there. Even if we leave aside the internal factors that contributed to that appeal and ascendancy, Africa has still to define its relationship with the global order that controlled its destiny in the past and continues to dominate it today.[3]

In conclusion, Ethiopia has been described as a classic case in which the noblest revolutionary goals can be betrayed.

NOTES

1. Marina Ottaway, ed., *The Political Economy of Ethiopia* (New York: Praeger, 1990).

2. John W. Harbeson, *The Ethiopian Transformation: The Quest for the Post-Imperial State* (Boulder, CO: Westview Press, 1988).

3. Bahru Zewde, "What Did We Dream? What Did We Achieve? And Where Are We Heading?" *Africa Insight: Ethiopia: Challenges from the Past, Challenges for the Future* no. 321 (October 1981).

7

Globalization and Other Postmodern Configurations: Ethiopia at Home and Abroad Since 1991

By the last quarter of the twentieth century, Ethiopian intellectuals and peasants have had enough of the imperial regime's slow pace of reforms. In what amount to a marriage of secularization with modernization goals, the intellectuals and activists associated Ethiopian backwardness with the regime's religious commitments and as a result began to campaign against the hegemony of the Solomonic dynasty. The revolution of 1974 declared a counter-hegemonic culture that was supposedly dislodged from the Ethiopian Orthodox Christian Church. The Derg legitimated its revolution by appropriating the theory of scientific authority from the intellectual and activists. Besides marginalizing the latter group from the realm of power and influence, the adoption of Marxism-Leninism also contributed to the repression of any sense of compulsion the Derg might have about enforcing the transition to secular modernity by any means necessary. Marxism also allowed the regime to focus on its radical projects of restructuring grassroots political networks. The new government consolidated its hegemony by expanding the military budget primarily designed to crush the Eritrean demand for independence from Ethiopia. It also established new institutions such as peasant associations, cooperatives, marketing boards, a nationwide worker's party, and mass education programs.

The Derg had also nationalized both urban and rural lands and distributed these properties to citizens on a usufruct right basis. Although the policy was driven by the desire to put an end to the imperial regime as well as restrain the emerging land market, such control installed a forced procurement of agricultural market surplus. The land policy also stifled individual and communal creativity and removed incentives for successful farmers. The most important failure in land reform was, however, embodied in the radical collectivization project called "villagization." Designed to force peasants to move their homesteads into planned villages that were clustered around utility supply points such as water, schools, and medical services, the program's results belied their earthy label and benevolent intentions. "Villagization" instead disrupted traditional organic relationships and ancestral linkages. In many cases, the social services that were promised simply failed to materialize. Beside the rapid decline in food production, the Derg regime was also accused of using famine as a weapon for weakening the opposition. Food aid was often withheld, especially in the Tigre region. Many peasants fled rather than embark on forced relocation or conscription. A large number of Ethiopians began to leave the country in greater numbers than what had been witnessed since the World War II Italian invasion, in search of material and emotional succor. Many young ambitious citizens also departed the country in search of upward mobility in the form of better economic and career opportunities. Although the "mass education," or *Zemecha,* program—a core part of the land reform program of 1975—was relatively successful in promoting literacy, it also produced numerous unintended consequences. The National Campaign for Education through Cooperation was established for the purpose of entrenching revolution, but the regime's exploitation of all available intellectual outlets (including art and music) as instruments of political propaganda provoked resistance from students and teachers. It became obvious that, through the program, the government had expanded its operations for the purpose of tracking the activities of average citizens, infiltrating not only village society but the family unit as well.

The onset of a major famine in 1984 and the death of more than a million Ethiopians exposed the failure of the regime's much-vaunted land reform beyond Ethiopian borders. Some of the hardest hit regions include central Eritrea, Tigre, Wollo, and parts of Begember and Shewa. Media activity in the West led to the launch of Live Aid organized by Bob Geldof and Midge Ure, which raised the international profile of the famine and helped secure international aid. In spite of its overwhelming challenges of fiscal and increasingly discernible moral bankruptcy, the state mobilized its officials and technocrats as they recycled a motley collection of vulgar Marxist-Leninist labels with the goal of harnessing more power and influence for a project in twilight. In this vein, the Workers Party of Ethiopia, or WPE, was created by the regime in 1984 as the civilian "vanguard" party. A new constitution was completed in 1986 to make provisions for a national *Shango* (assembly). In 1987, the ratification of the constitution of the *Shango* also proclaimed the birth of the People's Democratic Republic of Ethiopia, with Mengistu Haile Mariam as its president.

REQUIEM FOR THE DERG'S "MARXISM-LENINISM"

The failure of the Derg's policies and a growing wave of change and realignments in global relations encouraged radical opposition in domestic affairs. The erosion of international patronage, especially from the old Eastern Bloc, demoralized the officials and soldiers of the ruling government. The opposition, especially those engaged in guerilla warfare, saw an opportunity to escalate their insurgency against the unpopular regime. The rebel opposition included the Eritrean People's Liberation Front (EPLF), the Tigrean People's Liberation Front (TPLF), the Ethiopian Democratic Union (EDU), the Oromo Liberation Front (OLF), the Oromo People's Democratic Organization (OPDO), the Ethiopian Liberation Front (ENLF), and the Ethiopian Democratic Officers Revolutionary movement (EDURM). Four dominant insurgent groups—the Oromo People's Democratic Organization, the Amhara National Democratic Movement, the South Ethiopian People's Democratic Front, and the Tigrean People's Liberation Front—established an alliance in the form of the Ethiopian People's Revolutionary Democratic Front (EPRDF). With this step, these activists and guerillas that were mostly Marxists in orientation temporarily sacrificed unique and separate goals of self-determination for the purpose of overthrowing the Derg regime. The dominant partners in the new organization were the Tigrean People's Liberation Front (TPLF) and the Oromo Liberation Front (OLF).

With the expansion of military operations, the EPRDF secured strategic victory in the port of Massawa, Gondar, Wallo, and Dabra Tabor and was poised to secure the Ethiopian capital Addis Ababa. The Derg regime, realizing its precarious situation, made peaceful overtures and sought the assistance of foreign mediation from United States and Italy. High-level summits between the beleaguered president Mengistu Haile Mariam and representatives of EPRDF, however, left more unresolved issues on the table as the latter group threatened the government's hold on power through territorial victories while increasing their own influence over the public through a successful propaganda campaign. The resistance also received the tacit support of major Western powers, most of which had seen their strategic interests undermined by members of the old Eastern Bloc.

In May 1991, Mengistu Haile Mariam fled Ethiopia as the victorious EPRDF advanced upon Addis Ababa. The triumphant opposition immediately proceeded to consolidate its power and influence as a prelude to establishing an interim government. In this transitional phase, Ethiopia's army—one of the largest on the African continent—was demobilized and the major responsibilities of the military were taken over by the EPRDF fighters from Tigre, followed by a declaration that a new army would be conscripted with recruits drawn from across all Ethiopian nationalities. The new government also announced that it was seeking international assistance aimed at prosecuting those who committed human rights violations during Haile Mariam's regime.

POLITICAL TRANSITION AND MODERNIZATION: FROM MARXISM TO SOCIAL DEMOCRACY

As part of its new agenda, the interim authorities led by the EPRDF called a national conference of over 20 organizations with the goal of establishing a new administrative body. The Transitional Government of Ethiopia (TGE) was ultimately made up of many political organizations, with the EPRDF at the helm. EPRDF's leader, Meles Zenawi, was elected interim president of the transitional government and chairman of the transitional Council of Representatives, a position he occupied from 1991 to 1995. The three members of the junta who administered Ethiopia in this transitional phase included Meles Zenawi, who was president, Tamrat Layne, the prime minister, and Seeye Abraha, who was minister of defense. Zenawi was considered by many to be the dominant intellectual figure of the postwar administration.

A new constitution called for the election of 550 members to the Council of People's Representatives from all electoral districts on the basis of the size of the populations. Although Ethiopia had no prior experience with a popularly elected democratic government or legislature, over 60 political parties emerged to contest in regional elections held in 1992. By June of that year, the Oromo Liberation Front (OLF), the dominant party in Ethiopia's most populous region, had either backed out or was forced out of the political arrangement. The OLF also abandoned the cease-fire agreement as prescribed by the National Charter and instead dedicated itself to the idea of self-determination to be achieved through military means if such opportunity was not made available through civil negotiations. The ultimate political goal of the OLF was the creation of an independent state of Oromia.

The EPRDF reorganized the country as a federal state structured along ethnolinguistic lines. It also expressed the state's recognition of the unconditional right of every nation in the country to self-determination, cultural autonomy, and self-governance including a provision for special representation of minority nations. The objective was the selection of local representatives for communities and districts. The process of drafting a new constitution began on a nationwide basis between 1992 and 1993, with debates taking place not only in the major cities but also at the village levels.

Human rights and political activists were encouraged by the provisional steps towards a democratic dispensation marked by the restoration of a free press and a buoyant civil society. More than 50 new monthly magazines and 20 private newspapers emerged following the collapse of the socialist dictatorship. In June 1994, Ethiopia held its first series of elections to determine the membership of local governments. The government announced that the state media would give time and space for different political parties to carry on free discussions and inform the public about their views. This was, however, limited to the periods of election campaign. Both the print and electronic state media disseminated the government's policy most of the time.

In 1994, a new constitution stipulated that general elections were to be held in 1995, 2000, and 2005. Although opposition parties were encouraged, it was obvious that the Ethiopian People's Revolutionary Democratic Front (EPRDF) would emerge as the single dominant political party. In December 1994, a new constitution scheduled general elections for the following May. The document also established a new federal structure that allowed autonomy for nine major regional entities of Ethiopia. The policy of ethnic federalism endowed each autonomous state with the authority to evolve new constitutions and budgets and levy taxation for the purpose of developing its infrastructure. Opponents of the post-Derg regime have also responded with charges of official corruption and nepotism in governmental appointments and allocation of resources to favored groups, especially the dominant elements in the government's Tigre region. Some scholars and activists have, however, observed that in spite of the Tigrean sway over policies, the level of poverty for ordinary people in Tigrean and Amharan ethnolinguistic states is actually much higher than that of southern and Oromo ethnolinguistic regional states in spite of the historical marginalization of regional communities, especially the Oromo. The government, in defense of its policies, declared that the ideological basis for its policy of ethnic federation was based on the idea that central development policies in Ethiopia had historically been hegemonic and exploitative and were thus a major determinant in previous internecine strife and civil war. It accused leaders of the opposition of being antidemocratic and a threat to national security.

In spite of the above contradictory positions, the emergence of ethnic-based politics has alienated many experienced and budding political figures. Social critics and intellectuals argued that the new political structure was divisive and antidemocratic, as it fractured the opposition. They also believed that the policy would restrict economic adventures and risks necessary for modern political and economic activities. The administration on the contrary argued that ethnicity would become less of an issue as the economy grew and an organic process of assimilation into the Ethiopian body politic ensued. In spite of the initial government's overture towards various political and intellectual groups, it has also been accused of being too rigid in its disposition for a democratic order. The Zenawi-led government in its defense held that the constitutional guarantee of ethnic federalism favored autonomous existence for each ethnic group with the corollary of a higher level of recognition for local culture, history, and identities. In this regard, some scholars have amplified the governmental thesis by highlighting the introduction of local history and cultures in primary and secondary school syllabi as an improvement to the Solomonic era curricula. They stress that there are radio and television spaces for each of the major languages spoken in the country; and programs broadcasted on television now feature a variety of local customs and music.

The first major reform policy taken by the new administration led by the EPRDF was the weaning of Ethiopia from the Marxist-Leninist ideology of the Cold War era to embrace economic liberalization. The EPRDF adopted social democracy with pro-Western economic policies in what has been described as the pragmatic leadership style of Prime Minister Meles Zenawi. The government transformed Ethiopia from a centrally planned economy into a market-oriented one and in the process boosted the overall GDP growth rate to an annual 4.0 percent in 1991–2003 from 2.8 percent during the Derg rule (1974–91). In addition, the structure of the economy underwent a transformation, with agriculture's contribution to real GDP falling from 57 percent in 1991 to 42 percent in 2003. On the contrary, that of service rose from 34 percent to 47 percent. In spite of these changes, the contributions of industry and the private sector remained essentially unchanged as Ethiopia's growth potential, like that of most African states, remained largely unfulfilled.

In 1993, the Ethiopian government did not oppose Eritrea's demand for independence even though the change in territorial status and realignment transformed Ethiopia into a landlocked nation. Ethiopia and Eritrea signed cooperation agreements in which, among other provisions, 80 percent of Ethiopia's foreign trade passed through Eritrean ports. Ethiopia was also a market for about 80 percent of Eritrea's exports, and the two countries shared economic institutions such as a common currency, the birr, and a shared oil refinery at Assab port. When imported commodities pass through other countries, they are supposed to be in transit and thus free from custom taxes. An agreement on transportation also declared that Ethiopian Airlines would fly to Asmara. In addition, Eritrean nationals who resided in Ethiopia were allowed to live and work in their locations, and a similar status was bestowed on Ethiopians in Eritrea. The Ethiopian government also committed itself to the reconstruction and rehabilitation of the Eritrean economy, an agreement consummated by the former government's taking on a loan agreement from the International Development Assistance (IDA) group of the World Bank on behalf of the latter. The government and its supporters declared that the arrangement with Eritrea was a mutually beneficial arrangement; opposition to the bilateral agreements, however, emerged soon afterwards. The contrary position was that Eritrea took unfair advantage of an overly idealistic or politically naïve Ethiopian government. They highlighted the thesis that Ethiopia does not benefit from the agreement, which allows tax-free mutual importations of products from each country, because commodities that were sources of the much prized foreign exchange were excluded from the equation. Government critics mobilized public demonstrations from citizens who sought to express enlightened opinion on the Eritrean question. The Ethiopian government also complained that Eritrea did not adhere to the former's exchange rate for foreign currency, especially the U.S dollar. The two countries adopted varied development strategies as Eritrea was labeled as radical and outward oriented while Ethiopia was conservative and inward looking. Eritrea was also accused of buying coffee and oil seeds from Ethiopia for re-export, of selling untaxed commodities (imported as goods in transit) in Ethiopia, and of excluding Ethiopians from its growing market. Eritrea responded with accusations of Ethiopian protectionism and discrimination towards its citizens operating in the Ethiopian economy. In November 1997, Eritrea issued its currency, the *nakfa,* and Ethiopia subsequently revoked the special relationship, choosing to transact economic relationship with Eritrean using the normal international exchange of U.S. dollars and letters of credit. Ethiopia also refused to accept the Eritrean currency with a value at par with the birr. Many Ethiopians reacted to this turn of events by embarking on large-scale protests on university campuses that were summarily and often brutally suppressed. The government accused the opposition of anarchism and oppositional activists of being willful tools of those proffering political propaganda with little or no alternative paradigms. The University Teacher's Association that had begun to thrive after years of autocratic influence on campus during the imperial and Derg regimes found out that the new freedoms came at a price. Students and teacher were expelled and campus officials were purged as the government selectively renewed academic contracts.

In May 1998, Eritrean military forces invaded the border areas of Ethiopia, thus beginning a new era of conflicts between the two states. The Eritrean-Ethiopian War was to last from May 1998 to June 2000. Ethiopia launched air strikes against Eritrea's capital, Asmara. Eritrean aircraft also bombed the northern Ethiopian towns of Adigrat and Mek'ele. Ground troops from both countries fought on three fronts as the conflict rapidly spread due to Eritrean support for the Oromo Liberation Front, the rebel group seeking independence for Oromia. Both countries ultimately spent several hundred million dollars on new military equipment. By May 2000, Ethiopia occupied about a quarter of Eritrea's territory, displacing 650,000 people. It also destroyed key components of Eritrea's infrastructure. Ethiopia expelled 77,000 Eritreans, and some Ethiopians of Eritrean origin were also expelled. The estimated cost to Ethiopia in public and social infrastructure was more than 200 million dollars. Ethiopian goods were also looted in Eritrean ports. Eritrea claimed that 19,000 Eritrean soldiers were killed during the conflict, while Ethiopian casualties numbered in the tens of thousands. The refugee problem in the Horn of Africa was further compounded by drought and the displacement of citizens of both states. Diplomatic efforts by the United States, Rwanda, and the Organization of African Unity failed to bring peace. Finally, the two-year war ended following a peace agreement signed in Algiers in December 2000. The peace agreement outlined the establishment of a commission in the Hague to rule on the border issue. A U.N. peacekeeping force was established to guard the buffer zone between the two states. In 2001, a year after the war with Eritrea ended, Menes Zenawi began to face an internal revolt with the TPLF. Senior members of the Central Committee opposed some of the prime minister's reforms, and many resented his rapprochement with Eritrea. The war has also led to diversion of public expenditure.

GLOBALIZATION, MODERNIZATION, AND IDENTITY POLITICS

The fact that the EPRDF emerged on the national scene at a time in which socialism was being challenged in both domestic and international contexts combined with the fall of the Soviet Union and the domestic failure of the Derg regime helped influence the transformation of the new government's intellectual and political positions. Although the Tigre People's Liberation Front, a Marxist guerilla oppositional force that later dominated the core of the new government, was also socialist in its ideological roots, it had little choice but to jettison its intellectual pedigree. The government instead chose to embrace a political force rooted in another major grievance in Ethiopian history—ethnicity. The new administration, however, had to surmount incredible odds in its mission as it faced numerous obstacles in its attempt to carry out social, political, and economic reforms. In the last few decades of the twentieth century Ethiopia, like most African states, experienced major decline in foreign earnings due to a combination of factors including poor agricultural production, unequal international trade policies, warfare, and natural disasters. The famines of 1973–1974 and 1984 and 1986 were triggered by ecological crisis, social conflict, competition for resources, and human mismanagement of the natural environment. Besides excluding the private sector from participation in economic activity for close to two decades of Marxist dictatorship, the dictatorship had also wiped out almost an entire generation of productive youths, workers, and intellectuals. Ethiopia's defense budget at the height of military operations in the late 1980s was 26 percent of GDP. Between 1974/75 and 1989/90, growth decelerated to 2.3 percent, and per capita growth was estimated at 0.4 percent. Ethiopia was also on the verge of bankruptcy, and its foreign debt was almost $9 billion.

The above domestic factors have contributed to what some scholars have described as the internationalization of public welfare, a development of major ramifications for local and global politics. The importance of external factors in the political and economic instability in Ethiopia and the rest of the African continent cannot be overemphasized, as they have combined with domestic forces to shape contemporary political traditions. Two major schools of thought exist in modern African narratives on the intersection of politics and social reform. The first paradigm, favored by historically marginalized "nations" within Ethiopia, argues that European colonial powers operating in the Horn enabled Emperor Menelik to establish and entrench Amhara aristocracy. In addition to subjugating pastoral and peasant communities, a centralized political structure was imposed on disparate communities in the region. The Euro-Ethiopian relationship, it is argued, not only marked the beginning of the prioritizing of the center over the communities, it also placed the interests of exports over domestic consumption. Thus globalization, according to most ethnonationalists, undermined the system of collective responsibility and old forms of social security, a situation that could be redeemed through devolution of power and full recognition of self-determination for subnationalities. The pan- nationalism school also acknowledge historical grievances of cultural communities but often accuse ethnonationalist political activists and intellectuals of rewriting history by romanticizing peasant life and ancient traditions for the sake of elite-driven politics. Theorists and adherents of pan-nationalism argue that there is a need to understate cultural and ethnic differences in a competitive and often prejudiced world for markets and resources. In Ethiopia, the latter school indicted past and present administrations, including the imperial state, the Derg, and the EPRDF government, of riding to power behind thinly veiled ethnic projects. They also emphasized that Ethiopian history, culture, and political independence provide lessons, resources, and, above all, national security and unity. Ethiopia, it is argued, has always been culturally diverse due to thousands of years of continuous interaction, intermarriages, trade, migration, and other social activities in Ethiopian history. Both the pan-Ethiopian nationalists and their ethnonationalist counterparts also agree that since Ethiopia has more than 80 ethnolinguistic groups, its weakness lies in the fact that political leadership is a major culprit in the perennial conflict and competition over resources.

Critics of the Zenawi regime's decentralization policy (that is, the federal system organized along ethnolinguistic federal states) have described it as bogus and hyprocritical. They accused the state of protecting Tigrean ethnic interests, since the center retained resources for dispersal to the periphery. The accusation came mostly from the central and southern parts of the country where the Amharic and Oromigna speakers dominate. Others argued that the constitutional affirmation of the rights of any ethnolinguistic group to secede had negative ramifications for private economic activities, especially investors skeptical that their investments were going to be fully protected in regions farther away from their ethnic "home" base. In a similar vein, they suggested that an administrative framework based on an ethnolinguistic basis is incompatible with the existence of the market paradigm. The constitutional guarantee for secession, it was argued, was likely to limit labor and capital mobility across the ethnic enclaves. The government's position was that the centralized disbursement of resources was imperative, since the bulk of national income comes from import duties, a situation that can only evolve when the various regions begin to generate tax revenue through the cultivation of the agricultural and mineral sectors of the economy. The breakdown of Ethiopia's communities and ethnolinguistic groups and their interactions, however, reveals a more complex reality.

In Ethiopia, two groups—the Oromo (32 percent) and the Amhara (30 percent)—account for 62 percent of the population. Four ethnolinguistic groups—the Tigrawie (6 percent), Somalis (6 percent), Guragie (4 percent), and Wolaita (3 percent)—account for another 19 percent of the population. Sixty-one percent of Ethiopia's population is Christian (51 percent Ethiopian Orthodox and 10 percent other), while Muslims make up an additional 33 percent. Forty-two percent of the total and 81 percent of the urban population speak Amharic as either their first or second language. The cycle of revolt and conflict might appear on the surface to be grounded in ethnicity, but domination and inequality have always been regional and class based. According to economist Alemayehu Geda, two major historical factors are responsible for this age-old trend. The first factor was the "king of kings" system, in which the strongest regional-based king became the king of all regional kings and occupied central power. This king of kings came from one regional group and maintained his power by drawing officials from different regions, often consolidating such relationships through marriage to his offspring. Second, peasants of all ethnic groups have faced subjugation by the ruling elite. This fact, according to Geda, does not negate the historic domination of the northern highlander's language and culture over the others, but this fact, he concluded, was but a secondary factor. He suggests that conflict in Ethiopia is primarily the result of a violent power-sharing mechanism, which had a deleterious effect on economic performance and thus made the state unproductive and militaristic. Civil wars, he continued, were one of the root causes of the country's poverty and backwardness, as they contributed to the increase of endogenous factors that negatively impacted the growth rate of GDP. In addition, the "ethnic" card only functions as an ideological tool for mobilization for elites to secure political and economic power.

Modern Ethiopia also presents an interesting case study for evaluating the intersection between international power politics and domestic economic reform. It has been argued that Ethiopia has been a victim of "market fundamentalism," that is, the idea that markets work perfectly and demand must equal supply for labor as well as other goods and factor. Such programs are quite unpopular for many reasons, the most important of which is the simultaneous and dogmatic application of a single model to dozens of countries at once. The structural adjustment policy imposed by the International Monetary Fund (IMF) usually emphasized social and economic policies that encouraged internal savings and primary exports, often displaying a clinical detachment from the ability of African states to successfully address the needs and welfare of their citizenry. In this regard, Joseph E. Stiglitz, former senior vice president and chief economist of the World Bank, who had been actively involved in Ethiopia's efforts at liberalizing its economy, provided a sample of what he described as Ethiopia's struggle between "power politics and poverty." He highlighted the pitfalls of transnational financial institutions imposing economic policies on "developing" societies. Stiglitz credited Ethiopian leader Meles Zenawi for his efforts at democratic political reform combined with policies influenced by a deep understanding of economic principles tailored to the political and economic circumstances in his country. The IMF, on the other hand, frowned upon Ethiopia's independent action and suspended its subsidized loan program to the country. This action by extension threatened Ethiopia's sovereignty in economic management and political reform. The IMF, according to Stiglitz, failed to acknowledge Ethiopia's political or macroeconomic success. These included a reduction in the country's military budget in favor of poverty-alleviation programs and the effort directed at keeping borrowing and lending rates relatively low as opposed to relying on international market forces as the major determinant for social and economic policies. The IMF had instead recommended a program of "financial market liberalization," adding that rather than investing resources recouped from international assistance towards the construction or maintenance of social welfare infrastructures such as schools and health clinics, Ethiopia should instead secure such assistance in a rainy-day account usually kept in U.S. Treasury bills. According to critics, this policy was the embodiment of the internationalization of welfare, in which social democracy is a utopian goal for Africa and other "developing" states. The debt-ridden states, they argue, are prevented from establishing local welfare institutions but are in turn coerced to finance the well-being of richer societies. Neoliberal restructuring of the welfare state attempts to stimulate market reform while reconfiguring safety nets as contractual or project agreements linking donors and nongovernmental organizations (NGOs).

Ethiopia was ultimately able to present its plan for economic reform, especially its plan to liberalize certain sectors of the economy as opposed to the central control the previous government imposed on private sector. The government was, however, opposed to the privatization of selective strategic sectors of the economy. It devalued the currency, but as part of fulfilling this requirement of international finance, it was able to negotiate a caveat that allowed for the subsidization of fuel imports. Between 1990/91 and 1999/2000, total and per capita GDP on average grew at 3.7 percent and 0.7 percent per year respectively. This figure, it is argued, could have been even more impressive but for the sporadic conflicts with Eritrea. Critics of liberalization have pointed to the negative effect on local food, leather, and tobacco industries due to stiff foreign competition from producers in the "developed" world, many of whom are the beneficiaries of better technology and immense subsidies from their home governments. Ethiopian goods also faced the obstacle of high tariffs, which usually do not favor the African producers who have to secure foreign exchange.

Other measures taken to mitigate the shocks associated with economic reforms and transition, however, continue to face criticism from both domestic and international experts. One such critique lies in the fact that the Ethiopian government as stipulated by its new constitution does not allow private ownership of land. In what has remained a controversial policy with major political ramifications, land is only available through grant usage and long-term lease. Economists have argued to the contrary that an active land market is a prerequisite if any meaningful and dynamic social and economic transformation is to be effected. The government defended its policy as one dictated by a need to assuage the collective memory of the peasants, whose access to land and production have been historically and systematically exploited. In addition, according to the government, such a policy was guided by the fact that land not only remains the only social security for the peasants but also was also necessary for increasing agricultural productivity.

There are also major controversies surrounding Ethiopian development policies including its culture and record of international aid and its disbursement. Ethiopia's revenue comes from taxes and foreign assistance, and the latter has been a more stable form of income. Some observers have ascribed Ethiopia's crisis as one typical of Africa's underdevelopment due to corruption and misrule. Economist Jeffrey Sachs, who is renowned for his work on the alleviation of global poverty in Africa in general and Ethiopia in particular, suggests a nuanced perspective for analyzing events and policies in Africa. Sachs argues that economic stagnation has engendered cultural despair and political pathologies in Africa. Sachs acknowledges the relevance of the argument made by critics of African corruption and misrule on the one hand and those who accuse the West of meddling in African politics on the other. More important, he argues, is the recognition of Africa's prolonged crisis since the era of the Atlantic slave trade and the colonization of the continent, followed by the exploits of cold warriors and CIA operatives and their counterparts in Europe who opposed Africans who preached nationalism, sought aid from the Soviet Union, or demanded better terms on Western investments in African minerals and energy deposits. Sachs continues: "The one thing that the West would not do, however, was invest in long-term African economic development. The die was cast in the 1960s, when U.S. policy makers decided that the United States would not support a Marshall Plan type of policy for Africa, even though such an effort was precisely what was needed to build the infrastructure for long-term growth. It was not that U.S. officials rejected the diagnosis—they knew it was needed—but the political leadership was not willing to pay the price."[1]

The condition described above was the historical background in which the transnational financial bodies, who are often "lenders of last resort" and who hold the keys to global economic and financial system, stepped into postcolonial African social and economic development. The IMF and World Bank dictated economic policies and measures and thus have often been accused of monopolizing the power to sustain the enigma of enduring debt as a political and ideological tool.

International activists such as Bob Geldof and Bono have laid special emphasis on Ethiopian poverty while leading campaigns that call on the world's richest countries to do more in the global fight against poverty in Africa. Nongovernmental Organizations (NGOs) have also been critical of the tepid and meager contributions of the rich nations, most of whom are accused of a failure to deconstruct the international framework that perpetuates economic and political inequalities. The above activists argue that democracy is more than elections. True democracy, they argue, is a matter of sequence that includes the building of free institutions, free press, and so forth. Democracy, they argue, must also be an agenda of economic opportunity, since poverty gives rise to cultural despair and political pathologies.

Other scholars have drawn attention to the fact that Ethiopia's economy has also suffered from the vagaries of nature, weak institutions and public policies, and risk to property rights engendered by war. Since coffee constitutes 65 percent of Ethiopia's total trade, the economy's dependence on a single product for its major export makes the country vulnerable to the terms of trade shocks and other exogenous factors. It has also been suggested that food aid to Ethiopia has created a dependency syndrome among Ethiopian farmers. The perennial presence of foreign food crops as "humanitarian aid," critics argue, stifles innovative and inventive techniques and undermines national sovereignty. Others argue, however, that the contributions of donors and Nongovernmental Organizations (NGO) like Oxfam in Ethiopia are critical and inevitable. The NGOs and civil society organizations create an avenue to work for and on behalf of Ethiopian citizens outside of the government framework.

In perhaps the strongest indictment of the structure of Western aid to Africa, scholar William Easterly described contemporary approaches as mainly a rehash of the nineteenth century concept of "The White Man's Burden," in which humanitarian instincts and genuine goodwill on the part of many often intersected with less than altruistic and propagandist motives by state and regional policymakers. The result of colonial modernization projects, he argued, was less than fruitful because it was dictated by external interests, needs, and by "planners" as opposed to "searchers." He argue that some of the activists listed above should be commended for their efforts and for drawing attention to the problems in Africa and other parts of the poor regions of the world, but their efforts have been less than constructive and successful. One of the distinctions Easterly observed is that the dominant group of aid workers are planners as opposed to searchers. While the former raise expectations but take no responsibility for meeting them, the latter group would accept responsibility for their actions. Other examples he gave included the fact that planners determine what to supply but searchers find out what is in demand, planners apply global blueprints, while searchers adapt to local conditions. Perhaps of most importance, he concluded, planners think they already know the answers, they think of poverty as a technical engineering problem that their answers must solve. On the other hand, seekers admit they don't know the answers in advance and believe that poverty is a complicated tangle of political, social, historical, institutional, and technological factors. Easterly's campaign is for aid agencies to follow the model of the British NGO called Water Aid, who in the Great Rift of Ethiopia successfully inaugurated a water project that was run entirely by Ethiopians, with representatives from the villages sitting on the board of the agency. In spite of the above variety of approaches, Ethiopian economy in the immediate future requires foreign assistance and the state must also look inward for solutions.[2]

The Ethiopian government has in recent years faced intense criticism at home and abroad for what is considered as its autocratic and violent conduct. In 2000, more than 40 professors and lecturers were expelled from Addis Ababa University. In 2001, a student movement protesting for academic rights further aggravated the political authorities. The protests of 10,000 Addis Ababa University students gained the support of students from universities and colleges throughout the country and led to a virtual standstill of public higher learning in Ethiopia. The students called for the removal of police from their campus and their rights of freedom of expression. The government accused members from the two main opposition parties, the All Amhara People's Organization (AAPO) and the Ethiopian Democratic Party (EDP), of instigating the protests. The state was, however, more concerned about the general public's sympathies with the student's calls for the removal of police from their campus and their rights of freedom of expression.

Although many observers had initially lauded Ethiopia's contribution to the resolution of Sudan's political conflicts and social dislocations, human rights groups have accused the Ethiopians of carrying out ethnocentric attacks on their unfortunate southern neighbors who seek refuge in the former's territorial enclaves such as the Anuak cultural communities. Human rights activists have accused the Ethiopian state of carrying out systematic cleansing of the refugees accused of "occupying" a potential breadbasket such as the southwestern region of Gambella. Others claimed that the persecution of these communities was due to the question of cultural "difference" or their darker skin phenotypes. The government has responded to these accusations by arguing that its military activities in the region bring stability to the countryside where pillaging and brigandage threaten Ethiopian citizens' welfare, communication, and commercial activities. The residents of southern Ethiopia have been subjected to acts of injustice, alienation of land, and military and political subjugation. The sense of righteous anger and the struggle for freedom have inadvertently led to an assertion of guilt by association even when select officials and associations have benefited from the historical inequality of Ethiopia.

On May 15, 2005, Ethiopia held general elections for seats in its national and four regional government councils. The government promised free and fair elections, as it welcomed international observers from the European Union and the U.S.–based Carter Center. The government also imposed a general ban on protests throughout the election period, a step it claimed was necessary for peace and social stability. Systematic campaigns against the EPDRF government have been most strong in the urban region. Addis Ababa, the national capital, is also home to many of Ethiopia's unemployed youth and hundreds of thousands of people who fled from the rural areas to the city in search of livelihood but found none and were thus a potential constituency for political uprising. The theatre of politics including the televised debates geared towards creating awareness among the Ethiopian public is also often the preserve of urban dwellers where issues of unemployment and hunger had been an issue of great concern. By early May 16, 2005, initial results had the opposition heading towards winning a majority in the national parliament, with only about a third of the constituencies with complete tallies. By the end of the day the ruling party released statements indicating that it had won more than 300 seats, while the two major opposition parties, the Coalition for Unity and Democracy (CUD) and the United Ethiopian Democratic Forces (UEDF), subsequently announced their party's victory in 185 of the approximately 200 seats for which the National Election Board of Ethiopia (NEBE) had released preliminary results. This result was a radical shift in political equations since the previous elections. By evening, the prime minister declared a state of emergency, outlawed any public gathering, and assumed direct command of the security forces. The last measure was an indication of the replacement of the capital city police with federal police and special forces drawn from elite army units. The electoral board, NEBE, also ceased tabulating results for almost a week. The actions by the established authorities began to fuel organized resistance to the election results. The opposition parties not only increased their representation in parliament significantly during the elections, but the Coalition for Unity and Democracy (CUD), which comprises the Ethiopian Democratic League, the All Ethiopian Unity Party, the United

Ethiopian Democratic Party–Mehin Party, and Rainbow Ethiopia: Movement for Democracy and Social Justice, won by big margins all 23 seats in the capital, Addis Ababa. The CUD, chaired by civil engineer Hailu Shawil, says it offers a liberal alternative to the EPRDF and has been campaigning for, among other things, the privatization of land for commercial and other economic reasons. The CUD has at least four factions; the smaller United Ethiopian Democratic Forces (UEDF) is also comprised of several parties and has also been gaining seats in the parliament, especially from Oromiya and southern Regions. CUD supporters are largely Amharas from the north, and some of its members, it is argued, are resentful of what is considered the Tigreans' lock on power. Its leaders include Dr. Marara Gudina, a writer and professor at Addis Ababa University, and Dr. Beyene Petros, a leading opposition legislator in parliament. The UEDF is comprised of the Oromo National Congress, the Ethiopian Social Democratic Federal Party, the Southern Ethiopia People's Democratic Coalition, the All-Amhara People's Organization, and the Ethiopian Democratic Unity Party. Other members include the Afar Revolutionary Democratic Unity Front (ARDUF), the All Ethiopia Socialist Movement (MEISON), the Ethiopian People Federal Democratic Unity Party, the Ethiopia People's Revolutionary Party (EPRP), the Gambella People's United Democratic Front (GPUDF), the Oromo People's Liberation Organization (OPLO-IBSO), SEPDC, and the Tigre Alliance for Democracy (TAND).

The political events in Ethiopia have increasingly reflected an urban-rural disconnect, with the state investing its energy in pacifying the massive rural region. In cities like Addis Ababa, which has grown to over 5 million people, there is a high level of opposition to government policies such as city management measures that demolished large slums, an action that turn many destitute. In contrast to the situation in the cities, the government's electoral success is usually cemented in the rural areas. Critics argue that the government is both landlord and benefactor to the residents of the rural areas. The government provides fertilizer and farm implements on loan and also distributes food aid to rural regions whenever famine and drought strike. The EPRDF, however, continues to draw from the well of public goodwill of many of its supporters who still acknowledge its role in the ousting of the Derg socialist regime and in delivering social amenities to many over the past decade.

Eritrea also continues to serve as a lightning rod for opposition to the Ethiopian government. There has been call to reclaim "Ethiopia's Red Sea territories," which in essence refers to Eritrea.

In 2004, Meles Zenawi was named one of the members of Prime Minister Tony Blair of Great Britain's Commission for Africa. This body has declared good governance and the reduction of poverty on the continent as its goals.

At the end of the twentieth century and the beginning of the twenty-first, scholars and observers of Ethiopia have attempted to understand what some describe as the vicious cycle of crisis arising from the modus operandi of the ruling Ethiopian political groups. Ethiopia, it is argued, has explored the "trinity ideology" in modernity through Emperor's Haile Selassie's conservatism, the Derg's socialism, and the EPRDF's liberalism and has been ineffective in addressing the state's crisis because the political leaders have been misguided by these respective ideologies.

CONCLUSION: AFROMODERNITY AND THE ETHIOPIAN CENTURY

Prologue to African Conscience

Tamed to bend
Into the model chairs
Carpentered for it
By the friendly pharos of its time
The black conscience flutters
Yet is taken in.
    It looks right
It looks left
It forgets to look into its own self:
The broken yoke threatens to return
Only, this time
In the luring shape
Of luxury and golden chains
That frees the body
And enslaves the mind.
    Into its head
The old dragon sun
Now breathes hot civilization
And the wise brains
Of the strong sons of the tribes
Pant
With an even more strange suffocation.
    Its new self awareness
(In spite of its tribal ills)
Wishes to patch
its torn spirits together:
Its past and present masters
(With their army of ghosts
That remained to haunt the earth)
Hook its innermost soul
And tear it apart:
And the african conscience
Still moans molested
Still remains drifting uprooted.

Tsegaye Gabre-Medhin (1936–2005)[3]

Africans are victims of the largest forced migration in human history, and people of African descent make up what has been described as a multifaceted, shifting diaspora. For Ethiopia, the social and political instabilities created by internal and regional wars have resulted in negative social, psychological, political, and economic consequences for the citizenry, often followed by migratory redistributions. Such odysseys have also included journeys from rural to urban zones, across territories, cultures, and time zones. Other journeys have been necessitated by the pursuit of economic opportunity and to escape from the social upheavals conditioned by war, famine, and political and cultural oppressions. One might also add that the average citizens, the poor and the vulnerable, often pay the price for international power games and strategic calculations of local and global powers. Ethiopians contributed a great bulk of the post–Atlantic slave trade African Diaspora that began in the late nineteenth century and reached its apogee in the second half of the twentieth. Elizabeth Harney argues that since the fall of the Marxist military regime, many artists have returned from imposed exile to visit or in some cases relocate to Ethiopia. Harney situates Ethiopian history and artistic, intellectual manifestations from the medieval to the modern and postmodern or transnational experiences within the broader African Diaspora history. African histories, she argues, have always been shaped by histories of migration. Lucrative trade in resources coupled with the great river systems and ports of Africa have all shaped the political and cultural history of the continent. In this vein, Ethiopian traders, artisans, artists, intellectuals, and religious and political leaders have responded to local and external stimuli and been forced to reconsider and renegotiate affiliations to home, identity, and community. In the 1960s, the Ethiopian elite and their children went abroad in search of Western education. Between the 1970s and the 1980s, the fall of Haile Selassie's regime led to the dispersal of a number of members of his regime, who sought refuge outside of the country.

Ethiopians and Eritreans are the largest African group to resettle in the United States under the Refugee Act of 1980, the first refugee policy for African asylum seekers. Between 1981 and 1984, about 45,000 Africans entered the United States as refugees, with the majority coming from the Horn of Africa. In the late 1980s, drought, famine, and economic deprivation and political irredentism forced a number of rural populations into the global flows of migration. The flow of ideas between Ethiopia and the broader world, she continues, has also increased in the second half of the twentieth century. Within the Diaspora, Harney concludes, generations of migrants carry with them their own histories and imaginings of home, and Ethiopian artists in their rich contributions to modern art have made different choices about their relationships to a broader Ethiopian Diaspora community.

Ethiopian artists have built on the foundations laid by pioneers of modern arts such as Alexander "Skunder" Boghossian, Gebre Kristos Desta, and Afewerk Tekle. The new generation of Ethiopian intellectuals and artists embrace and exploit the universal medium of the Diaspora to represent Ethiopia's rich cultural heritage and articulate their unique modern experiences. In addition, one must pay attention to local commodities, which are also the product of a time-tested impressive creativity. The local Ethiopian cultural productions have suffered from neglect due to hegemonic political propaganda and the inability or unwillingness of modern scholars to place these productions within the common understandings and critical appreciation of African art, ideas, creativity, and subjectivity. The gap between the postmodern configurations of the Ethiopian Diaspora and the aspirations of modern conveniences for domestic Ethiopian communities must be bridged. It has been argued that many Ethiopians, like most Africans in both transnational and national contexts, still carry the scars of modernity and remain afflicted by the ruthless exhibition of power and destructive ideological and material products of modernity. Ethiopia remains one of the poorest countries in the world, with major obstacles to development such as frequent drought and food shortages. Inadequate roads and communications also hinder economic activities in the state.

The voices of local and global Ethiopian citizens, intellectuals, and artists could help mitigate those news items and images that do little beyond showcasing the pathologies of the country. There is need for a progressive lobby to help ameliorate the poor social and economic conditions in Ethiopian communities. In the domestic context, the rehabilitation of social services and infrastructures and state support for economic enterprises for local development could also speak to the yearnings and aspirations of Ethiopia and the African continent. The most important development has been the growth of the Ethiopian Diaspora in the United States, Europe and the Middle East. It is estimated that there are over one million Ethiopians in the Diaspora with more than 500,000 Ethiopians in North America alone. Ethiopians represent a significant number of immigrant populations in some major cities of North America. The greater Washington area has the world's largest concentration of Ethiopians outside of Africa, many of them left their country for a variety of social, political, and economic reasons. Besides the Washington metropolitan area, there are major Ethiopian communities in the San Francisco Bay region, Atlanta, Boston, New York, Houston, Dallas, Los Angeles, San Diego, Seattle, and Minneapolis/St. Paul. .The term Little Ethiopia refers to Fairfax Avenue in the Carthay district of Los Angeles, California, between Olympic and Pico Boulevard. Ethiopians have displayed economic strength and achieved educational laurels and successes in professional and entrepreneurial activities. One can find an Ethiopian restaurant in virtually every large American city, and Ethiopian Orthodox churches are also common. In most of the cities where they reside, Ethiopians have invested in properties and open businesses that cater to both general populations and the unique needs of its cultural communities. They have also invested in the establishment of service sectors and cultural centers. .Ethiopians abroad continue to have a deep attachment to their country of origin. Many send home remittances that sometime rival the annual income earned by the home state from foreign export. The country's biggest export is coffee, which, for example, earned $267 million in 1999 by exporting 105,000 metric tons. Ethiopian government officials have also organized campaigns and workshops aimed at exploiting Diaspora resources to fill the skill gap in the economic development of the home country. Sources indicated that several thousands émigrés had returned to Addis Ababa, and that they were launching an aggressive campaign to woo more, offering tax breaks on importing belongings and flexible land-ownership laws. In Washington, some embassy officials had been going door-to-door in Ethiopian-American neighborhoods, urging patriotic entrepreneurs to move back. In September 2006, the National Bank of Ethiopia (NBE) announced that total remittance from Ethiopians abroad had increased to $371 million, an increase of close to 60 percent in the past three years alone. It is claimed that the actual figure of incoming resources would increase manifold if the informal transactions were factored into the equation.

Ethiopian communities meet on a regular basis in real and virtual spaces to organize for civic, cultural, and social activism. Ethiopian associations emphasize mutual aid and welfare associations, sports, arts, and recreational engagements. The Ethiopian American Council and the Ethiopian Sports Federation of North America organize the annual Ethiopian Soccer and Culture Festival in Los Angeles. The above excursions, however, have not been devoid of less-favorable experiences such as those associated with immigrant populations who are sometimes restricted to the margins of modern and postindustrial economies. Like many first-generation migrants in these societies, Ethiopians encounter discrimination and occupational hazards in their new abodes. Ethiopian enterprises have also lost some grounds to postmodern development and gentrification projects across the Diaspora. Tensions have also flared up between Ethiopians migrants and native communities, with many in the latter group unhappy about losing ground to the new migrants. Many Ethiopians possess advanced academic and professional qualifications but are resigned to menial labor and service jobs. As this Diaspora population grows, it is also increasingly likely to visit Ethiopia by taking advantage of the direct Ethiopian Airline flights from Washington and Newark to Addis Ababa. The political and economic significance of the Diaspora on the Ethiopian-American relationship has yet to be fully realized.

Ethiopian literature, historical documentaries, and home movies have critiqued the failure of the socialist revolution as well as the influence of modernity in the form of unbridled capitalism and Westernization to the detriment of Ethiopian culture. Germachew Tekle Hawariat calls for a resolution of the conflict between tradition and modernity through a secularization process to be effected by separating the spiritual from the temporal. Kebede Mikael in *Silitane Mininech? (What is Civilization?)* also blames the failure of modernization on alienation, loss of identity, moral standards, and conspicuous consumption. On the less than positive side, diasporas have also been found to fan the flame of conflicts, and this has also been the case with the Ethiopian Diaspora. Diasporas, it is argued, harbor grievances much longer, finance conflicts, and provide ideological guidance for rebellion. Diaspora residents, some have argued, also yearn to define their identity in relation to new locations where they are protected from the violence and strain from such conflicts.

Global, continental, and subregional developments have continued to influence Ethiopia's history. The Horn of Africa has again in the beginning of the twenty-first century acquired its age-old geopolitical preeminence. The region has always been in close proximity to global political and diplomatic discourse, especially the perennial conflicts over identity, resources, and real estate in the Middle East, although popular narratives have often in a simplistic fashion highlighted political instability and misrule in the region as a variant of power play between local leaders. Towards the end the twentieth century, the spread of transnational religious and political radicalism presented new challenges that warrant new analytical frameworks. The 1993 Battle of Mogadishu between Somali guerrilla fighters (loyal to warlord Mohamed Farrah Aidid) and the forces of the United States brought the region to the attention of mainstream audiences. In the clash famously cemented in global popular imagination due to a movie and publications titled *Black Hawk Down*, between 1,000 and 1,500 Somali militiamen and civilians lost their lives in the battle, with injuries to another 3,000–4,000. Eighteen American soldiers also died, and 73 were wounded.

At the end of the Cold War, Ethiopia's strategic position in the Horn of Africa became close to irrelevant in the eyes of the superpowers. The violent conflicts between Ethiopia and Somalia were fueled by suspicion of territorial expansionism and political extremism in both states. For several decades both Ethiopia and Somalia also engaged in proxy wars as part of the ideological battle between the United States and the former Soviet Union. The conflict resulted in an overwhelming loss of life, disruption of the socioeconomic organization of society, and undermined economic performance. Ethiopia has since emerged as a long-term ally of President Abdullahi Yusuf of Somalia, helping him to defeat the threat of Islamist militia who gained momentum in the last decade of the millennium. Somalia has since experienced anarchy as rival warlords divided up the capital into separate fiefdoms. Ethiopia's interest in Somalia is also influenced by the existence of its own active rebel groups—namely the Oromo Liberation Front and the Ogaden National Liberation Front (a group of Somali origin). Since September 2001, the Horn has again been the focus of attention in the U.S. conflict with radical Islam led by the leaders of the al-Queda movement. The developments have brought to the fore the strategic value of secular political administrations in Africa such as the Zenawi-led Ethiopia. In other instances, covert Western support has been provided for amenable, albeit illiberal, religious elites. In July 2006, Ethiopian troops crossed its border to intervene in the unstable events in neighboring Somalia. The Somali Islamic militia subsequently threatened to embark on a holy war against Ethiopia. Observers have expressed hope that the mutual tolerance that has existed for several generations between Christian and Muslims would not be undermined by growing pressures on the state. By extension, they stress that U.S. antiterrorist interests must not outweigh Ethiopia's modernist aspirations for viable social infrastructures and sustainable economic development. More important, perhaps, Ethiopians at home and abroad also would not like their interest for good governance and human rights to be sacrificed by the self-serving needs of world political and economic powers. Some have called on the Western governments to help impose some restrictions on the Ethiopian ruling party. They accuse the Zenawi-led administration of being dictatorial and imprisoning social and political activists whose only crimes were efforts aimed at establishing the framework in a growing democratic dispensation.

It has become very difficult to maintain the international political profile of Africa. Although Prime Minister Menawi is one of the members of Tony Blair's Commission for Africa, which has brought poverty reduction to the fore, it remains to be seen if Ethiopia will receive any major support for its struggling economic initiatives and political conflicts over power and resources. If the framework established in post–World War II geopolitics prevails, the West would focus on expanding or consolidating its spheres of influence through military as opposed to development means and supplies. In a post–Cold War era, however, the relevance of progressive transnational political lobbying for international welfare has been undermined by market and geomilitary rationalism and political corruption, thus the military option remains very popular. In August 2006, it was announced that the Pentagon and the U.S. military were close to approving plans for an African Command with emphasis on proactive, preventative measures rather than maintaining a defensive posture designed for the Cold War. The post–World War II reconstruction projects that failed to develop African economies in the tradition of the program for European recovery (Marshall Plan) has not only helped to consolidate the image of a prostrate continent but now reveal it is also one susceptible to radical and extremist activities. In this regard, the importance of the Horn of Africa, its problems, and the interminable military option is visible in a speech given by U.S. General John Abizaid to the Senate Armed Services Committee in March 2005. The general stated that:

> The Horn of Africa is vulnerable to penetration by regional extremist groups, terrorist activity, and ethnic violence. Al Qaeda has a history of planning,

training for, and conducting major terrorist attacks in this region, such as the bombings of U.S. Embassies in Kenya and Tanzania. The volatility of this region is fueled by a daunting list of challenges, to include extreme poverty, corruption, internal conflicts, border disputes, uncontrolled borders and territorial waters, weak internal security capabilities, natural disasters, famine, lack of dependable water sources, and an underdeveloped infrastructure. The combination of these serious challenges creates an environment that is ripe for exploitation by extremists and criminal organizations.[4]

In addition to the above statement, General Abizaid added that the Central Command from its military base in Djibouti called Combined Joint Task Force-Horn of Africa (CJTF-HOA) have worked with the U.S. Embassy personnel in the region to deny terrorists access and propaganda value in the region. Such activities, he continued, include training local security and border forces, low-level civic projects such as digging wells, building schools and distributing books, and holding medical and veterinary clinics in remote villages.

In spite of the laudable goals highlighted above by General Abizaid, the track record of using a combination of military interventions and social engineering to promote peace, democracy, and development is far from being a reputable one. Such efforts have led to the development of what many describe as new forms of "trusteeship," liberal imperialism, or postmodern imperialism. The above international factors, however, pale in significance when compared to the need for Ethiopia to address what some have described as its culture of extremism and the chronic problem of uneven access to resources and power. Prime Minister Menawi had proven to be unsophisticated and outright brutal in dealing with the opposition. Ethiopian political dialogue and activity is also often filled with passionate diatribes and vituperations. The above equation only serves as an obstacle to the development of mature and sophisticated political culture.

Also of importance to Ethiopia's growth is the governmental responsibility to develop a mixed economy that guarantees entrepreneurial activities while developing mechanisms for the economic, political, and social integration of different social entities. This may prove problematic in light of the fact that the Ethiopian economy has grown at an annual rate of 2.6 percent over the past four decades while the population has grown more than 2.6 percent in the same period. The onset of environmental challenges such as pollution and the thinning of the ozone layer also threaten to wreck more havoc on the quality of life for Ethiopians.

Scholars and students of Ethiopian history have been looking back to the modernist imperial regime first in acknowledgement of the foundation laid for the modern state and second for inspiration for new aspirations of political stability and a better quality of life. Emperor Tewodros was credited with being the first to acknowledge Ethiopia's arrested development. He began his modernization project by uniting the fragmented polities of Ethiopia under the banner of *ser'at* (ordered governance), after which he sought the assistance of the technologically superior European states, particularly England. Emperor Menelik consolidated imperial authority, defended Ethiopian independence, and began the process of creating and supporting a modern Ethiopian educated elite with requisite infrastructures. Emperor Haile Selassie is also recognized for his role in the introduction of modern facilities, infrastructure, and administrative bureaucracies to Ethiopia. In spite of major shortcomings, the imperial regime experienced relative stability when compared to the social and political upheavals triggered by successive regimes in the last decades of the twentieth century. The imperial regime has been credited with establishing the legislative framework for modern civil and commercial activities. Some scholars have argued that the continuity and steadfastness of institutions such as Ethiopian Airlines, the civil service, the National Bank, and the Ministry of Finance combined with the nation's long and unique history and indigenous institutions and social norms have protected Ethiopia from total collapse as a result of an unstable political environment, violent regime shifts, and bad governance. Haile Selassie was finally laid to rest in at the Holy Trinity Cathedral 25 years after his death. Among those who attended his burial ceremony in Addis Ababa was Rita Marley, the widow of the famous reggae icon, singer Bob Marley. She had come pay to her respects while representing the millions of Rastafarians in Jamaica, most of whom still considered Selassie the earthly embodiment of God and place him at the top of the iconography of modern African social and political thought.

One of the greatest tributes paid to Haile Selassie's status and foresight as one of the twentieth century's greatest statesman and by extension, the important role of Ethiopia on the global stage can be found in "War," a song by Bob Marley. The song is derived from a speech made by Emperor Selassie at the 1963 U.N. conference in New York City. Selassie's speech called for world peace and equality among all without regard to race, class, or nationality. In his song, Marley asserts that until the day of an equal society, there is war. Besides the lyrics Marley uses in the song, during his speech in 1963 Selassie also urged U.N. officials and country representatives to disarm nuclear weapons and to end international exploitation (specifically with Africa). In this song, Bob honors Haile Selassie I while calling for action against racial inequality and international injustice.

Here is the part of Haile Selassie's speech that Marley uses in "War":

On the question of racial discrimination, the Addis Ababa Conference taught, to those who will learn, this further lesson: That until the philosophy which holds one race superior and another inferior is finally and permanently discredited and abandoned: That until there are no longer first-class and second class citizens of any nation; That until the color of a man's skin is of no more significance than the color of his eyes; That until the basic human rights are equally guaranteed to all without regard to race; That until that day, the dream of lasting peace and world citizenship and the rule of international morality will remain but a fleeting illusion, to be pursued but never attained; And until the ignoble and unhappy regimes that hold our brothers in Angola, in Mozambique and in South Africa in subhuman bondage have been toppled and destroyed; Until bigotry and prejudice and malicious and inhuman self-interest have been replaced by understanding and tolerance and good-will; Until all Africans stand and speak as free beings, equal in the eyes of all men, as they are in the eyes of Heaven; Until that day, the African continent will not know peace. We Africans will fight, if necessary, and we know that we shall win, as we are confident in the victory of good over evil.

—Haile Selassie I[5]

The attributes of traditional Ethiopian culture and the indigenous Orthodox Church have remained largely underappreciated. Philosopher Messay Kebede blames this phenomenon on the indoctrination of Ethiopia's intellectual elites with Western social theories that pair secularization with modernization. He conceives of a remodernization of Ethiopia in which traditional Ethiopian culture is applied to the realities of a modern economic and political world. Beside the achievements in religious, artistic, and intellectual production, Ethiopian traditions have been responsible for the maintenance of the organic continuity of communities in urban, rural, and even Diaspora contexts. For example, the indigenous money markets and self-help associations have helped create and sustain a dual market system in diverse environments and circumstances. The *Iquib* is an association established by a small group of people in order to provide substantial rotating funding for members in order to improve their lives and living conditions. The *Idir* is an association established among neighbors or workers to raise funds that will be used during emergencies, such as a death within these groups and their families. These two socioeconomic traditions are informal, bottom-up, and widely practiced among Ethiopians. The institutions are national phenomena that transverse Ethiopian lives across linguistic, religious, or ethnic backgrounds. These centuries-old economic, social, and psychological support networks and cooperatives have also functioned as a source of social security and stability outside of national welfare or international donor spheres of influence.

In the twentieth century, Emperor Haile Selassie had helped established a salaried bureaucracy that supported government functionaries and helped provide avenues where creative energies for developing local industries, market outlets, and civil society started to emerge. It has also been stressed that Selassie's economic program in the 1960s was accompanied by the highest contribution of capital, as a partial result of the three development plans, of the imperial regime. The investment in capital-intensive commercial farms and food-processing industries had the potential of transforming the age-old feudal aristocratic group into a nascent entrepreneur class. In spite of these progressions, the socioeconomic regime during the imperial regime was "feudal," with two distinct classes, the aristocracy and the peasantry. The monarchy was at the pinnacle of the society. Feudalism restricted wealth to only a select few, whose control of peasant production from the land restricted the idea of individual risk taking. The monarchy, the regional chiefs, and their officials (with the support of the church) were largely concerned with the consolidation of military and economic hegemony and privileges. It is a consensus among most observers of modern Ethiopian history that unless and until there is real political reform in the country that would make government accountable to the people, there are bound to be more conflicts and violence in the history of Ethiopia. It has also been argued that democracy or political reform could not thrive in conditions of economic stagnation. Market fundamentalists would only help entrench the Horn as a breeding ground for adventurous, political opportunists and radical religious fundamentalists.

Many Ethiopians are, however, unhappy about the essentialist and often recycled images of Ethiopian people as helpless victims in global media. These images, they argue, pathologize conditions in Africa by providing little or no political or economic contextual analysis of the continent's underdevelopment. It is also suggested that the frozen negative image of Ethiopia is predicated on a restrictive view of Western modernism that excludes most Africans even as the continent remains subjected to the political and economic interests of the powerful. Similarly, others contend that such images form part of an ideological construct that reifies unequal power relationships between the rich and the poor in the globalized economy.

Ethiopia remains a target for aid as opposed to foreign investment in spite of its size and potential for growth due to its untapped human and natural resources. The flow of foreign direct investment (FDI) to Ethiopia has been described as negligible in spite of political reform and the liberalization of its economic sector. It is often highlighted that the only major foreign excursion in the Ethiopian economy is by MIDROC, a company owned by Sheikh Mohammed Hussein Al-Amoudi, a Saudi Arabian tycoon with maternal roots in Ethiopia. The company has invested in industrial development, services, and agro-processing, making Al-Amoudi the largest individual employer in the country. Much has been made of Ethiopia's isolated communities and rugged terrains, which have been a major hindrance to the establishment of a successful economy, and by extension, a modern society. Economic insecurity, it is argued, pervades the system as rule of law, enforcement of contracts, and property right's security were configured on shaky political bases. Regardless of the impact of these shortcomings, it is also notable that Ethiopia's raw materials, especially coffee, continue to makes their way from rural farmlands to the global markets, especially the United States and Western European communities.

In the words of historian Bahru Zewde, Ethiopia's future is intimately linked with that of Africa in general and the Horn of Africa in particular. He emphasized his thesis by highlighting the ethnic links of the peoples of the subregion such as the Afar, who are found in Djibouti, Eritrea, and Ethiopia; the Somali in Djibouti, Ethiopia, and Somali/Somaliland; and the Tigrinya-speaking people in Eritrea and Ethiopia. With this background, Zewde calls for the relaxation of colonial boundaries in the larger region. Zewde foresee a future where Ethiopia's geographical location, material, and human resources could be the core for a subregional confederation. In the meantime, he continues, Ethiopia must embark on rehabilitating its political culture and public infrastructures. It must also develop its private sector and protect domestic and foreign investors. Only such steps could help stem the loss of Ethiopian skilled intellectual and technical labor through the movement of such labor to more favorable geographic, economic, or professional environments.

The nature of the second wave of globalization contributed to the failure of the project of modernity in Ethiopia, shaped by external incursion into the Horn of Africa region that included resource and market-driven expansion by European powers accompanied by strategic geopolitical considerations and religious expansionism. Between 1868 and 1896, external interventions featured three encounters with the Egyptians, four with the Dervishes, five with Italy, and one with the British. The protracted conflicts aggravated internal conflicts and further reinforced the militarization of the modern Ethiopian political culture. The conflicts also had negative effect on the economic development of the country.

Although many European officials cited domestic slavery as a reason for the political incursion into the area in the late nineteenth and early twentieth century, evidence shows that colonial enterprise in the Horn was dictated by thinly veiled European political and economic nationalism, often with the subtext of an international Social Darwinist theory that relegates African cultures, ideas, and welfare interests . One must also acknowledge the contributions of religious and secular expatriates who, even in this era, were motivated to help Ethiopian poor and underprivileged through material and moral support. These latter groups are reminiscent of modern-day NGOs and individual activists who campaign on behalf of Ethiopia and its underprivileged citizens. We are now living in another era of globalization with its own peculiar yet somehow familiar tendencies.

This project has explored two major eras of globalization in the evolution of modern Ethiopian history, both of which have failed to address the need of the ordinary folk in Africa. In the words of philosopher Olufemi Taiwo, scholars and policymakers have overemphasized the importance of structure-driven globalization at the expense of subjectivity-driven globalization. Doing globalization right the second time around, he concludes, requires the commitment of substantial resources to other parts of the world in order to enable Africans not merely to live as humans but more importantly to free up their energies for common survival and a flourishing society with commercial and free political activities. The relevance of this analysis for the study of Ethiopian modernity can hardly be overemphasized.

With the above narrative on the vicissitudes of Ethiopian social and political existence as background, there have been recent calls that Ethiopian intellectuals abandon the tendency to draw a dichotomy between tradition and modernity. In the project of redefining the concepts of freedom, identity, and history, Ethiopia, it is argued, should be taken as a subject with unique foundations rather than as a society that has to be remodeled on an external icon. In this regard, I highlight the recent careers of four Ethiopian intellectuals who have been successful in projecting Ethiopian and by extension African culture on the global stage: Skunder Boghossian, born in 1937, a major figure in modern African art history who made his first sojourn to the West in 1955 when he immigrated to England to study on a government scholarship; Mulatu Astatqe, a musician and arranger, also known as the "Father of Ethio-Jazz," born in 1943 in the western Ethiopian city of Jimma and trained in London, New York City, and Boston; Haile Gerima, filmmaker, producer, and university professor who came to the United States in 1968; and Aster Aweke, a successful musician born in 1961 in Gondar, a product of the Hager Fikir Theatre in Addis Ababa, considered not only one of the best but also the oldest indigenous theatre in Africa.

Skunder Boghossian, who died in 2005, had a career that took him around the globe during which he interacted with African artists and intellectuals who were part of the Negritude movement. He also critically engaged the work of the French surrealists and African American jazz artistes. Against this background, Skunder masterfully synchronized aspects of Ethiopia and Africa's cultural heritage within his works. His skill, it is argued, derives from the insightful manner in which he is able to recall broad-ranging visual motifs, myths, and calligraphic forms. He is said to have shifted them into a textured universe that is purely his own, and yet one that can be experienced by Ethiopian and global audiences alike.

Mulatu Astatqe is Ethiopia's leading contemporary composer, arranger, conductor, and musician. He successfully fused Ethiopian music with a wide variety of influences he encountered while studying abroad. At the height of the Cold War, the American State Department had organized a global trip with a stop in Ethiopia for legendary jazz musician Duke Ellington. The result, according to Penny von Eschen, was a musical collaboration between Ellington and Astatqe recorded by the U.S. officials as the most successful of the tour. Von Eschen quotes a U.S. Information Service press release: "The saxophone, trumpet, and trombone met the traditional Ethiopian *masinko* and *washint* musical instruments, and according to one Ellington bandsman, 'music may never be the same again.'"

From his well-received films including *Sankofa* (fiction, 1993), *Mirt sost shi amet* (*Harvest 3,000 Years*, 1975), and *Adwa: An African Victory* (documentary,

2000) Haile Gerima has emerged as one of the premier filmmakers who explore Ethiopian and African Diaspora history, subjectivity, and identity through his movies and cultural production.

Aster Aweke began singing professionally in her late teens in Addis Ababa clubs and hotels with such bands as the Continental Band, Hotel D'Afrique Band, Shebele Band, and the Ibex Band. She later launched a solo career, but felt stifled by the lack of political and artistic freedom in her homeland. By 1981, Aweke relocated to the United States and settled in Washington, D.C. She restarted her career by performing in local Ethiopian restaurants, in the process building up a following. She later toured Europe and the United States in 1985. Aweke is now immensely popular with the Ethiopian community across the Diaspora. She has been described as a voice for her people and perhaps the most famous female singer in Ethiopia.

Ethiopian history and civilization have been invaluable as a counternarrative to popular representations that exclude Africa from the narratives of modernity or set the continent beyond the pale of common humanity. The cultural production of the above intellectuals and artistes represents some modern dimensions of an Ethiopian renaissance. Perhaps the epitome of this spirit was Tsegaye Gabre-Medhin, (1936–2005), described as Ethiopia's greatest playwright and acclaimed Poet Laureate. According to historian Richard Pankhurst, Tsegaye was most proud of Ethiopia's long history of independence and of her unique cultural heritage. He also used the theatre to teach stories of Ethiopian past heroes and was described as being very concerned with questions of peace, human rights, and the dignity of humanity in his twilight years. During his lifetime, Tsegaye enjoyed great popularity, both in Ethiopia and around the world. One of his passionate interests revolved around the struggle to regain Ethiopia's looted treasures. Together with activists in Ethiopia and around the world, including Pankhurst, Tsegaye helped galvanize popular support for the Ethiopian demand for the return of the Aksum obelisk looted by fascist Italy on Mussolini's personal orders in 1937. In April 2005, the Axum obelisk, a 1,700-year-old stone monolith measuring 24 meters (78 feet) high and weighing 160 tons, returned home after more than six decades adorning a square in the Italian capital of Rome. The ancient monument was met at Addis Ababa airport by a delegation of priests, state officials, and jubilant citizens. The request that Britain should return the manuscripts, crosses, tents, and other historical artifacts seized from Emperor Tewodros's mountain citadel of Magdala in 1868 is pending. Some of these objects are currently in the British Museum and British Library, as well as in Britain's Royal Library in Windsor Castle, which currently holds six remarkably finely illustrated Ethiopian manuscripts. Ethiopian athletes such as Abebe Bikila, Muruse (Miruts) Yefter, Mamo Wolde, Addis Abebe, Derartu Tulu, Haile Gebrselassie, and Fatuma Roba have also represented and placed Ethiopian names on global pedestals.

Much of this study has been focused on modern Ethiopia's political, economic, intellectual and cultural history. The book also includes a critical evaluation of globalization and modern forms of international liberal development and welfare regimes. The new millennium offers a competitive paradigm to the western dominated discourse on economic modernization. New ideas of South-South and intra-African cooperation are gaining grounds and, unlike post-World war II liberal internationalism, these new propositions are rooted less in the legacy of racial or economic ideological orthodoxies and more in mutual exchange and complementary national interests. The year 2006, for example, marked the 50th anniversary of Sino-Africa diplomatic ties, a feat that was celebrated at a Summit of African head of states in Beijing China. A summit declaration called on wealthier nations to give more aid to Africa to fight poverty, halt desertification and combat natural disasters. Reading part of the declaration at the conclusion of the summit, Ethiopian Prime Minister Meles Zenawi declared that China and Africa have common goals and converging interests that offer a broad prospect for cooperation. Similarly, United Nations Secretary General Kofi Annan expressed the hope that Africans could benefit greatly from the experience of china, which has had much success in sustaining growth and reducing poverty. Many trade experts including the World Bank have also expressed that China and India's growing trade in Africa holds great potential for African economic growth. In 2006, Asia received 27% of Africa's exports, triple the amount as in 1990. As a corollary, Asian exports to Africa are equally growing at a rate of 18% annually, faster than any other global region.

Both western and select African officials have however also expressed concern that china's role in Africa portends the risk of a new colonialism, but, according to former Nigerian finance Minister Ngozi Okonjo Iweala, there is more to the China-Africa relationship than meets the eye. She acknowledged that African countries must be wary that old trappings of bondage are not exchanged for shiny new ones. At the same time, she added that when it comes to economic growth and transformation, China has much to offer that is relevant to present day Africa. China, Okonjo Iweala continued, knows what it mean to be poor, and has evolved a successful wealth creation formula that it is willing to share with African countries. China is also being courted to assist with Africa's infrastructural investment need, which is estimated at 20 billion dollars for the next decade. It has been suggested that while the dominant liberal paradigm of African development seem mired in foreign aid and less in foreign economic investment, China Seems willing to invest in railways, roads, ports and rural telecommunication projects as part of its formula for access to resources alongside economic development in Africa. Based on the above reasons, Okonjo Iweala concluded, China should be left alone to forge its unique partnership with African countries and the West must simply learn to compete (*BBC News*, October 24, 2006).

It must also be acknowledged that economic relations between China and Africa are, at the moment, far from being equal. In 2004, Chinese exports to Ethiopia made up over 93% of the two nations' bilateral trade. Yet in the first half of 2005, Chinese purchases from the Horn of Africa (Djibouti, Eritrea, and Somalia/Somaliland) were negligible. This imbalance could ultimately alienate these African countries from China's influence. It is often emphasized that Chinese firms are a little less "ethically constrained" than their western counterparts in their economic activities in Africa. This maxim, however, only marginally holds true since Africa's engagement with the West has been schizophrenic at best. Studies have shown that progressive ideas inherent in modern liberalism are often sacrificed for more seductive universalist projects hinged on current "national interests" of Africa's more powerful partners. The relevance of issues of human rights, democracy, freedom and economic growth cannot be overemphasized as part of the necessary tools for Africa's survival and growth in the new millennium. In this regard, Western Nongovernmental organizations can continue to play important role in education and lobbying on behalf of Africa's young democracies such as Ethiopia. In synopsis the thesis that the individual and the community needs ought not be sacrificed for the sake of economic expansion must be emphasized to all foreign investors and their domestic partners in Africa. In the absence of professional opportunities, creative outlets, and a viable obligatory citizenship arrangement between the state and its denizens, the theocratic or other forms of revolutionary option invariably becomes attractive alternatives. Mainstream modern media have been accused of being less interested in critical evaluation of developments outside of the pathological in the South and especially Africa. At the end of the 2006 Sino-African Summit, Ethiopian Foreign Minister Seyoum Mesfin declared that the leaders at the gathering were dismayed at "tainted" media coverage in the West that cast the summit as a gathering of "African dictators who have found a new homeland and friendship to escape Western pressures, to escape accountability and respect for human rights." (Seattle Times, November 06, 2006) On a positive note, scholars have highlighted increased academic output, the proliferation of alternative media on Africa and a decade of peace in the Horn region as the onset of a new generation of global engagement between ancient civilizations and modern nations, a category to which Ethiopia firmly belongs. Ethiopia is thus benefiting from increased tourism with the major tourist destinations including the northern historical route encompassing Bahir Dar, Gondar, Axum, Makalle and Lalibela. Addis Ababa, the principal economic and administrative capital in its own right, also remains a major destination. In addition, Ethiopia is also reaching out to the world. In 2006, Ethiopia made overtures to recruit from Nigeria six hundred professors to reach in its twelve new universities. Ethiopia's interest in Nigeria was encouraged by the performances of Nigerians who served as members of the Technical Aid Corps

(TAC), an international volunteering program set up by the Nigerian government in 1987 to serve as a practical demonstration of south-south cooperation.

Over time, Ethiopians have invested in the notion of civilization and modernity, embracing new ideas while resisting in many ways the imposition of a hierarchical and exclusionary modernist canon from the outside. The history of Ethiopia allows us to appreciate the subjectivity of Africans, the complexity of the container called the nation-state, the drama of the globalization phenomenon, and the debate over the relevance of historical and cultural particularisms in the application of what we might consider universal narratives of modernity.

NOTES

1. Jeffrey Sachs, *The End of Poverty: Economic Possibilities for Our Time* (New York: Penguin Press, 2005).

2. William Easterly, *The White Man's Burden: Why the West's Efforts to Aid the Rest Have Done So Much Ill and So Little Good* (New York: Penguin Press, 2006).

3. Richard Pankhurst, *An Ethiopian Hero: Tsegaye Gabre-Medhin (1936–2005)*, Open Democracy, www.opendemocracy.net/xml/xhtml/articles/3347.html.

4. U.S. General John Abizaid, speech to the Senate Armed Services Committee, 24 August 2006, *New York Times*.

5. War (Bob Marley song), Wikipedia entry, http://en.wikipedia.org/wiki/War_(Bob_Marley_song).

Notable People in the History of Ethiopia

Abraha, Seeye, was one of the more eminent figures of the last quarter of the twentieth century. In the 1980s he was the wartime leader of the Tigrean People's Liberation Front (TPLF), and in the 1990s as minister of defense under the new president, Meles Zenawi, he was one of the three members of the Ethiopian People's Revolutionary Democratic Front (EPRDF) junta that ran Ethiopia from 1991 to 1995 before elections entrenched the new democracy.

Afawarq, Gabra Iyasus (1868–1947) as an Ethiopian writer and possibly Ethiopia's first novelist to gain repute. He was one of the first Ethiopians to receive an art education abroad. Early in the nineteenth century, he worked on the church of Maryam at Entoto and was later sent to Italy by Emperor Menelik to study with the Italian envoy Count Antonelli. Afawarq studied art at the Academia Albertino in Turin, Italy, but soon abandoned art for literature and politics. He is controversial due to statements he made during the second Italo-Abyssinian War suggesting he was not opposed to some aspects of the modernist mission of the fascist regime.

Afewerk, Tekle (1932–) is one of Ethiopia's most celebrated artists, particularly known for his paintings on African and Christian themes as well as his stained glass. Born in Ankober, he grew up in a war-torn country largely occupied by Italian fascists during World War II. Following the war, in 1947, he decided that he wanted to help rebuild Ethiopia and elected to travel to England to study mining engineering. Before departing, he and other students leaving to study overseas were addressed by Emperor Haile Selassie. Afewerk recalls being told "you must work hard, and when you come back do not tell us what tall buildings you saw in Europe, or what wide streets they have, but make sure you return equipped with the skills and the mindset to rebuild Ethiopia."

Ahmed, Mahmoud, for over 30 years has deftly combined the traditional Amharic music of Ethiopia (essentially a five-note scale that features jazz style singing offset by complex circular rhythm patters which gives the music a distinct feel with pop and jazz influences. Ahmed has been a star in Ethiopia almost since the day he began recording. He has been credited with a style that fuses the past and present.

Ali, Yeshimebet, daughter of Woizero (later Ima-hoi) Wolete Giorgis and Ali Abba Jifar of Wollo, was the wife of Ras Makonnen and mother of Emperor Haile Selassie. She died during the emperor's infancy. Her mother and her sister, Woizero Mammit, helped care for her young son as he grew to adulthood.

Amda-Seyon I, Emperor, was an Ethiopian ruler (1313–1344) who reestablished suzerainty over the Muslim kingdoms of the coastal lowland regions. According to Edward Ullendorf, "Amde Tseyon was one of the most outstanding Ethiopian kings of any age and a singular figure dominating the Horn of Africa in the fourteenth century." Some of the earliest works of Ethiopian literature were written during Amda-Seyon's reign. Perhaps the best known is the *Kebra Nagast,* which was translated from Arabic at the request of Yaebika Egzi'e, governor of Enderta. Other works from this period include the *Mashafa Mestira Samay Wamedr (The Book of the Mysteries of Heaven and Earth),* written by Yeshaq of Debre Gol, and the *Zena Eskender (History of Alexander the Great),* a romance in which Alexander the Great becomes a Christian saint. Also, four of the Soldiers Songs, the earliest existing examples of the Amharic language, were composed during the reign of Amda-Seyon.

Amlak, Yekuno, Emperor (throne name Tasfa Iyasus) was *negusä nägäst* of Ethiopia (1270–1285) and founder (or some say restorer) of the Solomonid dynasty. He traced his ancestry through his father, Tasfa Iyasus, to Dil Na'od, the last king of Axum. Traditional history further reports that Yekuno Amlak was imprisoned by the Zagwe king Za-Ilmaknun ("the unknown, the hidden one") in Malot, but managed to escape. He gathered support in Amhara provinces and in Shewa, and with an army of followers, defeated the Zagwe king. Yekuno Amlak ordered the construction of the Church of Gennete Maryam near Lalibela, which contains the earliest surviving dateable wall paintings in Ethiopia.

Asfaw, Menen, Empress (Baptismal name *Wolete Giyorgis*) (1889–1962) was the wife and consort of Emperor Haile Selassie I of Ethiopia. Empress Menen was the daughter of Asfaw, Jantirar of Ambassel, a direct descendant of Emperor Lebna Dengel. Empress Menen was active in promoting women's issues in Ethiopia and was patroness of the Ethiopian Red Cross and the Ethiopian Women's Charitable Organization. Following her death in 1961, the empress was buried in the crypt of Holy Trinity Cathedral in Addis Ababa alongside the tombs of her children.

Ashenafi, Senait (1966–) is an Ethiopian-born actress in the United States who played Keesha Ward on *General Hospital* from 1994 to 1998. She has also worked as a dancer, singer, and model. Born in Addis Ababa, she moved to the United States with her family, where she studied at Florida State University. She has since been involved with activism and Ethiopian Diaspora issues

Astatke, Mulatu (1943–) is an Ethiopian musician and arranger. He is known as the "Father of Ethio-Jazz" and was born in 1943 in the western Ethiopian city of Jimma. Astatke was musically trained in London, New York City, and Boston, where he was the first African student at Berklee College of Music. He would later combine his jazz and Latin music influences with traditional Ethiopian music. In 2005, his music appeared on the soundtrack to the Jim Jarmusch film *Broken Flowers*.

Aweke, Aster (1961–) A native of Gandor, a small town near Lake Tara, Aweke is one of Ethiopia's best loved performers. Raised in the capital city of Addis Ababa, this daughter of senior civil servant in the imperial government, began singing professionally in her late teens in Addis Ababa clubs and hotels with such bands as the Continental Band, Hotel D'Afrique Band, Shebele Band, and the Ibex Band. She later launched a solo career but felt stifled by the lack of political and artistic freedom in her homeland. By 1981, Aweke relocated to the United States, and settled in Washington, D.C. She restarted her career by performing in local Ethiopian restaurants, in the process building up a following. She later toured Europe and the United States in 1985. Aweke is now successful throughout the world. She has been described as a voice for her people and perhaps the most famous female singer in Ethiopia.

Bayyana, Alamawarq, was a veterinary doctor, educated in Britain, and president of the Black Lions, a resistance political movement to the fascist invasion of Ethiopia in 1935. Alamawarq Bayyana was a conservative intellectual, albeit one who was interested in the political evolution of Ethiopia. He died shortly after Ethiopia's liberation.

Bedaso, Aragaw (1934–) is a longtime Ethiopian traditional singer who has won praise for his Gurage songs. His most popular song is "Alem Bire." He has been performing since 1957 and still performs and is active in the Ethiopian music scene.

Benti, Tafari (1921–1977) was the president of Ethiopia (November 28, 1974–February 3, 1977). Along with Aman Mikael Andom and Mengistu Haile Mariam, he led the military coup of September 12, 1974, which deposed Emperor Haile Selassie. Following the death of Andom 2 months later, and a 10-day period in which Mengistu was president, Benti became president. His was later assassinated based on the command of Mengistu, who succeeded him as leader and completed Ethiopia's transformation into a Marxist country until the fall of the military regime in 1991.

Betul, Taytu, Empress (died February 11, 1918) married King Sahle Maryam of Shewa, later Emperor Menelik II of Ethiopia. Taytu is acknowledged to have wielded considerable political power as the wife of Menelik, both before and after they were crowned emperor and empress in 1889. She led the conservative faction at court that resisted the modernists and progressives who wanted to develop Ethiopia along Western lines and bring modernity to the country. Deeply suspicious of European intentions towards Ethiopia, she was a key player in the conflict over the Treaty of Wichale with Italy, in which the Italian version made Ethiopia an Italian protectorate, while the Amharic did not do so. The empress held a hard line against the Italians, and when talks eventually broke down and Italy invaded the empire from its Eritrean colony, she marched north with the emperor and the imperial army, commanding a force of cannoneers at the historic Battle of Adwa, which resulted in a humiliating defeat for Italy in March 1894. Taytu is believed to have been somewhat active in the plot that eventually removed Emperor Iyasu V from the throne in 1916 and replaced him with her stepdaughter, Empress Zauditu. She lived out the rest of her life at Entoto Maryam Church near Addis Ababa. She is buried next to her husband at the Taeka Negest Ba'eta Le Mariam Monastery in Addis Ababa.

Bikila, Abebe (1932–October 1973) was born in the town of Jato about 130 kilometers away from Addis Ababa. Oral traditions held that he spent most of his childhood as a shepherd and student. At the age of twelve, he completed the traditional, *"qes"* schooling. By that time, Abebe had already distinguished himself as an exceptional *"gena"* player. In 1952, he was hired by the Imperial Bodyguard, with whom he participated in both athletics and "Gena" games. Abebe spent several years with the Imperial Guard before he distinguished himself as a fine athlete. Inspired by the athletes who represented Ethiopia in the Olympics, he was determined to be one of them. In 1956, at age 24, Abebe participated in the national armed forces championships, where he easily won his first major race. He went on to break the 5K and 10K records held by another Ethiopian. Abebe's race in the Rome Olympics established him as a legend as he set a new world record, becoming the first African to win an Olympic medal. Four years later, during the Tokyo Olympics, Abebe's overcame appendicitis and won the race barely six weeks after his surgery. Although Abebe trained for the Mexico City Olympics of 1968, he had to withdraw from the race due to poor health after running 15 kilometers. His compatriot, Mamo Wolde, later finished the race victoriously. Abebe competed in more than 26 major marathon races in his illustrious athletic career. The world championships he won in 1960 and 1962 deserve special recognition. In 1968, Abebe Bikila was involved in a car accident in the city of Sheno about 70 kilometers from Addis Ababa that left him paralyzed below the waist. Over the next nine months, he was treated both in Ethiopia and abroad. Even while in a wheelchair, his competitive spirit and desire to see his country's flag hoisted high and proud helped him compete and win several races. In 1970, he participated in a 25-kilometer cross-country sled competition in Norway where he won the gold medal. In the same tournament, he won a 10-kilometer race where he was awarded a special plaque. When he died, he was buried in the grounds of St. Joseph Church in the presence of Emperor Haile Selassie and a huge crowd.

Boghossian, Alexander Skunder (1937–2003), a native of Ethiopia, made his first sojourn to the West in 1955 when he immigrated to England to study on a government scholarship. He later moved to Paris, where he remained for nine years. While in Paris he interacted with African artists and intellectuals who were part of the Negritude movement, and he encountered the work of the French surrealists. Some of the artists who influenced Boghossian include Paul Klee, Roberto Matta, and the Afro-Cuban artist Wilfredo Lam. In 1972, Boghossian was appointed as a faculty member at Howard University in Washington, D.C. His work, described as "a perpetual celebration of the diversity of blackness," has been on display throughout the world including the Smithsonian Institution's National Museum of African Art. Upon Boghossian's death, Sharon F. Patton, director of the Smithsonian's National Museum of African Art, released a statement that captures his contribution: "Only days ago, Skunder was with us—surrounded by fellow artists, colleagues from Howard University, members of the Ethiopian community and friends from the National Museum of African Art—to celebrate the opening of 'Ethiopian Passages: Dialogues in the Diaspora.' We were fortunate to have Skunder participate in this exhibition. As a major figure in modern African art history, he opened the way for others to follow and left an important body of work behind. 'Ethiopian Passages' celebrates his legacy. His spirit will endure at the Museum."

Buli, Mulugeta, Major-General Instructor at Holata Military School, commander-in-chief of the imperial Bodyguard from 1941 to 1955. A popular military official who was initially designated by the 1960 coup planners as chief of staff of the armed forces but was later killed by Brigadier-General Mangestu Neway, the leader of the failed coup.

Chole, Eshetu (1945–1998) was Ethiopia's leading economist prior to his death. His work encompassed an extraordinary breadth: agriculture, industrial and social development, fiscal policy, macro- and microeconomics, and human development at national and regional levels. He was also a budding poet. He was born in Negele Borena, Eshetu, where he obtained his elementary education. He completed his education at the General Wingate Secondary School in Addis Ababa. He then joined the Department of Economics at University College Addis Ababa (later Haile Sellassie I University and now Addis Ababa University) and earned his first degree in economics (1966), winning the Chancellor's Gold Medal of the Arts Faculty. After his employment as a graduate assistant in his parent department, Eshetu obtained his M.A. from the University of Illinois-Urbana Champagne (1968), and his Ph.D. from the University of Syracuse (1973). In a keynote address at a symposium held in honor of Eshetu Cole, Ethiopian prime minister Meles Zenawi called Dr. Eshetu Chole "an academic and a scholar of a unique caliber" and a man of "great intellectual achievements." The prime minister added, "The fact that some of us did not agree with him on a number of fundamental issues does not diminish our respect for his intellect and our appreciation of his achievements." In addition to being an economist, he was also a fighter for social justice and democracy. Another speaker noted that Eshetu was a representative of a generation of Ethiopians who were committed to fighting poverty and accelerating socioeconomic development in Ethiopia, one of the finest personalities of his generation, an activist, a professional teacher, and a scholar responsible for producing many of the current generation of economists.

Damtaw, Dastaw, Ras, Desta Damtew was a son-in-law of Emperor Haile Selassie. Ras Destaw was a member of the prominent aristocratic Addisge clan and was given the Province of Sidamo as his governorate. Ras Destaw and Princess Tenagnework would become the parents of two sons, princes Amha and Iskinder Desta (later Rear Admiral), and four daughters, princesses Aida, Seble, Sophia, and Hirut. Ras Destaw Damtew was appointed governor-general, first of Kaffa and Limo, and then of Sidamo. In 1935, fascist Italy invaded Ethiopia and the imperial family were forced to flee. Ras Destaw, however, remained behind to command the imperial forces fighting in the south of the country. After battling valiantly, Ras Destaw was captured and summarily executed by the fascist forces.

d'Andrade, Antonio, born of Portuguese father and Ethiopian mother, played a crucial for the beginning of Ethiopian Studies. A member of the small Ethiopian community of priests and scholars at the Vatican. Andrade and other Ethiopian informants like abba Gorgoryos, an exiled Catholic priest from Mekane Sillasé in Amhara, assisted German Orientalists such as Hiob Ludolf whose *Historia Aethiopica* of 1681 and other works were the precursors of modern ethnological research. They laid the foundation for more independent exploits of future generations of scholars of religious literatures such as Dabtera Kefle Giorgis, Abba Abraham, Onesimos Nessib.

Dengel, Sarsa (Amharic "Sprout of the Virgin"; throne name Malak Sagad I) (1550–October 4, 1597) was *negusä nägäst* of Ethiopia (1563–1597) and a member of the Solomonid dynasty. He was the son of Menas. He was the first emperor of Ethiopia to confront the encroachment of the Oromo, who had defeated Nur ibn Mujahid, as he returned home from killing his uncle Gelawdewos in battle. In 1573, the tenth year of his reign, Sarsa Dengel defeated the Oromo in a battle near Lake Zway. He also battled them in 1578 and 1588. He campaigned against the Falasha in Semien in 1580, then again in 1585; and he confronted the Agaw in 1581 and 1585. He campaigned against the Gambo who dwelled in the lands west of the Coman swamp in 1590. He made a punitive expedition against the Ottoman Turks in 1588 in response to their raids in the northern provinces and made similar expeditions in Ennarea in 1586 and 1597.

Desta, Gebre Kristos (1932–1981) created paintings that have been described as remarkable not only for their technical and formal achievements, but also for their symbolic power and psychological insight. He observed and commented upon the political strife of Ethiopians in a symbolically expressionistic way. He is generally acknowledged as one of those responsible for introducing nonfigurative and abstract art into Ethiopia. His works such as *Mother and Child*, *Not far from Ambassador Theater*, *Golgotha*, *Shoe Shine Boys*, and *Black Music* capture Ethiopian national history, religious myths, legends, cultural issues, and social problems while also reflecting the political climate of the country. He fled from Ethiopia in 1979 during the era of the Derg. He died in the United States less than two years after settling as a political refuge in Lawton, Oklahoma.

Dinsamo, Belayneh (1965–) rose to international fame when he set a new world record in the marathon in Rotterdam, Holland, on April 17, 1988. His record of 2 hours, 6 minutes, and 50 seconds stood until 1998.

Ejigayehu Shibabaw, or **Gigi** as she is popularly known, is one of the most successful contemporary Ethiopian singers worldwide. Coming from an ancient tradition of song originating in the Ethiopian Church, she has brought the music of Ethiopia to wider appreciation and developed it in combination with a wide variety of styles. Gigi and her husband, producer Bill Laswell, have recently worked with American jazz legends including Herbie Hancock, Wayne Shorter, and Pharoah Sanders in recent musical collaborations.

Endalkachew, Makonnen Lij (1927–November 24, 1974) was an Ethiopian politician. Born in Addis Ababa, his father, Ras Betwoded Makonnen Endelkachew, served as Prime Minister of Ethiopia in the 1950s. Endalkachew Makonnen was a member of the aristocratic Addisge clan that were very influential in the latter part of the Ethiopian monarchy. He would be the last imperial prime minister appointed by Emperor Haile Selassie. Endalkachew himself served as prime minister from February 28, 1974, to July 22, 1974. During this period, the imperial government was under assault by protesting students and striking workers who demanded investigation of corruption in the highest levels of government, reforms in land tenure, and political reforms. Endalkachew Makonnen attempted to address these demands by presenting reforms that began to change the very nature of the Ethiopian monarchy. Under his urging, Ethiopia experienced its first (although brief) experience with freedom of the press. However, before any further constitutional reform could take place, the Derg, a military committee investigating corruption, arrested Prime Minster Endalkachew as a member of the previous cabinet of Prime Minister Tsehafi Tezaz Aklilu Hapte-Wold, on July 22, 1974. The Derg then asked Lij Mikael Imiru to assume the prime minister's office. In September 1974, Emperor Haile Selassie was overthrown in a military coup by the Derg and 61 officials of his previous governments, including Endalkachew, were executed on November 23, 1974.

Endalkachew, Betwoded Makonnen, Ras (1890–1963) was an Ethiopian nobleman and high official under Emperor Haile Selassie. He was head of the powerful aristocratic Addisge clan. Makonnen accompanied Haile Selassie during his tour of Europe from April 16 to September 4, 1924. He fought against the Italian invasion in 1936 and then spent some time in exile in Jerusalem between 1936 and 1941, returning with the emperor upon the fall of the liberation of the country. He served as Ethiopia's first prime minister, beginning when Haile Selassie created the position in 1942 shortly after retaking control of Ethiopia after the Italian invasion, and ending when he retired on November 1, 1957. He led the delegation that represented Ethiopia at the summit in San Francisco that created the United Nations. Ras Bitwoded Makonnen Endelkachew was also a noted author of both historical and fictional topics.

Eshate, Hakim Warqenah (also known as Dr. Charles Martin) was a surgeon, educator, provincial governor, and Ethiopian Minister to London at the outbreak of the Italo-Ethiopian War in 1935. Hakim Warqenah Eshate was a social and political progressive; in 1924 he was placed in charge of reforming feudal slavery.

Eshete, Alemayehu, a native of Addis Ababa, Alemayehu was one of the first to record music to vinyl in Ethiopia. As a young man, his talent for imitating popular singers had earned him the nickname "Alemayehu Elvis." Since 1961, Alemayehu has formed numerous modern bands, performing in Ethiopia's premier clubs and hotels. He has recorded both romantic and political songs that campaign against local and global injustices. His music remains very powerful and popular in modern Ethiopia. In 1984, he won a Tchaikovsky composition award at the International Music Festival in Dresden, Germany.

Fasilidas or **Basilides, Emperor** (1603–October 18, 1667) was born at Magazaz, Shew. He was *negusä nägäst* of Ethiopia (1632–October 18, 1667) and was a member of the Solomonid dynasty. He was the son of Sissinios and Empress Sultana Mogassa, and he became the heir apparent on June 14, 1624. He was proclaimed emperor in 1630 (throne name Alam Sagad) during a revolt led by Sersa Krestos, but did not actually reach the throne until his father abdicated in 1632. Fasilides immediately acted to restore the power of the traditional Ethiopian Orthodox Church. He confiscated the lands of the Jesuits at Dankaz and elsewhere in the empire and relegated them once again to Fremona. He founded what became the city of Gondar in 1636 and established it as the capital. Fasilides died at Azazo, five miles south of Gondar. His body was interred at St. Stephen's Monastery on Daga Island, located in Lake Tana.

Fremnatos or **Frumentius of Tyre** (d. 383? A.D.) was the most famous Christian saint of Ethiopia. As the founder of the Ethiopian Church and the first bishop of Axum, he is attributed with the introduction of Christianity into Ethiopia. According to the fourth-century historian Rufinus, Frumentius and Edesius accompanied their uncle Metropius on a voyage to Ethiopia. When their ship stopped at one of the harbors of the Red Sea, people of the neighborhood massacred the whole crew, with the exception of the two boys, who were taken as slaves to the king of Axum. The two captives soon gained the favor of the king, who raised them to positions of trust and shortly before his death gave them their liberty. The widowed queen, however, prevailed upon them to remain at the court and assist her in the education of the young heir Erazanes and in the administration of the kingdom during the prince's minority. Frumentius and Edesius remained and used their influence to spread Christianity, with the former especially playing a more pivotal role. They encouraged the Christian merchants present in the country to practice their faith openly; later they also converted some of the indigenous communities. The Roman Catholic Church celebrates the feast of Frumentius on October 27, the Eastern Orthodox on November 30, and the Coptic on December 18. Ethiopian tradition credits him with the first Ethiopian translation of the New Testament.

Gabre-Medhin, Tsegaye (1936–2005) was poet laureate of Ethiopia as well as a poet, playwright, essayist, and art director. Born in Boda, near Ambo,

Ethiopia, Tsegaye graduated from the Blackstone School of Law in Chicago in 1959, but by 1960 he had studied experimental theatre at the Royal Court Theatre in London and the Comedie-Francaise in Paris. Between 1961 and 1971, Tsegaye was artistic director for the Ethiopian National Theatre and in the late 1970s he founded the department of theatre at Addis Ababa University. However, in the 1970s he was imprisoned by the Derg regime, who also banned his writings. Tsegaye wrote numerous poems, plays, essays, and song lyrics, primarily in Amharic. Many Ethiopians regard him as their Shakespeare. Tsegaye translated Shakespeare (*Hamlet* and *Othello* being the most popular of these works) as well as Moliere's *Tartouffe* and *Doctor Despite Himself* and Bertolt Brecht's *Mother Courage.* Tsegaye died in Manhattan, where he had moved in 1998 to receive treatment for kidney disease. He was buried in Addis Ababa in the national cathedral where the body of Emperor Haile Selassie lies.

Gebru, Senedu, was an Ethiopian intellectual who studied in Switzerland and, during the fascist occupation, was kept for a time in detention in Italy. She was a member of the women's antifascist resistance movement in western Ethiopia. Senedu and other women wore uniforms and hats with Red Cross marks and served the cadets as "impromptu Red Cross Units," tending not only the fighting men but also the civilians suffering from bullets, burns, and poisonous gas. Her work (published in 1949–1950) was described as the first important piece of creative writing about the experience to be printed in Addis Ababa.

Gerima, Haile (born March 4, 1946) is an Ethiopian filmmaker who came to the United States in 1968. At the University of California in Los Angeles he was an important member of the Los Angeles School of black filmmakers. He has been a professor of film at Howard University in Washington, D.C., since 1975. His best-known film, *Sankofa* (1993), is about slavery.

Gugsa of Yejju (died May 23, 1825) was a Ras of Begemder (ca. 1798 until his death) and regent of the emperor of Ethiopia. He was the son of Mersu Barentu and Kefey, the sister of Ras Aligaz. He married one of his daughters to Dejazmach Meru of the house of Fenja; and his other daughter married Hirut to Dejazmach Haile Maryam. Upon becoming regent, Ras Gugsa reasserted the central power of the empire (although keeping the emperor as a figurehead) by dispossessing the nobility of the parts of Ethiopia he controlled, primarily Begemder. He accomplished this by proclaiming in 1800 in the name of the emperor that the legal title of land tenure would be converted from freeholds to state property, held at the will of the emperor. At first the peasantry welcomed this egalitarian measure, believing that they would benefit from the loss of their masters. However, as Ras Gugsa proceeded in dispossessing the great families each year under one pretext or another, the peasants lost their last defenders. Gugsa was buried at the church of Iyasus in Debre Tabor.

Gutu, Waqo (ca. 1924–2006) was an Ethiopian rebel figure and military general and leader of the United Liberation Forces of Oromia (ULFO) since the 1960s in Bale, South Oromia, Ethiopia. He was elected chairman of the ULFO in 2000. Between 1963 and 1970, he liberated Bale from imperial occupation, but according to Oromo accounts surrendered to Selasie's forces to prevent a massacre of his people. Between 1975 and 1991, his guerillas controlled several towns in Oromia. He also visited several countries, including Somalia, to raise funds and arms and to galvanize the struggle. In 1989, he established the United Oromo People Liberation Front (UOPLF) to join the struggle against deposed leader Mengistu Haile Mariam. He later joined the victorious Tigrean People's Liberation Front (TPLF) coalition of prime minister Meles Zenawi, which ousted Mengistu, but he bolted out in 1992 to return to the jungle, citing betrayal by the new rulers. He died in the Nairobi West Hospital.

Gwangul, Abba Seru (died 1778) was a chieftain of the Yejju Oromo, an ethnic group of Ethiopia. He claimed to be a descendant of an Arab named Omar, who had served in the armies of Ahmad Gran. He was reputed to have met and provided information for the Scottish explorer James Bruce in 1770 in his account of travels in Ethiopia.

Habte-Wold, Aklilu (1912–1974) was an Ethiopian politician under Emperor Haile Selassie. He was foreign minister of Ethiopia from 1947 to 1958 and prime minister from 1961 until shortly before his death. He and his brothers, Makonnen Hapte-Wold and Akalework Hapte-Wold, were the beneficiaries of imperial patronage from Emperor Haile Selassie, who had them educated in the country and abroad in his efforts to create a new Western-educated intelligentsia and professional class in his country. Aklilu Hapte-Wold was French educated. Aklilu Hapte-Wold was among those who joined Emperor Haile Selassie during his exile following the second Italo-Abyssinian War. He acted as a fundraiser for the beleaguered exile community and for the resistance inside Ethiopia. In 1958 the Emperor appointed Aklilu to replace him as Minister of the Pen, giving him the title of "Tsehafi Taezaz." When student protests, military mutinies, and an economic downturn caused by the oil embargo erupted in 1973 into a popular uprising against the government, calls went out for Tsehafi Taezaz Aklilu to be dismissed. When Emperor Haile Selassie was deposed in 1974 by the Marxist military junta that would rule the country for almost two decades, Tsehafi Taezaz Aklilu Hapte-Wold and his brother Akale Work Hapte-Wold were both executed with 60 other ex-officials of the emperor's government without trial, in November 1974.

Haymanot, Abune Takla, was the Third Patriarch of the Ethiopian Orthodox Tewahido Church. He was enthroned following the forcible removal from the patriarchal throne of the previous patrarch, Abune Tewophilous, by the Marxist Derg regime in 1977. Following the patriarch's arrest, the Derg ordered that an assembly of clergy and laity of the church along with the Holy Synod elect a new patriarch to replace the arrested Abune Tewophilos. All archbishops were disqualified from being elected for having been too close to the recently deposed Ethiopian monarchy. The church assembly was made to elect a hermit bahitawi monk by the name of Abba Melaku as the new patriarch of the Ethiopian Orthodox Church.

With little formal education and little exposure to temporal affairs, Abba Melaku had spent the bulk of his life as a hermit praying in a cave and preaching to the people of the Wollaita district. It is believed that the Derg hoped that such a man would be easy to control. He was enthroned, and, within a year, he was made to appoint 14 new bishops to replace the old ones who were deemed to have been close to the government of Emperor Haile Selassie. A government-appointed administrator was put in place to place the church under the tutelage of the Derg. The Derg eventually executed Abune Tewophilos but the Coptic church refused to recognize the removal of patriarch and declared that as far as the church of Egypt was concerned, he remained the canonical patriarch of Ethiopia.

Abune Takla Haymanot presided over the church during a tumultuous period of Ethiopian history. As Ethiopia weathered the Derg's misrule and a series of natural disasters, Abune Takla Haymanot embodied the Church's devoutness and dignity, and he became the most popular of all the men to have sat on the patriarchal throne in Ethiopia. Upon his enthronement, he had refused to don the black robes traditional to high-ranking hierarchs of the Orthodox churches. Instead he adopted robes that were bright yellow, the color of the bahitawi hermits, and a color that in Ethiopian tradition symbolized penance and suffering. Indeed the Patriarch spent the entire 11 years of his reign in almost constant penance. He prayed constantly, refused to eat anything but the simplest boiled and roasted grains and beans, slept on the bare floor, and wore the thinnest of sandals, in an act of constant self mortification. His personal allowance was spent on educating a group of famine orphans that he was personally raising in the patriarchate itself. Although never directly confronting the communist government for fear of increasing the persecution of his flock, Patriarch Abune Takla Haymanot preached to his people to be strong and to pray, joining them in this endeavor with all his heart. Sources indicated that he later voiced opposition to the violent actions of the Derg.

The patriarch suffered from poor health due to his constant fasting and penance. He ceased making public appearances other than to attend Mass at the church within the patriarchate. He made one final public appearance at the inauguration of a new church in Wollaita and visited the cave where he had once lived. He returned to Addis Ababa and was almost immediately admitted to the hospital, where he died in late May 1988. The government ordered a full state funeral for Patriarch Abune Takla Haymanot, complete with military escort, gun salutes, and flags at half staff throughout Ethiopia. The open casket was carried from St. Mary's church in the Patriarchate to Holy Trinity Cathedral on the same carriage that was once used by the fallen imperial regime for royal funerals. The patriarch lay in his coffin wearing a patriarchal crown and in his robes of office, draped with the Ethiopian flag.

Heruy, Emailaf, was an early twentieth-century Ethiopian artist and one of the first to make extensive use of photography to achieve more accurate portraiture. Following traditional Ethiopian practice, he learned to paint by helping his father, most notably at the great church of Maryam at Entoto. He subsequently decorated the churches of Selassie and Giyorgis in Addis Ababa and that of Selassie at Assabot, as well as the Menelik palace and the parliament, opened by Emperor Haile Selassie in 1931. His paintings in these buildings include decorative portraits of the principal nineteenth- and early twentieth-century Ethiopian rulers and of Emperor Haile Selassie surrounded by his principal courtiers and ministers.

Imru, Haile Selassie, Ras (1892–1980) was cousin to Emperor Haile Selassie and appointed Governor of Harar in 1916. The emperor appointed Ras Imru Haile Selassie as prince regent in his absence, departing with his family for Djibouti on May 2, 1936, during the Italo-Ethiopian war. Ras Imru maintained an underground government in western Wolega. He was later was appointed Ethiopian ambassador to the United States.

Imru, Yodit (1943–) became the first Ethiopian woman ambassador to the United States in the twilight years of Haile Selassie's reign. Her father, Ras Imru, was also earlier appointed Ethiopian ambassador to the United States. Yodit Imru is the sister of former prime minister Ras Michael Imru. For her activist campaigns against the postimperial administration, she has been described as helping improve Ethiopia's human and political rights. Her cause received some international claim when she was detained and held under military guard together with her two sisters, Hirut Imru, a former university lecturer, and Mammie Imru, an architect.

Iyasu V, also known as **Lij Iyasu** (February 4, 1887–November 25, 1935), was the designated but uncrowned monarch of Ethiopia (1913–1916). His baptismal name was Kifle Yaqub. Lij (meaning one born of royal blood) Iyasu was a grandson of Menelik II of Ethiopia and son of Menelik's daughter Shewaregga, who was a half-sister of Menelik's eldest daughter Zauditu. Because he was never crowned emperor, he is usually referred to as "Lij Iyasu." His excommunication by the Ethiopian Orthodox Tewahido Church prevented him from being referred to publicly as Iyasu V. His name is sometimes also written as Eyasu, an Amharic/Ge'ez version of the biblical name Joshua. He was proclaimed heir apparent in 1909. Iyasu's deposition in favor of Empress Zauditu in 1916 was met by the former's military resistance. He was captured in 1921 and cultivated by Italian forces during the 1935 invasion of Ethiopia. The Italian Air Force scattered fliers asking the population to rebel against Haile Selassie and support the "true Emperor Iyasu V." Historians have described Iyasu's reign as impressive albeit often contradictory. His imperial mother allowed him to claim descent from King Solomon and the Queen of Sheba, and through his father, he claimed decent from the Prophet Mohammed. His flirtation with Islam led many of this followers to desert him while providing ammunition for his detractors who accused him of being a traitor to Ethiopia and the Coptic Christian faith. Some historians in retrospective highlight Iyasu's reformism as a continuation of Menelik's program of modernization. Programs such as the establishment of the first police force in Addis Ababa and his overtures to the Muslim inhabitants of Ethiopia have been described as precursors to postrevolution efforts at recognizing Ethiopia's multicultural makeup.

Lalibela, Emperor, was a thirteenth-century monarch renowned for the construction of the great monolithic churches of Lasta (now called Lalibela). Lalibela was *negus* of Ethiopia and a member of the Zagwe dynasty. He is also considered a saint by the Ethiopian church. Details about the construction of the churches has been lost, but the *Gadla Lalibela*, a hagiography of the king, states that he carved these churches out of stone with only the help of angels.

Lamma, Mangistu, is an Ethiopian playwright best known for writing *Yalaccha Gabbiccha (Marriage of Unequa)*.

Lucha, Girma Wolde-Giorgis (December 1924–) is president of Ethiopia. He was elected president on October 8, 2001, by a unanimous vote of the Ethiopian parliament. The Ethiopian presidency is a largely symbolic office with little power over a six-year term. He served in the military and as a politician under Emperor Haile Selassie, serving first in parliament and then being elected speaker of the lower house. After the emperor was overthrown in 1974, he worked under the military Derg regime, particularly in Eritrea, as the local Red Cross representative. After the ouster of Mengistu Haile Mariam in 1991 he became a businessman, in addition to returning to parliament.

Makonnen, Ras (May 8, 1852–March 21, 1906) was a general and the governor of Harar province in Ethiopia. He was the father of Tafari Makonnen, later known as the Emperor Haile Selassie I. Ras Makonnen's father was Fitawrari Woldemikael Guddessa. Makonnen was a grandson of King Sahle Selassie of Shoa through his mother, Princess Tenagnework Sahle Selassie. As such, he was a first cousin of Emperor Menelik II and a member of the

Solomonic Dynasty. He was given the governorship of Harar after it was incorporated into the Ethiopian Empire by his cousin, the emperor. Ras Makonnen served other posts including temporary governor of Tigre after the removal of the rebellious Ras Mengesha Yohannes; general during various military campaigns including during the First Italo-Abyssinian War; and diplomat and de facto foreign minister. He had a leading role at the Battle of Adowa where Abyssinian forces routed the Italians.

Mariam, Mengistu Haile Lt. Col. (1937–) was head of state from 1977 to 1991. He formally assumed power as head of state and Derg chairman in 1977, although he had wielded behind-the-scenes power long before that, leading a coup in 1974. The transition of power resulted in the execution of two of Mengistu's predecessors as head of state. Under Mengistu, Ethiopia received aid from the Soviet Union, other members of the Warsaw Pact, and Cuba. From 1977 through early 1978, a rebellion against the new government ensued and was suppressed, resulting in many casualties. In response to guerrilla attacks from the anti-Mengistu Ethiopian People's Revolutionary Party (EPRP), Mengistu declared that the EPRP had begun a campaign of "White Terror." Anti-Mengistu forces, however, accused Mengistu's Workers Party of waging a campaign of "Red Terror." On September 10, 1987, Mengistu became a civilian president under a new constitution, and the country was renamed the People's Democratic Republic of Ethiopia. Mengistu's government was faced with enormous difficulties throughout the 1980s in the form of droughts, widespread famine (notably the Ethiopian famine of 1984–1985), and insurrections, particularly in the northern regions of Tigre and Eritrea. In 1989, the Tigrean People's Liberation Front merged with other ethnically based opposition movements to form the Ethiopian People's Revolutionary Democratic Front (EPRDF). In May 1991, EPRDF forces advanced on Addis Ababa. Mengistu himself blames the collapse of his government on Mikhail Gorbachev for letting the Soviet Union collapse and hence cutting off its aid to Ethiopia. Mengistu fled the country with 50 family and Derg members. He was granted asylum in Zimbabwe as an official "guest" of Robert Mugabe, the president of that country. He left behind almost the entire membership of the original Derg and the Workers Party of Ethiopia (WPE) leadership, which was promptly arrested and put on trial upon the assumption of power by the EPRDF. Mengistu still resides in Zimbabwe, despite attempts by Ethiopia to extradite him to face trial by the current Ethiopian authorities. Several former members of the Derg have been sentenced to death in absentia by the new regime. The trial against him, started in 1994, is ongoing as of 2006.

Matte, Lucien s.j. (1907–1975) was born in Quebec City in 1907 and attended the universities of Montreal and Laval where he earned degrees in philosophy, natural science, theology, and education. In 1930 he entered the Jesuit Order and was ordained in 1938. Fr. Matte came to Sudbury in 1962 when he was appointed president of the University of Sudbury. He was the driving force behind the creation of the Sudbury Teacher College at Laurentian University. Education was a special focus in his life. In 1945 he was asked by the emperor of Ethiopia, Haile Selassie, to reorganize Ethiopia's school systems. Haile Selassie wanted his schools to be based on the Canadian system. Fr. Matte reorganized the primary and secondary schools, founded the University College of Addis Ababa in 1954, and in 1961 became president of the newly formed Haile Selassie University. In recognition for the work Fr. Matte did for his country, Haile Selassie donated $10,000 toward the University of Sudbury's building fund.

Menas, Emperor (throne name Admas Sagad I) was *negusä nägäst* of Ethiopia (1559–February 1, 1563) and a member of the Solomonid dynasty. He was a brother of Gelawdewos. During Ahmad ibn Ibrihim al-Ghazi's invasion of Ethiopia, Menas was captured but treated well as a valuable prisoner. Ahmad ibn Ibrihim al-Ghazi (ca. 1507–February 21, 1543) was a Somali Imam and general who defeated several Ethiopian emperors and wreaked much damage on that nation. He is also known as Ahmad Gran (or Gurey), "Ahmed the left-handed." The clemency granted Menas came to an end in 1542, when the Imam, desperate for help from his fellow Muslims, included Menas in an assortment of extravagant gifts to the sultan of Yemen in return for military aid. However, Imam Ahmad's son was later captured in the aftermath of the Battle of Wayna Daga, and Gelawdewos used his prisoner to recover his brother Menas. Following his elevation, he campaigned against the Falasha in Semienr. He banished the Jesuit bishop Andre da Oviedo and his companions to a village between Axum and Adowa called Maigoga, which the Jesuits optimistically renamed Fremona, after the missionary Frumentius. One year into his reign, Bahr negus Yeshaq rose in revolt in Tigre proclaiming Tazkaro, the illegitimate son of Emperor Menas' brother Yaqob, as negus. This revolt occupied Menas' attention for the remainder of his short reign. He died while trying to regroup for another assault on the rebelling Bahr Negash.

Menelik I, Emperor, is traditionally believed to be the son of King Solomon of ancient Israel and Makeda, Queen of Sheba. According to Ethiopian legends, he was born in the province of Hamasien in Eritrea. Tradition credits him with bringing the Ark of the Covenant to Ethiopia, following a visit to Jerusalem to meet his father upon reaching adulthood. According to the *Kebra Nagastr,* King Solomon had intended on sending one son of each of his nobles and one son each of each temple priest with Menelik upon his return to his mother's kingdom. He is supposed to have had a replica made of the ark for them to take with them, but the son of Zadok the high priest secretly switched the replica with the real ark and brought it into Ethiopia, where it is said to remain to this day in the ancient town of Axum. Upon the death of Queen Makeda, Menelik assumed the throne with the new title of emperor and king of kings of Ethiopia. He founded the Solomonic Dynasty of Ethiopia, which ruled Ethiopia with few interruptions for close to 3,000 years and 225 generations and ended with the fall of Emperor Haile Selassie in 1974.

Menelik II, Emperor (1844–1913) is considered to be the founder of modern Ethiopia. He was the son of the Queen of Sheba and King Solomon and is regarded as the founder of the Aksumite Empire as stated in the *Kebra Negast*, or *Book of the Glory of Kings*. Before his death in 1884, Yohannes IV named his son, Ras Mengesha Yohannes, as his heir. Although a group of Tigrean nobles led by Ras Alula attempted to promote the claim of Yohannes' son, Ras Mengesha Yohannes, as emperor, many of the dead monarch's other relatives on both the Enderta and Tembien sides of his family objected and went into open rebellion against Mengesha. Tigre was torn asunder by the rebellions of various members of the Emperor's family against Mengesha and each other. Menelik of Shewa took advantage of Tigrean disorder, and after allowing the Italians to occupy Hamasien, Serai, and Akale Guzai, districts loyal to Yohannes IV, he was proclaimed esmperor of Ethiopia as Menelik II.

Mentewab, Empress (born ca. 1706 at Qwara, died at Qusqwam Palace, near Gondar, June 27, 1773) was empress of Ethiopia, the consort of Emperor Bakaffa, mother of Iyasu II, and grandmother of Iyoas I. She was also known officially by her baptismal name of Welete Giyorgis ("Daughter of St. George"). Empress Mentewab wielded significant authority throughout the reign of her son and well into the reign of her grandson as well. She built several significant structures in Gondar, including her own castle in the Imperial Precinct as well as a large banqueting hall. Most significantly, she built a church dedicated to the Virgin Mary at Qusquam (named for a site in Egypt where the holy family had stayed during their exile) in the mountains outside of Gondar. In 1730, Empress Mentewab was crowned co-ruler upon the succession of her son—a first for a woman in Ethiopia—and held unprecedented power over government during his reign. (She descended in her own right from emperors who reigned two centuries earlier.) Her attempt to continue in this role following the death of her son in 1755 led her into conflict with Wubit (Welete Bersabe), his widow, who believed that it was her turn to preside at the court of her own son, Iyoas.

Nega, Berhanu (1958–) was elected mayor of Addis Ababa, Ethiopia in the Ethiopian general elections, 2005. He is a founding chairman of the Rainbow Ethiopia: Movement for Democracy and Social Justice and an Deputy Chairman of Coalition for Unity and Democracy (CUD), for whom he served as chief election campaign strategist. He attended Addis Ababa University where he participated in the student movement against the ruling Derg government in his freshman year. When the government acted against political dissidents in 1977, Berhanu fled with other radical student activists to Mount

Asimba in northern Ethiopia. After a division within the Ethiopian People's Revolutionary Party, he was detained for openly criticizing killings within EPRP. After a few months, he was released by his captors and crossed into the Sudan where he lived for two years until he was granted political asylum in the United States. He returned to Ethiopia in 1994 and became an entrepreneur and academic. He was president of the Ethiopian Economic Association from 1996 to 2000. He has also served as the head of the Ethiopian Economic Policy Research Institute, a nonprofit organization that he helped to establish. He had also worked as a consultant including for the United Nations Economic Commission for Africa (ECA). During the 2005 elections, Dr. Berhanu contributed to the opposition movement against Meles Zenawi with remarkable performances at the pre-election debates with the ruling party. Despite the postelection political impasse, CUD met on August 20th and elected Dr. Berhanu mayor of Addis Ababa. Dr. Admasu Gebeyehu and Assefa Habtewold were elected deputy mayor and speaker of the city assembly, respectively, at the same meeting. If the CUD decides in favor of taking over the task of running the city, these people would be the first elected public administration in Ethiopia.

Neway, Garmame, Mengistu's U.S.-educated brother and the 1960 coup's radical intellectual leader. He had obtained a B.A. from the University of Wisconsin and an M.A. from Columbia. He was largely considered a progressive social reformer who was ahead of his time in his sensitivity to the national question and social welfare reform. He was reputed to have recruited his brother to join the attempted coup to overthrow Emperor Selassie. He died fighting forces loyal to the triumphant emperor.

Neway, Mangestu, the commander of the Imperial Bodyguard who, together with his brother, led an unsuccessful coup against Emperor Selassie in 1960. He was injured, captured, and subsequently tried and hanged.

Pankhurst, Richard (1927–) was born in London, the son of the renowned activist Sylvia E. Pankhurst who was one of the more vocal antifascist activists in Europe during the 1920s and 1930s. Sylvia's antifascist activities led her to take interest in Ethiopia. Dr. Pankhurst lives and works in Ethiopia. His career as a historian of Ethiopia has entered its fifth decade. As a constant champion of Ethiopian causes, Dr. Pankhurst has earned the respect and admiration of many in Ethiopia and abroad. Further, as part of his active participation in the national committee for the return of the Axum Obelisk, Dr. Pankhurst is currently among a group of concerned professionals forming a national committee for the return of treasures looted by the British expeditionary force sent to free British prisoners from Magdala in 1868.

Pankhurst, Sylvia Estelle (May 5, 1882–September 27, 1960) was a campaigner in the suffragette movement in the United Kingdom and a prominent

Left communist. She was born in Manchester, England, a daughter of Dr. Richard Pankhurst and Emmeline Pankhurst, members of the Independent Labour Party and much concerned with women's rights. Her sister, Christabel, would also become an activist. In 1906 she started to work full-time with the Women's Social and Political Union with her sister and her mother. But in contrast to them she retained her interest in the labor movement. In the mid-1920s Pankhurst drifted away from communist politics into antifascism and anticolonialism. She responded to the Italian invasion of Ethiopia by renaming the *Workers Dreadnought* as *The New Times and Ethiopia News* in 1936 and became a supporter of Haile Selassie. She raised funds for Ethiopia's first teaching hospital and wrote extensively on Ethiopian art and culture. Her research was eventually published as *Ethiopia, a Cultural History* (London: Lalibela House, 1955). Having moved to Addis Ababa in 1956 with her son, Richard Pankhurst, she founded a monthly journal, *Ethiopia Observer*, which reported on many aspects of Ethiopian life and development. Upon her death, she was buried in front of Trinity Cathedral in Addis Ababa.

Paulos, Abune (born Gebre Igziabiher Wolde Yohannes, 1935) is Abuna (our father) and Patriarch of the Ethiopian Orthodox Tewahedo Church (1992–). His full title is "His Holiness Abune Paulos, Fifth Patriarch and Catholicos (re-ese Liqane Papasat) of Ethiopia, Echege of the See of St. Tekle Haymanot, and Archbishop of Axum." Patriarch Abune Paulos was born in Adwa in the province of Tigre in northern Ethiopia. His family was long associated with the Abune Gerima monastery near the town, and he entered the monastery as a young boy as a deacon trainee, eventually taking monastic orders and being ordained a priest. He continued his education at the Holy Trinity Theological College in Addis Ababa under the patronage of Patriarch Abune Tewophilos. He was sent to study at the St. Vladimir Othodox Seminary in the United States and afterwards joined the doctoral program at the Princeton Theological Seminary. In 1974, his education was interrupted by a summons from Patriarch Abune Tewophilos, and he returned to Addis Ababa shortly after the revolution that toppled Emperor Haile Selassie. He was anointed a bishop along with four others, assuming the name and style of Abune Paulos, and given responsibility for ecumenical affairs by the patriarch. But because the patriarch had named these new bishops without the permission of the new Derg regime, all five men were arrested and the patriarch eventually executed. Abune Paulos and his fellow bishops were imprisoned until 1983. Abune Paulos returned to Princeton in 1984 to complete his doctoral degree there and began his life as an exile. He was elevated to the rank of Archbishop by Patriarch Abune Takla Haymanot in 1986 while in exile. In March of 2006, Abune Paulos was elected to serve as one of the seven presidents of the World Council of Churches, during its summit in Brazil.

Roba, Fatuma (1973–), a 1996 Olympic gold medalist, is constantly reminded of her special place in the hearts of Ethiopians. She started running in her elementary school in the Arsi region that was once home to Olympic gold medalists Derartu Tulu and Haile Gebre Selassie. Roba won the gold medal in the marathon at the 1996 Summer Olympics. In 1997, she became the first African women to win the Boston Marathon, subsequently winning two more times, in 1998 and 1999. Her effort at a fourth title ended with a spirited second-place position. She has been a great role model for millions of young athletes.

Saffo, Dejazmatch Balcha (Abba Nefso), Menelik's loyal general, appointed Governor of Harar and later the wealthy province of Sidamo. He was a conservative foe to Emperor Haile Selassie who had him jailed. The emperor released Saffo during the Italian invasion and the latter formed a guerrilla force and fought the Italians valiantly until he was killed. He is respected as a martyr and patriot of modern Ethiopia.

Salomon II or **Solomon II, Emperor** (*negusä nägäst* of Ethiopia, April 13, 1777–July 20, 1779) was the son of Abeto Adigo. He may be identical with the Emperor Solomon, whom the traveler Henry Salt lists as one of the emperors still alive at the time of his visit in 1809–1810. Solomon was made emperor by Ras Gusho and Wand Bewossen after they deposed Tekle Haymanot II. Richard Pankhurst credits him with the construction of Qeddus Fasilides ("St. Fasilides," literally "Holy Fasilides") church in Gondar.

Sebestyanos (ca. 1703–March 6, 1719) was a ruler of Shewa, an important Amhara noble of Ethiopia. He was one of the sons of Negasi Krestos. Sebestyanos established his capital at Doqaqit. He was killed on March 6, 1719.

Seged, Wossen (ca. 1808–1813) was a *meridazmach* of Shewa, an important prince of Ethiopia. He was the elder son of Asfa Wossen by a woman of the Solomonid dynasty. He was the first ruler of Shewa to claim a higher title than Meridazmach, calling himself Ras. It was during the reign of Wossen Seged that the chronology of Shewa became stable. One mention that helps date the Meridazmach's reign is that of Henry Salt, who spoke of him as ruling Yifat (the contemporary name of Shewa) during his visit to Ethiopia in 1809–1810. As Asfa Wossen had sons by a second wife, who came from the aristocracy in Menz, Wossen Seged feared that he would be passed over in favor of his younger half-brother, and he rebelled against his father. Failing to attract support, Wossen Seged was defeated and imprisoned; yet the aging Asfa Wossen was reconciled to Wossen Seged and not only made him governor of Antizokia in northern Shewa, but also his successor. Abir mentions a tradition that during a battle against the Yejju Oromo he was captured by Chief Guji, the grandson of Gwangul, but ransomed by the head of the Shewan church, who had disguised himself as a Muslim sheikh to enter the territory of Yejju undetected. After he assumed control of Shewa, he joined in an alliance with Ras Wolde Selassie of Tigre to invade the territories of Ras Gugsa of Yejju.

Wossen Seged began a campaign of church building, restoring the Church of the Trinity in Debre Berhan and the Church of the Virgin in Debre Libanos as well as building a new church in Sela Dingay. Despite these works, members of the local Ethiopian church were dissatisfied with him due to his policy of religious toleration toward his Muslim subjects.

Selassie, Amha, Emperor of Ethiopia (1916–1997) was the last emperor of Ethiopia, proclaimed on the deposition of his father Haile Selassie. His brief reign ended when he was deposed and exiled after the abolition of the Ethiopian monarchy in March 1975. He was born Asfaw Wossen Tafari in the walled city of Harrar in August 1916 to Dejazmach Tafari Makonnen, then the governor of Harrar and future emperor of Ethiopia, and his wife Menen Asfaw. Amha Selassie became Crown Prince Asfaw Wossen of Ethiopia when his father was crowned emperor on November 2, 1930. In December 1960, the Imperial Guard launched a coup and seized power in Ethiopia while the emperor was on a visit to Brazil. The coup leaders compelled the crown prince to read a radio statement in which he accepted the crown in his father's place and announced a government of reform. However, the regular army and the Ethiopian Orthodox Church both refused to accept the new government, and the leader of the church, Patriarch Abune Baslios, issued an anathema against all those who cooperated with the coup leaders. The emperor returned to Ethiopia and the army stormed the palace, where members of the government were being held prisoner by the Imperial Guards. In 1973, Crown Prince Asfaw Wossen suffered a massive stroke and was evacuated to Switzerland for medical treatment. He was accompanied by his wife and daughters. In April 1989, Crown Prince Asfaw Wossen was proclaimed "Emperor of Ethiopia" in exile at his home in London by members of the exiled Ethiopian community. He took the throne name of Amha Selassie I. Amha Selassie died of longtime ailments in Virginia, in the United States, at age 80 on February 17, 1997. He had never completely recovered from the massive stroke he experienced in 1973. His body was flown back to Ethiopia and buried in the imperial family vaults.

Selassie, Haile Gebre (1973–) is regarded universally as the greatest long-distance runner of all time. He was born in the province of Arsi in central Ethiopia and was inspired by runners Abebe Bikila and Miruts Yifter. As a child he was said to have run 20 kilometers every day going to and from school. At age 16, without any formal training, he entered the Addis Ababa marathon and finished in 2:42. Haile rose to international prominence in 1992 when he won the 5K and 10K world junior championships. In 1993 at the Stuttgart world championships, he won gold in the 10K and silver in the 5K competition. Haile set his first world record in 1994 by breaking the six-year-old world record of Said Aouita. The year 1995 established Haile as an unparalleled long-distance runner. He broke Moses Kiptanui's world record in a two-mile race. Only a week later, he broke another world record. He won another victory in the world championship 10K by earning a gold medal. His fourth world record occurred in Zurich, Switzerland. At the Atlanta Olympics in 1996, he won a gold medal in the 10K race in an Olympic record time. In February 1997 in Stuttgart, Germany, he set a new world record in the 1,500-meter race. Gebre Selassie's seventh world record occurred in Stockholm, Sweden. In a 1997 competition, he won a prize of $1 million. On July 4, 1997, in Oslo, Norway, he had an outstanding 10K race in which he had a huge lead against his opponents and again set a new world record. In the following month, he earned another 10K world championship to be followed by another on August 13, 1997, where he once again won a 5K race by setting a new world record that was three seconds better than his previous time. In 2000, he won his second gold medal at the 10K in the Sydney Olympics. In 2004, Gebre Selassie came to the Olympic games seeking to become the first man in history to win three straight Olympic gold medals in the 10K run. He was unable to do so, however, he finished fifth in a race won by his fellow countryman and protégé, Kenenisa Bekele.

Selassie, Sahle (ca. 1795–October 22, 1847) was a *meridazmach* (and later *negus*) of Shewa (1813–1847), an important Amhara noble of Ethiopia. He was a younger son of Wossen Seged.

Sellassie, Sahle (1936–) is an Ethiopian author who has contributed to at least four books. *The Afersata* (1969) in the African Writers Series is perhaps the best known of these works.

Selassie, Zera Yacob Amha, appointed ceremonial crown prince of Ethiopia, is the grandson of Emperor Haile Selassie and son of Emperor-in-Exile Amha Selassie of Ethiopia. After the revolution of 1974, he lived in exile in the United Kingdom, where he had been attending school, and briefly in the United States. He is currently living in Addis Ababa. He is recognized as the head of the imperial house of Ethiopia at the present time.

Selassie I, Haile, Emperor (1892–1975) was born Lij Tafari Makonnen and served as Emperor of Ethiopia from 1930 to 1974. He was noted for his statesmanship and for introducing many political, economic, and social reforms. He is the religious symbol for God incarnate among the Rastafari movement.

Shawul, Hailu (also spelled Shawel; Shawil) (born 1936) is an Ethiopian engineer and the chairman of the Coalition for Unity and Democracy (CUD). He was born in Northern Shewa. As a result of the protests that followed the general elections of May 2005 the government placed Hailu Shawul under house arrest for a period. When the CUD led an initially peaceful protest in October, he and 23 other CUD leaders were arrested and imprisoned.

Sheba, Queen, was the ruler of Sheba, an ancient kingdom that modern archaeology speculates was located in present-day Ethiopia or Yemen. She is also called Makeda, and in Islamic tradition her name is Bilqis. Alternative names given for her have been Nikaule or Nicaula. Ethiopian Christians tell the story about Solomon and the Queen of Sheba, that the Queen was an Ethiopian sovereign named Makeda (Magda), and that she returned from her celebrated journey to the court of Solomon in Jerusalem bearing the king's son, David, who became the first king of Ethiopia, ruling as Menelik I. Makeda's tale is told in an ancient Ethiopian book, the *Kebra Negast*, or *Book of the Glory of Kings*.

Sissinios, Emperor (throne name Malak Sagad III) (born in 1572) was *negusä nägäst* of Ethiopia (1607–September 7, 1632). His father was Abeto (Prince) Fasilides the Confused, from Shewa, a grandson of Dawit II. As a result, while some authorities list him as a member of the Solomonid dynasty, others consider him the founder of the Gondar line of the dynasty.

Solomon, King (ca. 1000 B.C.) was a wise ruler of an empire during the biblical era. The royal magnificence and splendor of Solomon's court are unrivaled. Solomon was known for his wisdom and proverbs. People including queen Makedah, or Bilqis, of Sheba (identified with Ethiopia and modern Yemen) came from near and far "to hear the wisdom of Solomon." According to Ethiopian tradition, the son of King Solomon and the Queen of Sheba, Menelik I, became the first emperor of Ethiopia.

Tewodros II, Emperor (also known as Theodore II) (1818–1868) was an emperor of Ethiopia (1855–1868). His name at birth was Kassa Haile Giorgis, but he was most often referred to as Kassa Hailu. His rule is often marked as the beginning of modern Ethiopia, ending the decentralized Zemena Mesafint (age of the princes). He moved the capital city of the empire from Gondar, first to Debre Tabor, and later to Magdala. Tewodros ended the division of Ethiopia among the various regional warlords and princes that had vied for power for almost two centuries. He forcibly reincorporated the regions of Gojjam, Shewa, and Wollo under the direct administration of the imperial throne after having been ruled by local branches of the imperial dynasty (in Gojjam and Shewa) or other warlords (Wollo). Tewodros, fearful of these northerly powers, wrote a letter to Queen Victoria asking for British assistance in the region. After two years had passed and Tewodros had not received a reply, he imprisoned several British subjects in an attempt to get Victoria's attention. This led to a British invasion under Robert Napier, who, with the help of several of the warlords that Tewodros spent his life fighting against, defeated the Ethiopian army. As a result, Tewodros committed suicide on April 13, 1868.

Tulu, Derartu (1972–) is an Ethiopian long-distance track, road, and marathon athlete. She was born in Bokoji in Arsi province, the same village as the male running sensation Kenenisa Bekele. She is the first Ethiopian woman, and the first woman from sub-Saharan Africa, to win a medal in the Olympic Games. She rose to fame when she convincingly won the women's 10K race in the Barcelona Olympics in 1992. After giving birth in 1998 and 1999, she came back in 2000 in the best shape of her life. She won the 10K Olympic gold for the second time, the only woman to have done this in the short history of the event. She has a total of six world and Olympic gold medals. She also won a bronze at the Olympics in 2004 and many other medals in international competitions. She is an icon of the Olympic movement, and many will recall her victory lap in 1992 with white South African Elana Meyer, symbolically celebrating an African victory and the end of apartheid on the track.

Wale, Gugsa, Ras (b. at Marto, Yajju, April 1877–1930) Governor of Begameder (1916–1928) and Yajju (1928–1930). Gugsa Wale was a nephew of Empress Taytu and was married to regent Zauditu's. He was later opposed to the centralization policies and the enthronement of Haile Selassie and was defeated and killed at the Battle of Anchem in 1930 by forces loyal to the emperor.

Wolde, Mamo (1931–May 26, 2002) was born in the village of DreDele in the Ad-A district about 60 kilometers from Addis Ababa. He had a traditional upbringing, spending most of his childhood in DreDele where he attended a "qes" school. In 1951, he was hired by the Imperial Bodyguard. While in the prestigious armed forces, Mamo was able to further his education. In 1953, he was transferred to the Second Battalion of the Imperial Guard and sent to Korea as part of the U.N. peacekeeping mission. He spent two years in Korea where he had a distinguished military service. After returning from Korea, he got married and pursued his passion of athletics. He qualified to be a member of the Ethiopian Olympics team that participated in the Melbourne Olympics in 1962 and produced the best overall performance of the national Olympics team by placing fourth in a 1,500-meter race. In 1968, Mamo competed in the 10K race along with other favorite Kenyan athletes Kip Keno and Naphtaly Temo, at which time he won his first silver Olympic medal. He overcame athletes from 44 countries to win a third gold medal in a marathon event for his country. In 1972, at age 39, Mamo participated in the Munich Olympics where he won a bronze medal in the 10K competition. He has participated in a total of 62 international competitions.

Woldemariam, Mesfin (also spelled Mesfin Wolde Mariam; born 1930) is an Ethiopian peace activist who was active during the Meles Zenawi era. He is a founding member of the Ethiopian Human Rights Council (EHRC) and later founded Rainbow Ethiopia: Movement for Democracy and Social Justice.

Born in Addis Ababa, Mesfin received his B.A. from Punjab University, Chandigarh, in 1955 and his M.S. from Clark University in the United States in 1957. Mesfin was professor of geography at Haile Sellassie University (now Addis Ababa University or AAU) and for a time the head of the geography department. He was also a senior Fullbright scholar in 1971, 1986, and 1987. In December 2005, the government of Ethiopia detained Mesfin on charges of treason, genocide, and outrage against the constitution, along with other leading members of the Coalition for Unity and Democracy.

Worku, Asnakech (1935–) is a beloved Ethiopian vocalist. Her trademark is the *krar*, a traditional stringed instrument similar to a lyre. In 2003, Buda Musique released *Ethiopiques 16: The Lady With the Krar*, a compact disc that compiles her recordings from the mid-1970s.

Wossen, Asfa (ca. 1770–ca. 1808) was a *meridazmach* of Shewa, an important Amhara noble of Ethiopia. During his reign, Shewan's control over the tributary states of Geshe, Antzioka, Efratar, Moret, and Marra Biete was strengthened. He was said to have embraced, on the ground of religious and political exigencies, the Sost Lidet doctrine, which taught that Christ had three births: the first at Creation from the Father, the second at the Nativity from the Holy Virgin, and the third from the Holy Spirit at the Baptism. He was also described as a brave warrior and talented administrator whose achievements included tax reforms and the use of administrative liaisons in each district.

Yared was a fifteenth-century composer who established the Deggua, or liturgical music, of the Ethiopian Church.

Yeggazu, Mulugeta, Ras, was Minister for Finance under Emperor Menelik. He later became Minister of War and commander of the imperial troops at the time of Italian invasion. Ras Mulugeta was killed during a counteroffensive against the Italian invaders in 1936.

Yifrashewa, Girma (b. Addis Ababa, October 15, 1967) is the first Ethiopian classical pianist to perform widely in Africa. He has also given concerts elsewhere, including Europe and Australia. Married and the father of one child, he lives in Addis Ababa.

Yifter, Miruts (1938–) was born in the Tigre region of Northern Ethiopia in the district of Adigrat. He spent his youth working in different factories and as a carriage driver. His talent as a long-distance runner was noticed when he performed exceptionally in the 1,500- , 5,000- , and 10,000-meter events in Asmara of northern Ethiopia. Folklore held that Miruts saw athletes from the Ethiopian Air Force racing in the streets and begged the leader of the team to allow him to participate, eventually securing an impressive third-place position. Upon his request, he was allowed to practice with the national team in preparation for the 1968 Olympics in Mexico City. Miruts competed with athletes from Africa, Asia, the Americas, and Europe and he excelled in 5K and 10K races with outstanding results. His trademark was his ability to spring apart from the pack of runners around the last 200 meters. This unusual burst of energy that earned him numerous victories earned him the nickname "Miruts the Shifter." In the 1972 Munich Olympics, he took the bronze medal in the 10K but arrived too late for the 5K final. Miruts earned two gold medals for Ethiopia at the Moscow Olympics in 1980. Those two victories earned him wide respect and admiration in his country, which was looking to continue the legacy set by the legendary Abebe Bikila and Mamo Wolde. Miruts also had a high chance of securing a gold medal in the 1976 Olympics held in Montreal, Canada, had it not been for the boycott of the game by Ethiopia and other African countries protesting the participation of South Africa. In a long career, Miruts participated in more than 252 races and earned a gold medal in 221 of them. In recognition of his outstanding career, the World Sports Journalists' Association honored Miruts by awarding him the "Golden Shoe."

Yohannes, Mengesha (1868–1906) was the natural son of Emperor Yohannes IV of Ethiopia, Ras of Tigre, and as a claimant of the imperial throne is often given the title of prince. He was designated as heir by his father Yohannes IV on his father's deathbed at the Battle of Metemma. Fighting between various relatives of the slain emperor split Mengesha's camp and prevented him from making a viable bid for the imperial throne. The throne was assumed by Menelik of Shewa. Ras Mengesha refused to submit to Menelik and even flirted with joining the new Italian colony of Eritrea, hoping that they would support his rebellion against Emperor Menelik. However, encroachments by the Italians into his native Tigre, their previous enmity to his father Yohannes, and recognition that their ultimate goal was to conquer Ethiopia led him to finally submit to Menelik II and fight at his side against the Italians at the Battle of Adowa.

Yohannes IV, Emperor (ca. 1831–March 10, 1889), also known as Johannes IV or John IV, born Dejazmach Kassai or Kassa, was *negusä nägäst* of Ethiopia (1872–1889). Dejazmach Kassai was a sworn enemy of Emperor Tewodros II and gave logistical and political support to the British forces who arrived to defeat Emperor Tewodros in 1868. In gratitude, the British gave Dejazmatch Kassai a large number of modern firearms as they withdrew following their victory at Magdala. This helped him to control the province of Tigre, and he became one of the three most powerful princes in Ethiopia (the others being Wagshum Gobeze of Lasta and Wag, the future emperor Tekle Giyorgis II; and Sahle Maryam King of Shewa, the future emperor Menelik II), each of whom vied to become sole ruler and could claim to be descended from the Solomonic kings. Yohannes' life came to an end while he was dealing with another invasion by the followers of Muhammad Ahmad's successor, Abdallahi ibn Muhammad, at the Battle of Metemma on March 9, 1889.

Zar' a-Ya'qob, Emperor (1434–1468) was an Ethiopian ruler renowned for his excellent administration and deep religious faith. Ethiopian literature attained its greatest heights during his reign.

Zauditu, Empress (also spelled Zawditu or Zewditu) (April 29, 1876–April 2, 1930) was empress of Ethiopia from 1916 to 1930. She was noted for opposing the reforms of Tafari Makonnen (later Emperor Haile Selassie) and for her strong religious devotion.

Zenawi, Legesse ("Meles") (1955–) is prime minister of Ethiopia. Born in Adwa from an Eritrean mother and a Tigrean father in Tigre Province, he was appointed to the office of prime minister on August 22, 1995, after his governing party swept parliamentary elections that were boycotted by the opposition. He had previously been transitional president of Ethiopia, from May 28, 1991, until August 22, 1995. He has served as chairman of the OAU from June 1995 until June 1996. He is also serving as cochairman of the Global Coalition for Africa and has also been actively involved in IGAD's efforts to end the conflicts in Sudan and Somalia and African initiatives to seek a solution to the crisis in Burundi. Meles acquired a first class M.A. in business administration from the Open University in the United Kingdom in 1995 and an M.Sc. in economics from Erasmus University of the Netherlands in 2004.

Zewde, Bahru, is a distinguished historian of Ethiopia and Africa. He received his B.A. with distinction from the Haile Selassie I University (1970) and his Ph.D. from the University of London (1976). He has taught at the Addis Ababa University (Ethiopia), the University of Illinois-Urbana Champaign (United States), and Hamburg University (Germany). He has served as director of the Institute of Ethiopian Studies at Addis Ababa University; editor of the *Journal of Ethiopian Studies*, the *Eastern Africa Social Science Research Review*, and *Africa Review of Books*; member of the International Advisory Board of the *Journal of African History*; president of the Association of Ethiopian Historians; resident vice-president of the Organization for Social Science Research in Eastern and Southern Africa (OSSREA); and first vice president of the Association of African Historians. Currently, Bahru Zewde serves as the executive director of the Forum for Social Studies (Ethiopia) and a board member of Trust Africa. He authored widely acclaimed books including *A History of Modern Ethiopia 1855–1991* (2001) and *Pioneers of Change in Ethiopia: The Reforming Intellectuals of the Early Twentieth Century* (2002). He edited the book *Between the Jaws of Hyenas: A Diplomatic History of Ethiopia 1876–1896* (2002), co-edited *Ethiopia: The Challenge of Democracy from Below* (2002), and compiled *A Short History of Ethiopia and the Horn* (1998). He is also the author of more than 30 articles and book chapters.

Selected Bibliography

CHAPTER 1

Adera, Tadesse, and Ali Jimale Ahmed, eds. *Silence is Not Golden: A Critical Anthology of Ethiopian Literature.* Lawrenceville, NJ: Red Sea Press, 1994.

Boll, Verena, Kaplan Steven, and Andreu Martinez D'Alos-Moner, eds. *Ethiopia and the Missions: Historical and Anthropological Insights.* Germany: Lit Verlag, 2005.

Brooks, Miguel F., ed. *Kebra Nagast (The Glory of Kings): The True Ark of the Covenant.* Lawrenceville, NJ: Red Sea Press, 1995.

Chaillot, Christine. *Ethiopian Orthodox Tewahedo Church Tradition: A Brief Introduction to Its Life and Spirituality.* Paris: Inter-Orthodox Dialogue, 2002.

Chojnacki, Stanislaw, and Carolyn Gossage. *Ethiopian Icons: Catalogue of the Collection of the Institute of Ethiopian Studies.* Italy: Addis Abada University, 2000.

Hancock, Graham, Mohamed Amin, and Duncan Willetts, eds. *The Beauty of Addis Ababa: A Photographic Guide to Addis Ababa Highlighting the City's Architectural Heritage, Its Colourful Market Places and Historical Buildings.* Ethiopia: 1997.

Hancock, Graham, Richard Pankhurst, and Duncan Willetts. *Under Ethiopian Skies, A Photographic Introduction to Ethiopia Describing Aspects of Its Religions, Architecture, Natural World, and Its People.* Kenya: Camerapix, 1997.

Henze, Paul. *Layers of Time: A History of Ethiopia.* UK: Hurst & Co., 2000.

Kiros, Teodros, and Zara Yacob. *Rationality of the Human Heart.* Lawrenceville, NJ: Red Sea Press, 2005.

Lipsky, George A. *Ethiopia: Its People, Its Society, Its Culture.* New Haven, CT: Hraf Press, 1962.

Marcus, Harold G. *A History of Ethiopia*. Berkeley: University of California Press, 1994.

Markakis, John. *Ethiopia: Anatomy of a Traditional Polity*. Oxford: Clarendon Press, 1974.

Mathew, David. *Ethiopia: The Study of a Polity, 1540–1935*. London: Eyre & Spottiswoode, 1947.

Munro-Hay, Stuart. *Ethiopia, The Unknown Land: A Cultural and Historical Guide*. London: I B Tauris, 2002.

Pankhurst, Alula, and Dena Freeman, eds. *Peripheral People: The Excluded Minorities of Ethiopia*. UK: Hurst, 2003.

Pankhurst, Richard. *The Ethiopians*. Oxford: Blackwell Publishers: 1998.

Pankhurst, Richard, David Northrup, and Frederic A. Sharf. *Abyssinia, 1867–1868: Artists on Campaign*. CA; Tsehai Publishers and Distributors, 2003.

Trimingham, J. *Spencer Islam in Ethiopia*. UK: Cass, Frank, 1976.

Wendorf, Fred. *A Middle Stone Age Sequence from the Central Rift Valley*. Ethiopia, 1974.

CHAPTER 2

Adejumobi, Saheed A. "Ethiopia." In *Africa: Volume 1: African History Before 1885*, ed. Toyin Falola, 231–242. Durham, NC: Carolina Academic Press, 2000.

Baum, James E. *Savage Abyssinia*. London: Cassell, 1928.

Bredin, Miles. *Pale Abyssinian: The Life of James Bruce, African Explorer and Adventurer*. UK: HarperCollins Publishers, 2000.

Caulk, Richard, ed. *Between the Jaws of Hyenas: A Diplomatic History of Ethiopia (1876–1896)*. Germany, Harrassowitz: Verlag, 2002.

Crummey, Donald. "Initiatives and Objectives in Ethio-European Relations, 1827–1862." *The Journal of African History* 15, no. 3 (1974).

———. "Society and Ethnicity in the Politics of Christian Ethiopia during the Zamana Masafent." *The International Journal of African Historical Studies* 8, no. 2 (1975).

———. "Society, State and Nationality in the Recent Historiography of Ethiopia." *The Journal of African History* 31, no. 1 (1990): 103–19.

———. "Tewodros as Reformer and Modernizer." *The Journal of African History* 10, no. 3 (1969).

Harrington, Peter, Richard Pankhurst, and Frederic A. Sharf, eds. *Diary of a Journey to Abyssinia, 1868. With the Expedition of Sir Robert Napier, K.C.S.I. The diary and Observation of William Simpson*. CA: Tsehai Publishers and Distributors, 2002.

Lepsius, Richard. *Letters from Egypt, Ethiopia, and to Peninsula of Sinai*. London: H.G. Bohn, 1853.

Lewis, Herbert S. "Historical Problems in Ethiopia and the Horn of Africa." *Annals of the New York Academy of Sciences* 96, art. 2, 505.

Marcus, H. G. "The Black Men Who Turned White: European Attitudes Towards Ethiopians, 1850–1900." *Archiv. Orientalni*. no. 39 (1971).

Pankhurst, Richard. *The Ethiopia Borderlands: Essays in Regional History from Ancient Times to the End of the 18th Century*. Lawrenceville, NJ: Red Sea Press, 1997.

———. "Ethiopian Emperor Menelik II Repulsed Italian Invasion, 1895." *The Africa Reader: Colonial Africa*. Edited and with introductions by Wilfred Cartey and Martin Kilson. New York: Random House, 1970.

———. *The Ethiopians: A History*. UK: Blackwell, 2001.

———. "The Independence of Ethiopia and Her Import of Arms in the Nineteenth Century." *Presence Africaine* nos. 32/33 (1964).

———. *An Introduction to the Economic History of Ethiopia, From Early Times to 1800*. Lalibela House: 1961.

Ramos, Manuel Joao, and Isabel Boavida, eds. *The Indigenous and the Foreign in Christian Ethiopian Art: On Portuguese Ethiopian Contacts in the 16th 17th Centuries*. UK: Ashgate Publishers, 2004.

Rubenson, Sven, ed. *Correspondence and Treaties: 1800–1854*. Evanston, IL: Northwestern University Press, 1987.

Taiwo, Olufemi. "Prophets Without Honor: African Apostles of Modernity in the Nineteenth Century." *West Africa Review* 3, No. 1 (2002).

CHAPTER 3

Adejumobi, Saheed A. "Northeast Africa." In *Africa: Volume 3: Colonial Africa 1885–1939*, ed. Toyin Falola, 397–411. Durham, NC: Carolina Academic Press, 2002.

Araia, Ghelawdewos. *Ethiopia: The Political Economy of Transition*. Lanham, MD: University Press of America, 1995.

Bulcha, Mekuria. *Making of the Oromo Diaspora: A Historical Sociology of Forced Migration*. Minneapolis, MN: Kirk House Publishers, 2002.

Caulk, R. A. "Armies as Predators: Ethiopia c. 1850–1935." *The International Journal of African Historical Studies* XI, no. 3 (1978): 472–78.

Donham, Donald L., and Wendy James, eds. *The Southern Marches of Imperial Ethiopia: Essays in History and Social Anthropology*. UK: James Currey Publishers, 2002.

Erlich, Haggai. *Ras Alula and the Scramble for Africa: A Political Biography*. Lawrenceville, NJ: Red Sea Press, 1996.

Greenfield, Richard. *Ethiopia: A New Political History*. New York: Frederick A. Praeger Publishers, 1965.

Hanchard, Michael. "Afro-Modernity: Temporality, Politics, and the African Diaspora." *Public Culture* 11 (1999): 245–268.

Hansberry, Leo. *Pillars in Ethiopian History: The William Leo Hansberry Notebook*, ed. Joseph E. Harris. Vol. 1. Washington, D.C.: Howard University Press, 1974.

Hayford, Casely J. E. *Ethiopia Unbound: Studies in Race Emancipation*. London: Cass, 1969.

Jalata, Asafa. *Oromia and Ethiopia: State Formation and Ethnonational Conflict, 1868–2004*. Lawrenceville, NJ: Red Sea Press, 2005.

Marcus, Harold G. *Haile Selassie, I: The Formative Years, 1892–1936*. NJ: Red Seas Press, 1995.

McCann, James. "The Political Economy of Rural Rebellion in Ethiopia: Northern Resistance to Imperial Expansion, 1925–1935." *The International Journal of African Historical Studies* 18, no. 4 (1985).

McClellan, Charles W. "Articulating Economic Modernization and National Integration at the Periphery: Addis Ababa and Sidamo's Provincial Centers." *African Studies Review* 33, no. 1 (April 1990).

Norberg, Viveca. *Halldin Swedes in Haile Selassie's Ethiopia, 1924–1952: A Study in Early Development Co-operation*. Uppsala: University of Stockholm; Almqvist & Wiksell International, distr., 1977.

Schaefer, Charles. "The Politics of Banking: The Bank of Abyssinia, 1905–1935." *The International Journal of African Historical Studies* 25, no. 2 (1992).

Taiwo, Olufemi. "Reading the Colonizer's Mind: Lord Lugard and the Philosophical Foundations of British Colonialism." In Susan E. Babbitt and Sue Campbell, eds., *Racism and Philosophy* Ithaca, NY: Cornell University Press, 1999.

Tibebu, Teshale. "Ethiopia: The 'Anomaly' and 'Paradox' of Africa." *Journal of Black Studies* 26, no. 4 (March 1996): 414–30.

Time Magazine, August 9, 1926.

Time Magazine, November 3, 1930.

Time Magazine, November 10, 1930.

Waugh, Evelyn. *Waugh Abroad: Collected Travel Writing/Evelyn Waugh*. Introduction by Nicholas Shakespeare. New York: Everyman's Library, 2003.

Zewde, Bahru. *Pioneers of Change in Ethiopia: The Reformist Intellectuals of the Early Twentieth Century*. UK: James Currey Publishers, 2002.

CHAPTER 4

Ben-Ghiat, Ruth. *Fascist Modernities: Italy, 1922–1945*. Los Angeles, CA: University of California Press, 2004.

Ben-Ghiat, Ruth, and Mia Fuller. *Italian Colonialism*. NY: Palgrave McMillan, 2005.

Clapham, Christopher. *Haile-Selassie's Government*. Foreword by Dame Margery Perham. New York: Praeger, 1969.

Davis, Mary Sylvia Pankhurst. *A Life in Radical Politics*. London: Pluto Press, 1999.

Del Boca, Angelo. *The Ethiopian War, 1935–1941*. Chicago: The University of Chicago Press, 1965.

Diggins, John P. *Mussolini and Fascism: The View from America*. Princeton, NJ: Princeton University Press, 1972.

DuBois, W.E.B. "Inter-racial Implications of the Ethiopian Crisis: A Negro View." *Foreign Affairs* 4, no. 1 (October 1935): 85–86.

Esedebe, Olisanwu. *Pan-Africanism: The Idea and Movement, 1776–1963*. Washington DC: Howard University Press, 1982.

Falola, Toyin. *Nationalism and African Intellectuals*. Rochester, NY: University of Rochester Press, 2001.

Gaines, Kevin K. *Black Expatriates and the Civil Rights Era: American Africans in Ghana* NC: The University of North Carolina Press, 2006.

Gallo, Patrick J. *Old Bread, New Wine: A Portrait of the Italian-Americans*. Chicago: Nelson-Hall, 1981.

Gebrekidan, Fikru Negash. *Bond Without Blood: A History of Ethiopian & New World Black Relations, 1896–1991*. NJ. Africa World Press, 2005.

Goldberg, David Theo. *The Racial State*. MA: Blackwell Publishers, 2002.

Goodman, Madeline Jane. "The Evolution of Ethnicity: Fascism and Anti-Fascism in the Italian-American Community." Ph.D. dissertation, Carnegie-Mellon University, 1993.

Harris, Joseph E. *African-American Reactions to War in Ethiopia, 1936–1941*. Baton Rouge: Louisiana State University Press, 1994.

Jackson, John G. *Ethiopia and the Origin of Civilization*. MA: Black Classic Press, 1978, originally published in 1939.

Kelley, Robin. *Freedom Dreams: The Black Radical Imagination.* MA: Beacon Press, 2002.

Larebo, Haile. *The Building of an Empire: Italian Land Policy and Practice in Ethiopia.* NJ: Africa World Press, 2006.

Magubane, Bernard Makhosezwe. 'The Significance of Ethiopia in Afro-American Consciousness.' In *The Ties That Bind: African-American Consciousness of Africa,* ed. Magubane. Africa World Press, Inc., 1987.

Moses, Wilson J. "The Poetics of Ethiopianism: W.E.B. DuBois and Literary Black Nationalism." *American Literature* 47, no. 3 (November 1975).

Pankhurst, Richard "Italian Fascist War Crimes in Ethiopia: A History of Their Discussion, from the League of Nations to the United Nations, (1936–1949)." *Northeast African Studies* 6, no. 1-2 (1999).

———. *Sylvia Pankhurst: Counsel for Ethiopia.* CA: Tseha, 2003.

Rankin, Nicholas. *Telegram from Guernica: The Extraordinary Life of George Steer, War Correspondent.* UK: Faber, 2003.

Rogers, J.A. *The Real Facts about Ethiopia.* Black Classic Press, 1982, originally published in 1936.

Sbacchi, Alberto. *Legacy of Bitterness: Ethiopia and Fascist Italy, 1935–1941.* Lawrenceville, NJ: The Red Sea Press, 1997.

Scott, William R. "Black Nationalism and the Italo-Ethiopian Conflict, 1934–1936." *The Journal of Negro History* 63, no. 2 (April 1978).

Shack, William A. "Ethiopia and Afro-Americans: Some Historical Notes, 1920–1970." *Phylon* 35, no. 2 (1974).

Time Magazine, October 28, 1935.

Ventresco, Fiorello B. "Italian Americans and the Ethiopian Crisis." *Italian Americana* 6, no. 1 (summer 1980): 4–27.

Von Eschen, Penny M. *Race Against Empire: Black Americans and Anticolonialism, 1937–1957.* Ithaca: Cornell University Press, 1997.

Zewde, Bahru. "The Ethiopian Intelligentsia and the Italo-Ethiopian War, 1935–1941." *The International Journal of African Historical Studies* 26, no. 2 (1993).

CHAPTER 5

Agyeman-Duah, Baffour. *The United States and Ethiopia: Military Assistance and the Quest for Security, 1953–1993.* Lanham, MD: University Press of America, 1994.

Bahrey, Almeida, Huntingford, and Beckingham. *History of the Galla (Oromo) of Ethiopia: With Ethnology and History of South West Ethiopia.* CA: African Sun Publishing, 1993.

Clapham, Christopher. "The Ethiopian Coup d'Etat of December 1960." *The Journal of Modern African Studies* 6, no. 4 (1968): 495–507.

———. "Imperial Leadership in Ethiopia." *African Affairs* 68, no. 271 (April 1969).

Gudina, Merera. *Ethiopia: Competing Ethnic Nationalisms and the Quest for Democracy, 1960–2000.* Maastricht, Holland: N.P Shaker Publishing, 2003.

Iyob, Ruth. *The Eritrean Struggle for Independence: Domination, Resistance, Nationalism, 1941–1993.* Cambridge: Cambridge University Press, 2004.

———. "Regional Hegemony: Domination and Resistance in the Horn of Africa." *The Journal of Modern African Studies* 31, no. 2 (1993).

Kapuscinski, Ryzard. *The Emperor: Downfall of an Autocrat.* New York: Vintage, 1983.

Lefebvre, Jeffrey A. "The United States, Ethiopia and the 1963 Somali-Soviet Arms Deal: Containment and the Balance of Power Dilemma in the Horn of Africa." *The Journal of Modern African Studies* 36, no. 4 (December 1998).

Schwab, Peter. "Cold War on the Horn of Africa." *African Affairs* 77, no. 306 (January 1978).

Sellassie, Haile. *My Life and Ethiopia's Progress: The Autobiography of Emperor Haile Sellassie.* Translated from Amharic by Edward Ullendorff. 2 vols. New York: Frontline Books, 1999.

Tibebu, Teshale. *The Making of Modern Ethiopia: 1896–1974.* Lawrenceville, NJ: Red Sea Press, 1995.

Zewde, Bahru. *A History of Modern Ethiopia, 1855–1991.* 2nd ed. Athens: Ohio University Press, 2001.

——. "Intellectuals and Soldiers: The Socialist Experiment in the Horn of Africa." Paper prepared for CODESRIA 30th Anniversary Conference, Dakar, December 8–11, 2003.

CHAPTER 6

Brind, Harry. "Soviet Policy in the Horn of Africa." *International Affairs* 60, no. 1 (Winter 1983–1984).

Chege, Michael. "The Revolution Betrayed: Ethiopia, 1974–79." *The Journal of Modern African Studies* 17, no. 3 (1979): 359–80.

Donham, Donald L. *History, Power, Ideology: Central Issues in Marxism and Anthropology.* CA: The University of California Press, 1999.

——. *Marxist Modern: An Ethnographic History of the Ethiopian Revolution.* Berkeley: University of California Press, 1999.

——. "Revolution and Modernity in Maale: Ethiopia, 1974 to 1987." *Comparative Studies in Society and History* 34, no. 1 (January 1992): 28–57.

——. *Work and Power in Maale, Ethiopia.* UK: Columbia University Press, 1979.

Harbeson, John W. "Socialism, Traditions and Revolutionary Politics in Contemporary Ethiopia." *Canadian Journal of African Studies* XI, no. 2 (1977): 217–34.

James, Wendy, Donald L. Donham, Eisei Kurimoto, and Alessandro Triulzi, eds. *Remapping Ethiopia: Socialism & After.* UK: James Currey Publishers, 2002.

Kebbede, Girma. *The State and Development in Ethiopia.* Atlantic Highlands, NJ: Humanities Press, 1992.

Keller, Edmond J. "Ethiopia: Revolution, Class, and the National Question." *African Affairs* 80 (1981).

Keller, Edmond J., and Donald Rothchild, eds. *Afro-Marxist Regimes: Ideology and Public Policy.* Boulder & London: Lynne Rienner Publishers, 1987.

Marcus, Harold G. *History of Ethiopia.* CA: The University of California Press, 2002.

Ottaway, Marina, ed. *The Political Economy of Ethiopia.* New York: Praeger, 1990.

Pankhurst, Helen. *Gender, Development, and Identity: An Ethiopian Study.* London: Zed Books, 1992.

Pausewang, Siegfried, Kjetil Tronvoll, and Lovise Aalen, eds. *Ethiopia Since the Derg: A Decade of Democratic Pretensions and Performance.* London: Zed Books, 2002.

Tibebu, Teshale. *The Making of Modern Ethiopia, 1896–1974*. Lawrenceville, NJ: Red Sea Press, 1995.

Young, John. *Peasant Revolution in Ethiopia: The Tigray People's Liberation Front, 1975–1991*. Cambridge: Cambridge University Press, 1997.

CHAPTER 7

Abraham, Kinfe. *Ethiopia: From Bullets to the Ballot Box: The Bumpy Road to Democracy and the Political Economy of Transition*. Lawrenceville, NJ: Red Sea Press, 1994.

Adejumobi, Saheed A. "African Intellectual History: Contradictions in the African Encounter with Modernity." In *Intellectual News: Review of the International Society for Intellectual History* no. 11 (Winter/Spring 2004): 38–55.

Africa Insight: Ethiopia: Challenges from the Past, Challenges for the Future, no. 321 (October 1981): 519–49.

Chole, Eshetu. *Underdevelopment in Ethiopia*. East Lansing: Michigan State University Press, 2004.

Easterly, William. *The White Man's Burden: Why the West's Efforts to Aid the Rest Have Done So Much Ill and So Little Good*. New York: Penguin Press, 2006.

Geda, Alemayehu. "Does Conflict Explain Ethiopia's Backwardness? Yes and Significantly." Paper presented at Making Peace Work Conference at WIDER, Helsinki, Finland, June 2004.

———. "Macroeconomic Performance in Post-Reform Ethiopia." *Journal of Northeast African Studies* 8 no. 1 (2005): 159–85.

———. "The Political Economy of Growth in Ethiopia." *Cambride African Economic History* (forthcoming).

Gidron, B., P. Q. Ufford, and A. B. Kello. "NGOs dealing with refugee in Amsterdam." NIRP Research for Policy Series 12. Royal Tropical Institute, 2003.

Hammond, Jenny. *Fire from the Ashes: A Chronicle of the Revolution in Tigray, Ethiopia, 1975–1991*. Lawrenceville, NJ: Red Sea Press, 1999.

Harbeson, John W. *The Ethiopian Transformation: The Quest for the Post-Imperial State*. Boulder, CO: Westview Press, 1988.

Harney, Elizabeth. *Ethiopian Passages: Contemporary Art from the Diaspora*. New York: Palgrave Macmillan, 2003.

International Journal of Ethiopian Studies 1, no.2 (winter/spring 2004).

Kebede, Messay. *Survival and Modernization: Ethiopia's Enigmatic Present: A Philosophical Discourse*. Lawrenceville, NJ: Red Sea Press, 1999.

Lata, Leenco. *The Ethiopian State at the Crossroads: Decolonization and Democratization or Disintegration?* Lawrenceville, NJ: Red Sea Press, 1999.

Levine, Donald N. *Greater Ethiopia: Evolution of a Multiethnic Society*. Chicago: University of Chicago Press, 2000.

Mengisteab, Kidane. "New Approaches to State Building in Africa: The Case of Ethiopia's Ethnic-Based Federalism." *African Studies Review* 40, no. 3 (December 1997).

Pankhurst, Richard. "An Ethiopian Hero: Tsegaye Gabre-Medhin (1936–2005)." Open Democracy: Free Thinking for the World. http://www.open democracy.net/xml/xhtml/articles/3347.html.

Parker, Ben, and Abraham Woldegiorgis. *Ethiopia*. UK: Oxfam Publications, 2003.

Pausewang, Siegfried, Kjetil Tronvoll, and Lovise Aalen, eds. *Ethiopia Since the Derg: A Decade of Democratic Pretension and Performance.* London: Zed Books, 2002.

Poluha, Eva. *The Power of Continuity: Ethiopia Through the Eyes of Its Children.* Sweden Nordic Africa Institute, 2004.

Sachs, Jeffrey. *The End of Poverty: Economic Possibilities for Our Time.* New York: Penguin Press, 2005.

Sorenson, John. *Imagining Ethiopia: Struggles for History and Identity in the Horn of Africa.* New Brunswick, NJ: Rutgers University Press, 1993.

Stiglitz, Joseph E. *Globalization and Its Discontents.* New York: W.W. Norton & Co., 2002.

Taiwo, Olufemi. "Colonialism and its Aftermath: The Crisis of Knowledge Production." *Callaloo* 16, No. 3 (1993).

Taiwo, Olufemi. "Globalization: Doing It Right this Time Around." Forthcoming.

Turton, David, ed. *Ethnic Federalism: The Ethiopian Experience in Comparative Perspective.* Athens: Ohio University Press, 2006.

www.Wikipedia.com. Ethiopian people stubs is a popular resource for capsule information on select Ethiopian historical figures.

Von Eschen, Penny M. *Satchmo Blows Up the World: Jazz Ambassadors Play the Cold War.* Boston: Harvard University Press, 2004.

Zewde, Bahru. "What did we dream? What did we achieve? And where are we heading?" *Africa Insight: Ethiopia: Challenges from the Past, Challenges for the Future* no. 321 (October 1981).

Zewde, Bahru, and Siegfried Pausewang, eds. *Ethiopia: The Challenge of Democracy From Below, Alternative Voices.* Sweden: Nordic Africa Institute, 2002.

Index

About the Author

SAHEED A. ADEJUMOBI is Assistant Professor of History with the Global African Studies Program and Department of History at Seattle University. He has written widely on African and African Diaspora intellectual and cultural history and traditions.

Other Titles in the Greenwood Histories of the Modern Nations
Frank W. Thackeray and John E. Findling, Series Editors

The History of Argentina
Daniel K. Lewis

The History of Australia
Frank G. Clarke

The History of the Baltic States
Kevin O'Connor

The History of Brazil
Robert M. Levine

The History of Canada
Scott W. See

The History of Central America
Thomas Pearcy

The History of Chile
John L. Rector

The History of China
David C. Wright

The History of Congo
Didier Gondola

The History of Cuba
Clifford L. Staten

The History of Egypt
Glenn E. Perry

The History of Finland
Jason Lavery

The History of France
W. Scott Haine

The History of Germany
Eleanor L. Turk

The History of Ghana
Roger S. Gocking

The History of Great Britain
Anne Baltz Rodrick

The History of Holland
Mark T. Hooker

The History of India
John McLeod

The History of Indonesia
Steven Drakeley

The History of Iran
Elton L. Daniel

The History of Iraq
Courtney Hunt

The History of Ireland
Daniel Webster Hollis III

The History of Israel
Arnold Blumberg

The History of Italy
Charles L. Killinger

The History of Japan
Louis G. Perez

The History of Korea
Djun Kil Kim

The History of Mexico
Burton Kirkwood

The History of New Zealand
Tom Brooking

The History of Nigeria
Toyin Falola

The History of Panama
Robert C. Harding

CPSIA information can be obtained
at www.ICGtesting.com
Printed in the USA
LVOW08*1803130418
573310LV00003B/28/P